Vanishing Boundaries

The Religion of Mainline
Protestant Baby Boomers

Vanishing Boundaries

Dean R. Hoge
Benton Johnson
Donald A. Luidens

Westminster/John Knox Press
Louisville, Kentucky

Book design by Elizabeth Hickey and Susan E. Jackson

Cover design by Peyton Tabb Talbot III, Fearless Designs

First edition

Published by Westminster/John Knox Press
Louisville, Kentucky

This book is printed on acid-free paper that meets the American National Standards Institute Z39.48 standard. ∞

PRINTED IN THE UNITED STATES OF AMERICA

9 8 7 6 5 4 3 2 1

Library of Congress Cataloging-in-Publication Data

Hoge, Dean R., 1937–
    Vanishing Boundaries : the religion of mainline Protestant baby boomers / Dean R. Hoge, Benton Johnson, and Donald A. Luidens. — 1st ed.
        p.   cm.
    Includes bibliographical references and index.
    ISBN 0-664-25492-6 (alk. paper)

    1. Liberalism (Religion)—Protestant churches.   2. Protestant churches—United States—History—20th century.   3. Baby boom generation—Religious life.   4. United States—Church history—20th century.   I. Johnson, Benton.   II. Luidens, Donald A.   III. Title. IV. Title: Mainline Protestant baby boomers.
BR526.H64   1994
280'.4'097309045—dc20   93-31968

Contents

Preface

The decline of mainline Protestantism has been a central fact of religious life in the United States for a quarter of a century. Since the late 1960s, the Presbyterians, United Methodists, Episcopalians, and other denominations that formed the historical core of American Protestantism have experienced dropping membership, weakening financial support, and sagging confidence. In particular, the mainline denominations have lost the involvement of a substantial portion of the postwar generation—the Baby Boomers.

This book grew out of the authors' longtime concern for the current condition and future prospects of these religious bodies. In 1987 the Lilly Endowment sponsored a conference at Hartford, Connecticut, during which a variety of scholars—including the authors—exchanged views on why the mainline denominations were losing members. Although the conference participants were at no loss for theoretical explanations of the decline, it became clear that there was a lack of reliable information for assessing the theories. In particular, little information was available on the religious motivations and experiences of adults born after World War II, the generation most conspicuously absent from the churches.

With the assistance of the Lilly Endowment and the encouragement of John Mulder, President of Louisville Presbyterian Theological Seminary, we launched a pilot interview study of young adults who had, as adolescents, made confessions of faith in Presbyterian churches. This pilot study led to a larger, nationwide survey of persons who had been confirmed in Presbyterian churches and who were 33 to 42 years old in 1989—the Baby Boomers. The results of this nationwide survey form the basis of *Vanishing Boundaries*.

We have arranged the materials in this book to set the broad context of the decline of the mainline Protestant denominations and then to focus on the particular insights we gained from the Baby Boomers and other sources. The Introduction outlines the recent history of mainline Protestant membership trends and presents the major theories that purport to explain them. In chapter 1, four representative Baby Boomers whom we interviewed tell about their own spiritual journeys. Chapter 2 describes the methods we used in our survey and the basic characteristics of the people we interviewed. Chapter 3 sorts the interviewees into eight types that reflect their current religious participation. The four "churched" types are described in chapter 4, and the four "unchurched" types are described in chapter 5. Chapter 6 is a statistical analysis of the influences that led the respondents to their varied religious outcomes. In chapter 7 we evaluate the principal theories of the decline in mainline membership and offer an explanation of our own. Finally, in chapter 8 we explore the implications of our findings for the future development of the mainline Protestant denominations.

The main protagonists in the book are the hundreds of Baby Boomers who participated in our telephone interviews. Together with the forty who agreed to in-depth person-to-person interviews, they provided the data on which our analyses are based. We are grateful for their cooperation and we trust that we have accurately reflected their personal opinions and visions.

Many others also helped us in this project, and we wish to thank them. Our principal advisor throughout has been John Mulder, the codirector with Milton J Coalter and Louis Weeks, all of Louisville Seminary, of a recent multivolume study of the Presbyterian Church. During the pilot study we were assisted by an advisory committee consisting of Mark Noll, Wade Clark Roof, Steven Tipton, and Robert Wuthnow. Earlier versions of the manuscript were read by Dorothy Bass, Harvey Cox, William McKinney, Roger J. Nemeth, and Wade Clark Roof, and their comments were extremely helpful to us. Financial support for the study came from the Lilly Endowment, Inc., through the help of Craig Dykstra, Vice-President, and Fred Hofheinz, Program Officer in Religion. Finally, we thank the numerous presbytery executives, pastors, church secretaries, and parishioners, those who assisted us in the field, and the many who conducted telephone interviews or transcribed the taped person-to-person interviews.

Understanding Mainline Protestant Rise and Fall

For mainline Protestantism,[1] the 1950s appear to have been a heyday of church growth. Denominational memberships reached an all-time high. With little or no effort, it seemed, new churches were being planted at an unprecedented rate. Sunday schools were crowded with youngsters, contributions were pouring in, seminaries were bulging at the seams; in sum, the future looked bright.

According to the Gallup organization, 49 percent of all Americans said that they attended church or synagogue on a weekly basis in both 1955 and 1958. This figure represented a jump of 12 percentage points from the prewar low of 37 percent in 1940. In addition, roughly 73 percent of all Americans claimed membership in some church or synagogue, maintaining the high levels reached in the 1930s and 1940s.[2]

In 1955 *Time* magazine rhapsodized: "Everybody knows that church life is booming in the U.S., and there are plenty of statistics to prove it."[3] *Newsweek* dedicated its March 28, 1955 cover story to "Resurgent Protestantism." It pointed to "the vast resurgence of Protestantism" experienced in Sunday schools, lay groups, and seminaries:

> There are 35.4 million children in the Sunday schools of America, and almost 33 million are Protestants. Lay groups affiliated with various denominations have infused new blood into old congregations; the National Council of Presbyterian Men, for example, has grown from zero at its birth

in 1949 to a membership of 400,000 today. Protestant seminaries are attracting ministerial students of high caliber in numbers unimagined a decade ago. The Presbyterian Church in the U.S.A. (Northern) is a case in point. Fifteen years ago, the denomination was closing and consolidating some of its seminaries. Since then, the enrollment has doubled.[4]

Growth was recorded throughout the mainline denominations. During the 1950s the Methodist membership ballooned to almost 11 million from a prewar level of about 8 million; Episcopalians numbered 2.2 million in 1965, up from only 1.4 million in 1945; and the denominations that merged in 1958 to form the United Presbyterian Church in the U.S.A. grew from 2.2 million just after the war to 3.2 million by the early 1960s.[5]

This tremendous growth astonished many members of mainline churches. In 1955 Franklin Clark Fry, president of the United Lutheran Church, observed: "There is so much momentum in the United Lutheran Church these days that the leaders have to keep moving to avoid having their troops—the rank and file of pastors and congregations—run over them."[6] A pastor in Massachusetts told church historian Sydney E. Ahlstrom that "the people keep joining the church without my lifting a finger. . . . The thing's gotten out of hand and I don't know what to do."[7]

As a result of this unprecedented growth, many denominations set unrealistic expectations about the ease with which churches could be established and memberships built. A sense of euphoria prevailed in certain quarters of the Protestant scene. *Newsweek* quoted Liston Pope, highly regarded social analyst and Dean of Yale Divinity School, as predicting more of the same: "Dean Pope . . . believes that, in the next twenty years, American Protestantism will enlarge its numbers by one third."[8]

A Change in Fortunes

During the 1960s, however, the pattern of growth that marked the 1950s began to change. By the late 1960s memberships in the mainline churches were dropping precipitously, and this trend continued throughout the 1970s. The dimensions of the decline were as remarkable as had been those of the earlier membership growth.

United Methodist membership peaked in 1964 at 11.1 million members; by 1975 this figure had fallen by 11 percent to 9.9 million. Episcopalian membership decreased from a high of 2.3 million in 1967 to 2.1 million only eight years later. And the United Presbyterians lost 642,000 members (or 19 percent) in the decade after their 1965 crest of 3.3 million.[9]

In 1972 Dean Kelley, a United Methodist minister and an executive with the National Council of Churches, published his analysis of the impending crisis, *Why Conservative Churches Are Growing*. His book struck a sensitive chord in many of the mainline denominations. Perhaps Kelley should have titled his book *Why Liberal Churches Are Declining*, for it was to them that much of his discussion was addressed. He observed that

> at least ten of the largest Christian denominations in the country, whose memberships totalled 77,666,223 in 1967, had fewer members the next year and fewer yet the year after. Most of these denominations had been growing uninterruptedly since colonial times. In the previous decade they had grown more slowly, some failing to keep pace with the increase in the nation's population. And now they have begun to diminish, reversing a trend of two centuries.[10]

From a 1958 peak of 49 percent of all Americans attending church or synagogue in any given week, Gallup researchers found that the church attendance level fell to 40–41 percent for most of the 1970s.[11] Similar drops were reported among those claiming church membership (down from 73 percent in 1965 to 68 percent in the late 1970s), and among those saying that religion was "very important" in their lives (from 70 percent in 1965 to 52 percent in 1978).[12]

Invariably, questions were raised. What happened? Where did all the members go? Had a historic revival dissolved into mass disillusionment and defection? Had the churches not delivered on what was promised? Had they alienated vast numbers of people in some way? Along with Dean Kelley, much of the mainline Protestant world was struggling with these questions by the early 1970s.

A "Return to Normalcy"?

The church growth of the 1950s appeared to be so dramatic, and its subsequent reversal so precipitous, that it is necessary to ask whether the downturn in the 1960s was a *return* to some pre–World War II trend line that was temporarily skewed during the 1950s. Perhaps the 1950s were a sociological exception. Maybe the mainline denominations, like trees righting themselves after a gust of strong wind, were merely returning to the membership growth rates that had preceded the war. In short, was the 1960s downturn simply a "return to normalcy"?

In 1976 the Hartford Working Group,[13] consisting of researchers and executives from a number of mainline denominations, addressed the issue of the upturn of the 1950s and the subsequent downturn of the 1960s, but they found it bewildering. They concluded that, after the upturn of the 1950s, the most likely trends to expect would be downward; some slowdown after the rapid growth would appear to be "normal":

> But beyond this initial statement we were unable to apply the notion of "return to normalcy" with any explanatory rigor. In a period of rapid social

change the notion of normalcy may be unclear, and it seems so for the years under study here.[14]

During the 1980s, historian William R. Hutchison examined the question of a return to normalcy in his analysis of church trend studies covering the greater part of the twentieth century. In his opinion, the 1950s were indeed exceptional:

> [F]or the oldline churches it was the higher growth rates of the 1950s that were unusual, not the relatively lower ones that set in after the early sixties. The immediate postwar period was, for the oldline establishment, a brief shining moment that is not a particularly good benchmark for subsequent "decline."[15]

Hutchison maintains that "most of the elements of the so-called decline of Protestantism that people think of as having happened since 1960 were present and operating in the earlier 20th century, the previous 60 years."[16] In Hutchison's view, the cultural and religious hegemony once enjoyed by the mainline Protestant denominations was eroding throughout the entire twentieth century. What happened in the 1960s, he argues, was not a sharp break with the past; the conditions making for decline had been present for decades.

Hutchison's analysis reopens the question of an alleged "return to normalcy" after the 1950s. Some clarity can be achieved by carefully plotting membership trend data for selected denominations. By looking at pre–World War II figures and then following through to the 1980s, it is possible to shed some important new light on the "normalcy" issue. Figures I.1 and I.2 present membership data for the Presbyterian and Methodist denominations since the early twentieth century. They have been chosen in part because they are two of the principal mainline denominations and in part because they have had the most consistent data collection policies. Similar trends were experienced throughout the mainline denominations.

Figures I.1 and I.2 also compare denominational growth to that of the entire U.S. population. In each case a trend line has been calculated on the basis of the denomination's proportion of the total population in 1945. Using 1945 as the baseline for establishing this comparison seems reasonable on several counts. Much of the discussion about church growth has focused on the postwar years. Most of the U.S. population growth from the 1930s to the 1960s came from natural increase rather than from immigration, and 1945 represents a rough midpoint in that period. Furthermore, as indicated by infant baptism rates for the period, mainline Protestants did not differ greatly from the American average fertility rate, so it would be "normal" to expect that mainline church memberships would grow at roughly the same rate as the total population.[17]

Figure I.1 plots the trend in communicant membership of the Presbyterian Church (U.S.A.) (which was formed by merger in 1983) and its predecessor denominations. In 1945 Presbyterian membership was 2.03 percent of the total U.S. population. For purposes of long-term comparison, therefore, a "normal expectation" line representing 2.03 percent of the total U.S. population is included.

FIGURE I.1

Membership of the Presbyterian Church (U.S.A.) and Pre-Merger Denominations, Compared with U.S. Population Growth

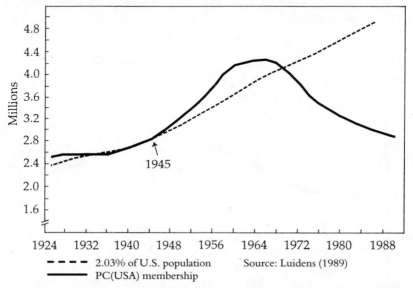

A comparison of the two trend lines indicates which periods of Presbyterian growth were "normal" relative to the U.S. population and which were not. During the 1920s and into the early 1930s, Presbyterian membership growth ran slightly ahead of the U.S. population; for the balance of the 1930s and most of the 1940s, the two sets of figures remained very close, with the Presbyterian growth rate outstripping the national one during the late 1940s. The "1950s revival" was highlighted by almost two decades during which church membership grew at a higher rate than the national population. By the early 1970s, however, an entirely new pattern emerged; relative to national growth, Presbyterians experienced extensive losses. Rather than returning to the prewar pattern, the proportion of the U.S. population affiliated with this denomination plummeted well below the prewar levels.[18]

For the Methodists (Figure I.2) the data are even more grim. Relative to the national growth figures, the "revival" that seems to have affected the Presbyterians did not occur in this church. As Figure I.2 shows, for most of the war and the early postwar period Methodist membership and U.S.

population growth rates were virtually the same. The rate of membership increase ran very slightly ahead of the general population increase for a few years during the early 1950s, but that did not last for long.

Methodist growth was sizable in absolute terms, but by 1955 it was only sufficient to *maintain* the same proportion—6.15 percent—of the nation's population that the denomination had boasted in 1945. By the late 1950s,

FIGURE I.2

Membership of the United Methodist Church and Pre-Merger Denominations, Compared with U.S. Population Growth

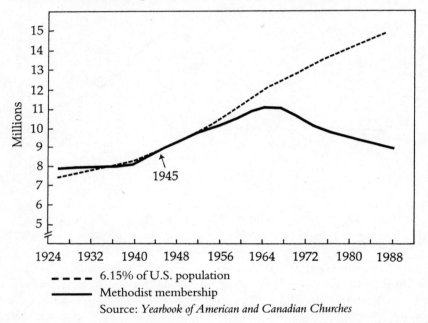

- - - - 6.15% of U.S. population

——— Methodist membership

Source: *Yearbook of American and Canadian Churches*

while the U.S. population continued to grow, Methodist growth leveled off. Even before Methodists began losing members, their share of the national population had dipped far below 6.15 percent. By the late 1960s Methodist membership figures were falling sharply while the U.S. population continued growing at a steady pace.[19]

From these figures and from comparable ones for other denominations, it is possible to draw several important conclusions. First, the downturns in membership experienced by these denominations after the 1960s *cannot* be seen as a "return to normalcy." On the contrary, the declines represent a major departure from "normal" expectations based on population growth. Second, our analysis shows that the much-touted "religious revival" of the 1950s was less extensive than many who experienced it believed. While some denominations, such as the Presbyterians and the Episcopalians, grew at rates slightly exceeding the rate of U.S. population growth during the 1950s, their growth lines descended and crossed the normal-expectation line by the early 1970s. The effects of the 1950s "revival" were fully erased by the late 1960s, leaving the extensive declines after 1970 to be explained in other ways.[20]

Greatest Change Among Young Adults

The question remains: What caused the membership figures to drop so dramatically? The Hartford Working Group on church trends made a discovery that is now beyond doubt and is central to our task in this book. They found that the downturn in membership during the 1960s and 1970s was not caused by the departure of large numbers of older adults from the churches. Rather, it was caused by the failure of the young adults within mainline Protestantism to become committed members, thereby replacing older members. This conclusion was based on the evidence of rising death rates in mainline denominations, on age-specific poll data on church attendance, and on reports of observers.[21]

Other studies have confirmed this finding. In an article published in 1976, Robert Wuthnow reviewed Gallup poll data from the 1950s through the middle 1970s, focusing on self-reported church attendance broken down by age groups. He found that the greatest decline in church attendance in the United States after 1957 was among those under 30 years of age. Wuthnow also presented data from 1959 and 1971 studies in Detroit and a 1973 study in the San Francisco Bay area. These, too, confirmed that young adults were dropping below the levels of older adults in measures of belief and attendance. The age differences were greater than any data reported in earlier nationwide polls. Wuthnow found that the most decisive cutting point for distinguishing younger adults from older adults in matters of belief and church attendance was 35 years of age.[22]

In 1981 Wade Clark Roof analyzed nationwide data from 1972 to 1976 to see which categories of adults who had been Protestants, Catholics, or Jews when they were sixteen years old now had no religious preference. Roof also found that the defections were disproportionately high among young adults. What caused the youth to leave in such numbers? He concluded that significant cultural changes had affected these religious dropouts:

> Secular influences in modern society are generally greater among the young, the educated, for men more than for women, and occur more in the West and North. Historically in the American experience these have been the collectivities most exposed to changing styles and cultural trends.[23]

In his 1976 article on religious trends, Robert Wuthnow also addressed the question of cultural changes affecting youth. He concluded that the youth counterculture of the 1960s made that decade a new period in American history. According to Wuthnow, "the downward shift in religious commitment during the 1960s was at least partly, if not largely attributable to the emergence of this [countercultural] generation unit."[24]

The finding that the mainline downturn is largely traceable to weak church commitment among young adults—and especially among the well-educated ones—has never been disputed. We accept it as proven. It is consistent with the repeated conclusions of sociologists that youth are commonly the forerunners of social and cultural change. This is especially true among college students, the most highly educated segment of young adults.[25]

During the last two decades, dozens of books have been written on the purported cultural shifts that began among college-age youth in the 1960s. One such book was Daniel Yankelovich's widely read *New Rules,* published in 1981.[26] Yankelovich points out that a large array of values centering around family, marriage, sexuality, and lifestyle shifted during the 1960s. While ably describing these value shifts, his book and many others like it do not seriously address the question of whether they were altogether new or simply the resumption of a series of long-term changes that had been briefly interrupted in the 1950s. Nonetheless, most observers of American life in the 1960s agree that significant cultural changes were taking place, and that the changes were spearheaded by the youth.

Young Adulthood: The "Impressionable Period"

Social scientists have tended to identify late adolescence and very young adulthood as the "impressionable period" during which social and political attitudes are formed. Karl Mannheim chose the years after seventeen as the impressionable period of the European youths he studied.[27] Others have picked ages ranging between fifteen and twenty-five as the most crucial ones.[28]

Young adults' impressionable openness to cultural influences means that college-age youths are much more volatile than older adults in their social, religious, and political viewpoints. They change more quickly from half-decade to half-decade. It also means that the directions of their changes are quite unpredictable. As a result, college observers have not been able to predict events on American campuses. For instance, no one predicted the radicalism of the 1960s, and no one predicted its abrupt demise in 1972. Nor are observers better equipped today to predict the course of student behavior for the next five or ten years.

To say that college students' values are subject to quick and unpredictable change is *not* the same as saying that individual college students will change *their own* views in the years after college. The latter statement has not been substantiated by researchers. On the contrary, most studies show that college students' values, including their religious beliefs, persist long after they have left academe.[29] As a result, we should expect that the liberal youths of the 1960s and 1970s will continue to be liberal for years to come—even if college students in more recent decades are different. Also, we should expect that religious values established during those college years will be crucial determiners of personal religious commitments throughout the lives of the 1960s generation.

These considerations—the attitudinal volatility of youth and the stability of values once they are established—will influence our analysis in the following chapters. Since the downturn in mainline Protestantism is mostly traceable to the actions of young adults, the problem for the church is that a large proportion of these youths from Protestant families formed no commitment to church life over a period of years.

The impermanence of value shifts among college students suggests caution in making predictions about future trends. Since past experience has been that values shift back and forth unpredictably, the safest prediction is that the future will see more changes. It is impossible to know what forms they will take. In the 1950s Liston Pope made the mistake of assuming that the "religious revival" would be permanent. In the 1990s we should not make the same mistake by assuming that the mainline Protestant churches will continue to lose members indefinitely. The most permanent residue of the low commitment of young adults during the decades after 1960 is that many of these people will probably be uncommitted their whole lives. As a result, the mainline churches may always have an underrepresentation of members born in the 1950s and 1960s.

Searching for Answers

One effort to seek answers to the dilemma of church decline was the creation of the United Presbyterian Special Committee to Study Church Membership Trends. It met from 1974 to 1976 and issued a report that was presented to the 1976 General Assembly of that denomination.

At its first meeting, the Special Committee set about its task by proposing theories about the reasons behind the decline. Members of the committee—including many veteran ministers, lay leaders, and church officials —generated dozens of insights, hunches, anecdotes, and theories. Within two hours, all four walls of the committee room were papered with newsprint crammed with notes, outlines, and cryptic summaries. There were theories about the alleged breakdowns of seminary training, of preaching, and of church leadership; there were theories about the dire effects of underfunding this or that program; there were theories about disastrous ventures into social action, about geographic and social mobility, about economic hard times; and there were theories about the challenges from the youth counterculture and from the collapse of Western civilization and the resultant growth of secularism. In sum, there was no shortage of explanations.

The task of the committee became clear. It needed to find ways to assess these explanations, rather than to seek additional ones. The committee set to work gathering evidence bearing on as many of them as possible. The result of the two-year study was that some progress was made, but the level of success was limited by the information available at the time.

Our own deliberations followed somewhat the same format. We first generated a series of possible theoretical explanations for the dramatic membership decline of the 1960s and 1970s. Then, using data collected from extensive interviews with a sample of Baby Boomers drawn from one of the mainline denominations, we endeavored to determine which, if any, of them provided the best explanation of membership decline.

Possible Explanations of Church Decline

As we noted above, the 1974–1976 Presbyterian Special Committee generated many possible explanations for church decline. One distinction was immediately obvious: most explanations were either *institutional* or *contextual* in nature. The institutional explanations were based on such things as changes in quality of denominational leadership, quality of clergy performance, effectiveness of decision-making by denominational judicatories and bureaucracies, social action programs, and so on. All of these focused on institutional resources and policies. Contextual explanations relied on trends and forces external to the denomination. They included the growth of cities, migration to the South and West, declines in birthrate, emergence of the counterculture on campuses in the 1960s, and high residential mobility.

A second dimension cut across the institutional/contextual one. It concerned whether the analysis should focus on local or national factors. These two dimensions became the basis of a fourfold typology of explanations. *National contextual explanations* reflected nationwide social changes, such as fertility trends, migration patterns, and cultural shifts. *Local contextual explanations* were related to changes in the immediate vicinity of the congregation, such as shifts in the racial or economic compositions of the local neighborhood or community. *National institutional explanations* dealt with denominational programs, decisions, and policies. *Local institutional explanations* referred to changes in congregational characteristics, such as satisfaction with leadership, amount of conflict in the congregation, and program emphases and strengths.

Researchers in the 1970s found local contextual explanations to be the most important ones in accounting for the growth or decline of specific congregations over a five- or ten-year period. In particular, neighborhood changes were powerful forces. For example, shifts in either racial or socioeconomic composition brought about church growth or decline, regardless of such local institutional factors as pastoral leadership or breadth of congregational programming. Hoge and Roozen estimated that local contextual explanations accounted for 50 to 70 percent of the growth or decline in individual congregations, with local institutional explanations accounting for the rest.[30]

Whether an entire denomination's trends could be explained by aggregating such local measures was doubtful. The decline in membership was so all-pervasive that it would be implausible to conclude that most congregations across the country were encountering the same kinds of local contextual changes. Broader issues had to be involved. Hoge and Roozen tentatively concluded that contextual explanations were more important than institutional ones for interpreting membership trends on the national level. However, they were unclear about the relative importance of local and national explanations in determining denominational growth or decline. Rather, they judged that local and national explanations might explain *different kinds* of trends.

Cultural, Structural, and Institutional Factors

More than fifteen years have passed since that earlier study, and the downturn in mainline membership still continues. In the current study we have analyzed overall denominational trends, not trends in particular congregations. Thus we have focused on national (that is, denominational) rather than local (congregational) explanations. This has left us with the single distinction between national contextual explanations and national institutional explanations. We have expanded this distinction by subdividing the contextual explanations into *cultural* and *social structural* ones.

National cultural explanations refer to changes in the meanings, values, beliefs, and sentiments held by the larger population. They include shifts in life priorities, views about one's own faith and other religions, and views on morality. National social structural explanations rely on patterns of social interaction and institutional life, for example, changing trends in gender roles, marriage rates, birthrates, and rates of participation in various forms of community life. While the distinction between cultural explanations and social structural explanations is not absolute and clear-cut, it does present a valuable rubric for distinguishing among major changes in recent U.S. history.

We therefore constructed a model of church membership decline using three explanatory categories: (1) cultural, (2) social structural, and (3) institutional. From our reading, we gathered a total of twelve factors. Each is held by some authorities to be crucial in the decline in church membership. Table I.1 presents the three categories and the purported causal factors related to each.

TABLE I.1

Hypothesized Explanatory Factors Behind Church Decline

Cultural Factors
C-1. Increase of liberal education
C-2. Rise in pluralism
C-3. Rise in individualism
C-4. Rise in privatism
C-5. Growing anti-institutionalism

Social Structural Factors
S-1. Decline of community
S-2. Changes in family life and the role of women
S-3. Decline of switching-in

Institutional Factors
I-1. Failure to be relevant
I-2. Too much social activism
I-3. Failure of leadership and programs
I-4. Loss of internal strength (Kelley's thesis)

Cultural Explanatory Factors

Cultural explanations of denominational decline focus on the dramatically shifting cultural scene of the recent past to account for changes in the levels of religious involvement in American churches.

C-1. Increase of Liberal Education. The relationship between people's intensity of religious commitment and their level of education has drawn considerable attention from researchers. It has generally been argued that there is a negative relationship between the two, with increased education resulting in growing religious relativism, skepticism, and liberalism. This is especially true among youth pursuing higher education. Robert Wuthnow has pointed to the burgeoning ranks of colleges and universities in the years since World War II to account for the declining levels of religious commitment among youth. He writes:

> In addition to dividing people on social issues and on religious attitudes, the role of higher education can also be seen in some of the longer range trends that have been mentioned. . . . For instance, . . . religious participation rates declined more rapidly in the 1960s among the better educated than in the rest of the population. The full extent of these changes can be seen more clearly in light of additional evidence from the 1980s. Between 1958 and 1982, the most serious declines in regular church attendance came about among younger people with at least some college education.[31]

In our study of Presbyterian Baby Boomers, we will look at the relationship between education, including higher education, and religious commitment.

C-2. Rise in Pluralism.   American culture has become increasingly pluralistic during the twentieth century. Increased travel and the availability of mass media are making Americans more aware of other cultures today than were their counterparts a half century ago. This awareness has inevitably had an impact on the religious community. For instance, it has introduced Presbyterians and other mainline Protestants to alternative religious experiences and interpretations. Some analysts have argued that encounters with pluralism weaken the Christian's belief in the teachings of his or her own church. The Baby Boomers have been reared in a pluralistic world; it would appear probable that this factor has played a role in molding their adult religious commitments.[32]

C-3. Rise in Individualism.   In their widely read *Habits of the Heart*, Robert Bellah and his colleagues argue that the rise of modern individualism has weakened Americans' ties to their community life. While affirming the heritage of a morally responsible individualism, the authors decry the prevailing forms of self-centered individualism that undermine "real community."[33] In the realm of religion, this self-centered individualism can result in "faith" without community. After their memorable description of "Sheilaism," the purely private faith devised by one of their interviewees, the authors conclude: "This suggests the logical possibility of over 220 million American religions, one for each of us."[34]

As the level of individualism has risen in America, many Presbyterians and other mainline Protestants have come to believe that churchgoing and church authority are optional. These traditional community-based involvements are no longer necessary for one to be a good Christian. Rather, contemporary individualism maintains that everyone has the right to maximal personal religious freedom. According to this model, Baby Boomers would find that their personal faith need not be exercised in the context of formal religious organizations. Dropping out of church would not necessarily imply a loss of Christian faith and commitment; these can be successfully maintained on an individual basis.

C-4. Rise in Privatism.   Closely related to issues of individualism are ones having to do with privatism. Bellah and his colleagues refer to the trend in American residential patterns toward "lifestyle enclaves," quasi-communities based on common socioeconomic characteristics rather than common histories. Lifestyle enclaves are retreats from public involvement; they are predicated on the assumption that individuals want privacy and can attain it best by living alongside others like themselves who are seeking the same privacy. Though people live in proximity with each other, they fail to develop interdependence or community. Rather, personal fulfillment and success are the hallmarks of privatism.[35]

In terms of religious commitments, the rising privatism has encouraged growth of a utilitarian perspective on faith and the church. Faith and church are seen to have importance to the believer to the extent that they contribute to personal success and fulfillment. In a privatist setting, *faith is good for you* because it helps you achieve your life goals. Gibson Winter and others have been concerned that the "suburbanization" of the mainline denominations, which got under way on a large scale during the 1950s when the Baby Boomers were being brought into the fold, has infused the church with these privatist goals.[36] In Winter's thinking, goals of personal advancement and success have displaced the collective purposes that have traditionally undergirded the organized church.

C-5. Growing Anti-Institutionalism. As suggested above, Wuthnow and others have pointed to the significant cultural shifts the Baby Boomers experienced during the 1960s as an explanation for their weakened religious involvements. A keynote in the counterculture movement was distrust—distrust of "anyone over 30" as well as of institutions more generally. Public opinion polls from the 1960s through the 1980s show a loss of public confidence in the leadership of most major institutions—including the church. As a result of this drop in confidence in the church, it has been argued, large numbers of believers left it.[37]

Social Structural Explanatory Factors

Explanatory Factors S-1 to S-3 hold that changes in the structure of American society during the last half century account for membership declines.

S-1. Decline of Community. During the 1920s and 1930s, Robert and Helen Merrill Lynd reported on life in "Middletown"—Muncie, Indiana.[38] In *All Faithful People*, their 1978 follow-up study of Middletown, Theodore Caplow, Howard Bahr, Bruce Chadwick, and others found no significant lessening of church involvement in comparison with that reported by the Lynds. However, they did find a significant shift away from the intolerance and rigidity that reinforced denominational and congregational loyalties during the earlier period. "On the one hand, Middletown people are extraordinarily attached to their faith; on the other hand, they are reluctant to impose it on others or even to assert that it ought to be imposed."[39]

This openness to the differences that formerly divided society the strata of society was broadly apparent in the Middletown of the 1970s. The authors describe it as a "new tolerance":

Elsewhere [in *All Faithful People*] we discuss the "new tolerance" in Middletown. A blurring of the sharp social boundaries that formerly divided the population into fairly homogeneous segments (business-class and working-class, Protestant and Catholic, upper income and lower income) is apparent in many aspects of community life.[40]

This "blurring of the sharp social boundaries" has tended to undermine the cohesiveness of the local community. This is because the "new tolerance" takes the form of greater isolation among the believers, each pursuing his or her own vision of truth:

> Devout Christians in Middletown, like happily married couples there, regard themselves as exceptional: surrounded by people just like themselves, they think they stand quite alone. This almost universal illusion explains, at least in part, why Middletown people are so reluctant to lay down the law or to expound the prophets for the benefit of their neighbors. In this sense, there is less community in Middletown today than there was in 1924 or in 1890, when it was customary for respectable people to perceive themselves as participating in a moral consensus.[41]

Finding themselves with fewer and fewer corporate allegiances, the Middletowners of today lack a model for social boundary-setting.

One symptom of the decline in the constraining role of local communities has been the major shift, since World War II, in acceptable Sunday behavior. The demise of Sabbatarianism is used by Benton Johnson as a sign of the erosion of traditional community values and ties.[42] The resulting tendency for individuals to go their own way, without the constraining influence of the church, further erodes the bonds of community. This pattern has been especially noted among the middle- and upper-middle class population that comprise the heart of the mainline Protestant denominations.

S-2. Changes in Family Life and the Role of Women.   In the recent past, the mainline churches could count on their young adults—who had left the church at the time of college or departure from home—returning to the fold in their early twenties, when they sought marriage for themselves and then baptism for their children. The establishment of a family brought with it a return to the church. Since the 1950s, however, changes of historic proportions have taken place in the structure of the family and the position of women. These structural changes—such as cohabitation of unmarried people, rising age of marriage, delay of first childbirth, decreasing numbers of children, and rising divorce rates—have had a pronounced impact on church involvement. The conventional life course has been disrupted: people are more reluctant to return to the ecclesiastical fold after experiencing longer years of absence; the ambivalence people feel because of their unconventional marriage patterns have made church participation awkward for many; and the reduction in number of children and the delay in bearing them have worked to diminish the attractiveness of church involvement for many others.

Parallel to changes in family patterns have been changes in women's roles. As more and more women become part of the workforce, fewer are available for the voluntary activities on which the churches have relied to maintain their programs. Furthermore, with the rise of the feminist movement in the 1970s, the teachings of the church and its language for worship have been widely criticized for being patriarchal. Most mainline denominations have reformed their rules and language in response to the critique, but no doubt the issue has caused some decline in church commitment.

S-3. Decline of Switching-In. In the mid-1960s, Rodney Stark and Charles Glock analyzed patterns of denominational switching (movement from one denomination to another). They found in a nationwide survey that "denominational changes among American Protestants follow a pattern of movement to churches with more liberal, modernized theologies and away from churches that are still foursquare for traditional orthodoxy."[43] In such a milieu, the more liberal mainline churches—including the Presbyterian Church—were growing at the expense of the more conservative churches.

However, subsequent studies have found less evidence of this source of migration into the mainline. In 1987 Wade Clark Roof and William McKinney reviewed recent data on switchers and came to the following conclusion:

> All evidence points to less upward switching, or conservative-to-liberal transfer of religious membership, now than in the past. Net gains resulting from switching for liberal Protestants are not as marked today as they were in previous decades; there seems to have been a falloff in what had once been an important source of their growth during the 1950s and 1960s.[44]

The pattern of upward switching, which reflected the upward economic mobility of the 1950s and 1960s, no longer prevails. In the past two decades the mainline churches have not been the recipients of much in-migration from conservative denominations. This drop in switching-in would be particularly evident among the young adults who are making their church membership choices.

Institutional Explanatory Factors

Institutional explanations of membership decline are quite varied. We have grouped them in four categories.

I-1. Failure to Be Relevant. During the late 1960s some church leaders predicted that the mainline churches would lose their youth unless they altered their teachings and program priorities to make them more "relevant" to the challenges of the modern world. Writing in 1967, William F. Starr observed that many students on college campuses had abandoned "the old 'church-on-Sunday-golden-rule-*status-quo*' Christianity." Instead, they were following the new breed of radical leaders in the churches who were involved in "civil rights, the war in Vietnam, the problems of poverty and the Negro ghetto," and who refused to reinforce "childish ideas about the church as a safe refuge from the world."[45] A similar sentiment was expressed in a communication from a student group addressed to the General Assembly of the Presbyterian Church U.S. in 1970. "We demand the church change," it proclaimed, "or it will be buried in future decades by all youth who have completely given up on the church."[46]

I-2. Too Much Social Activism.   Explanatory Factor I-2 is virtually the opposite of Factor I-1. Its advocates explain church decline as a negative reaction to an excessive denominational emphasis on radical social programs. In a widely read book published in 1969, Jeffrey Hadden warned of a "gathering storm in the churches" brought on by the political activism of a "new breed" of radical clergy in the face of mounting resistance from a laity that was preponderantly conservative.[47] It was Hadden's contention that the increasing political involvement of mainline pastors—especially those who were engaged in "specialized ministries" such as the campus pastorate—jeopardized the harmony of their denominations and therefore threatened their membership bases.[48]

Since Hadden's analysis, mainline denominational leaders have frequently been accused of being excessively concerned with social action projects. For instance, countless overtures to Presbyterian General Assemblies and letters to the editor of *Presbyterian Survey* have explained the denomination's membership loss as a negative reaction to the liberal political preoccupations of many church leaders. Sociologist Peter Berger, for example, has written that "the lay people most annoyed" with these preoccupations "just quietly stole away, taking themselves (and, not unimportant, their financial support) elsewhere."[49]

I-3. Failure of Leadership and Programs.   A theory often heard in church circles blames the decline on a failure of denominational leadership and program emphases. For example, some contend that denominational leaders are out of touch with their membership and thus are unable to generate a sense of denominational identity or to instill denominational loyalty. Current members become disillusioned and potential members are turned off; decline follows.[50]

Others contend that there was a grave failure during the postwar decades in the mainline denominations' programs, especially those designed for young people. In their opinion, the youth did not receive proper religious training, with the result that they failed to develop any long-term commitments to the church, and ultimately left.

I-4. Loss of Internal Strength (Kelley's Thesis). Dean Kelley's institutional explanation of the decline of the liberal Protestant denominations is the most influential one yet advanced, and it has stimulated a great deal of debate. Unlike the other institutional theories, which focus on denominational policies and programs, his theory focuses on the character of religious life at the level of the local church.

Kelley's 1972 book, *Why Conservative Churches Are Growing,* begins by documenting the fact that many theologically conservative Protestant denominations have continued to add members even while the mainline, and more liberal, denominations have suffered losses. He then divides churches (congregations and denominations) into two categories, the "strong" and the "weak." Strong churches grow, he argues, and weak churches decline. Strong churches (1) are characterized by a total, closed belief system that is deemed sufficient for all purposes and needs no revision. They (2) have a distinctive code of conduct that sets their members apart from nonmembers. They (3) exercise a strict discipline over their members in matters of belief and practice. They (4) demand a high commitment of time and energy from their members. Finally, they (5) maintain a missionary zeal and are eager to tell the good news to all persons. Weak churches, by contrast, are characterized by relativism, permissiveness, and individualism in matters of belief; tolerance of internal diversity and pluralism; lack of enforcement of doctrinal or behavior standards; tolerance of a limited commitment to the church; little effective sharing of convictions or spiritual insights within the church; and a preference for dialogue with outsiders rather than attempts to convert them.

Kelley bases his argument on the assumption that people are attracted to religious groups because they want compelling and clear-cut answers to questions about the meaning of human existence, including why we are here, how we should live, and what our destinies are. Churches that unequivocally provide answers to these questions and require a regime of conduct that brings believers together into a tight-knit fellowship of spiritual nurture will attract new members and retain those they already have. On the other hand, churches that preach an uncertain message, fail to attend to their members' spiritual needs, allow members to decide for themselves how they will live, and make few attempts to convert others not only will fail to attract converts, also will generate a high level of apathy within their own ranks. They are prime candidates for membership loss. According to Kelley, America's mainline Protestant churches have become weak, whereas most of its conservative churches remain strong. The former decline, the latter grow.

We will assess these cultural, structural, and institutional explanations for mainline Protestant membership losses in the following chapters. While not every explanatory factor will be fully evaluated, our evidence will speak to many of them. Before presenting in detail the methodology and findings of our study, let us listen to the voices of four of the Baby Boomers whom we interviewed in depth. Their different spiritual journeys are broadly representative of the diverse paths our interviewees have taken since they were confirmed as Presbyterians during the 1960s.

Chapter 1

Four Voices

In matters of religious faith our Baby Boom interviewees range all the way from orthodox Christians who are deeply involved in church life to outright skeptics who rarely if ever attend church. Some belong to fundamentalist churches, many more belong to mainline churches, a few have become Roman Catholics or Jehovah's Witnesses, and a large number claim no church affiliation at all.

In this chapter we will hear the stories of four of the people we interviewed in depth. Marcia Wilson is an active Presbyterian, Wayne Sanders has become a fundamentalist, Ann Brooks is a church dropout who is thinking about returning, and Calvin Caletti is an agnostic. These are not their real names, of course. We have obscured their identities by giving them new names and by altering some of the details of their lives. But we have changed nothing essential in the stories they told us, and we have used their exact words to bring out the highlights of their spiritual journeys. We will revisit each of these four at later points in the book and we will introduce a few other people by name along the way.

Marcia Wilson

Marcia Wilson attends Bryan Memorial Presbyterian Church every Sunday. As she sits in the well-furnished living room of her spacious house in San Antonio she recalls the joy she experienced when she first heard

Jack Earl, the minister, preach not long after she and her husband moved to Texas two years ago. "I remember thinking, 'Holy cow, where did this guy come from?' I just kept going back and going back, and he just got better and better."

Marcia has had a keen interest in religion for as long as she can remember. Her father, an independent businessman, was a Presbyterian deacon; her mother, a schoolteacher turned housewife, was active in the women's Bible and missionary circles. Marcia grew up in Masonville, one of North Carolina's many small cities, where her parents spent all their adult lives. She was devoted to them, and especially to her mother, who was "a powerful, kind, giving woman. Every time somebody was sick, my mother was there with food." For Marcia the Presbyterian Church was an extension of her warm and happy family. "I always had the special sense," she remembers, "that in my church there were adults that cared about me, watched over me, and loved me."

Last year, when she was thirty-eight, Marcia experienced that love once again, when she returned to Masonville for her mother's funeral. "My old friends, my family's friends were *all* right there for me. It was an incredible shock," she exclaimed, to "go into that funeral home and in walked *fifty* people from my church! That church was there, just like an anchor waiting for me and supporting me." Marcia has now found a new circle of Christian friends in Texas. Although she had only lived in San Antonio five months when her mother died, the women of her Bible study group brought dinner to her house every night for three weeks. And when she returned from her mother's funeral they were all at the airport to meet her.

As a child, Marcia learned to serve others as well as to be served. "To whom much is given, much is required," was her mother's guiding maxim. "My mother thought I had this *talent* for the piano and I needed to use it on Sunday morning for the glory of God, and I was right there every Sunday morning playing the hymns whether I wanted to or not." She also has memories of her parents discussing church affairs. She recalls vividly their debating whether it was right to spend money on a new church building when "there were starving people in Masonville." Her parents' concern for starving people was the main reason Marcia decided, at fifteen, to become a social worker. "I wanted to feed the hungry or place adopted children."

At college, Marcia found the required pre–social work courses "kind of fluffy," so she decided to become a schoolteacher instead. She had always made good grades and loved her studies and she now resolved to use her "fairly rare gift of learning as a form of social work to influence people's lives." After two years in the classroom, Marcia's father convinced her that her real calling was the law. On completing an intensive course of study she launched a successful career as a paralegal in Winston-Salem. There she met Randy, her future husband, a rapidly rising bank manager several years older than she. They were married when Marcia was thirty-one. She continued working after their two children were born, but when the bank gave Randy a substantial salary increase and transferred him to San Antonio Marcia resolved to quit work and devote her time to caregiving. Her career was exciting and lucrative, but "Being a mother and a wife is just the most wonderful role I've had so far. I thank Randy every week for putting us in a situation that I can stay at home."

Unlike others of her generation, Marcia did not drop out of church after high school and she never rebelled against her religious upbringing. Instead, her interest in the Bible increased. She had greatly enjoyed the Bible stories that her mother and Sunday school teachers had told her. She had even complained to her minister about the new curriculum her denomination adopted when she was fourteen because it had "*no* emphasis on the Bible." At college Marcia resumed her study of scripture and as a result, her interest in it took an intellectual turn. In San Antonio she brings a writing pad to church to take notes on Jack Earl's sermons and she is thinking seriously about attending seminary when her husband retires to North Carolina in fifteen years.

Marcia's faith has also grown deeper over the years. At college she experienced "a very quiet, intellectual sort of Nicodemus rebirth," thanks in part to the impressive scholarship and Christian faith of the "incredibly powerful" woman who taught the Old Testament survey course. Not long after graduation Marcia joined an informal Bible study group and at twenty-four she became a Young Life leader. In Young Life the real heart of the Christian message finally became clear to her. "It's a simple message that there is a God and He had a son who died for you and if you believe in Him you will live forever." Much as she loved her home church in Masonville, she now perceives that it failed to emphasize this simple message or make its meaning clear to young people.

Marcia believes that Masonville Presbyterian Church is typical in this respect. Most of her Young Life teenagers "came from churchgoing families in wonderful, healthy churches, but a lot of these kids just somehow didn't understand" what it means to be a Christian. Marcia's husband, Randy, does not understand, nor did most of her religion teachers at college. Randy was raised a Methodist, attends Bryan Memorial with her every Sunday, and thinks Jack Earl "is the coolest guy in the world," but he cannot make that simple affirmation of faith. Marcia did arrange, however, for Louise, Randy's twenty-one-year-old daughter by a previous marriage, to become involved with Young Life. Louise accepted Christ and will be leaving San Antonio soon for a year of missionary work in Africa with an interdenominational agency.

Today the real core of Marcia's religious life is her women's Bible study group, which meets for three hours every Tuesday morning. Being involved with it "is probably spiritually the single greatest thing that ever happened to me." She is in awe of the elderly woman who leads the group. "She's *unbelievable*. She knows the Bible like you've never seen in your life." Marcia is equally impressed with the members of the group, most of whom are about her age. They are all "dedicated mothers and dedicated wives and they are working Christians, daily Christians."

Marcia is firm in her conviction that to be a Christian means accepting Christ as one's savior, but everything else about religion "gets gray after that" for her and depends on how one interprets scripture. She believes that Christianity is truer than other religions, but she rejects the position that everyone is lost who dies without accepting Christ. She believes "that God is a kind, loving God, and that Muslims and Buddhists who are good people will have some salvation," though she does not know what sort of salvation that might be.

Marcia's views on controversial social issues are neither stereotypically conservative nor liberal. Ten years ago she left a Presbyterian church in Winston-Salem because the minister "would look at you like you couldn't possibly be a Christian and be pro-choice" on the abortion issue. "I could never have an abortion," Marcia explains, but "these fundamental Christian types, I just think they're sinning in a whole 'nother way, and what the Catholic Church has done recently on abortion is just sickening to me." She thinks it was "pretty neat" that Bryan Memorial's session voted to oppose arming the Nicaraguan Contras, and she is emphatically against a constitutional amendment banning flag burning. On the other hand, she generally supports Republican positions on economic issues, and she has "this huge problem" with the ordination of homosexuals because her study of the Bible has convinced her that "this is not what the Lord would have in mind."

Although Marcia has absorbed much of her mother's piety, even before adolescence Marcia had a mind of her own. At eleven she successfully challenged her mother's rule against attending movies on Sunday afternoons. "I really sort of won the argument with her about the whole issue of the Sabbath because I began to look at scripture and try to think that through for myself." Her reading of the Bible convinced her that "the Lord would really not have a problem with my going to see a healthy movie on Sunday afternoon as a form of relaxing. I didn't see any difference between that and sitting out on the front porch all Sunday afternoon like my mother's family did."

Marcia's mother would never have left the Presbyterian Church, but Marcia did leave it for a time. For her, quality of sermons and style of worship are more important than denomination. Marcia could never be a Roman Catholic, she finds charismatic worship services "just *offensive*," and she has "a whole lot of problems with what the Southern Baptist Convention stands for"; but she could be an Episcopalian and she joined her husband's Methodist church in Winston-Salem after they were married.

"It almost killed my mother," she jokes. "I left the Presbyterian Church and the Junior League in the same year, and I had to have a baby to make her happy!"

In San Antonio Marcia is a Presbyterian again only because she is enthralled with Jack Earl's preaching, which she discovered in the course of sampling the city's Protestant worship services. At first, she and her husband attended Oak Park Presbyterian Church, which is much closer to her own suburban neighborhood. Her young daughters attend preschool there and Marcia participates in the parents' support group, but she did not join Oak Park Church because "from the pulpit the minister just does not do it for me." Moreover, despite her enthusiasm for Jack Earl, Marcia is not entirely happy with Bryan Memorial Church. For one thing, "You've got to stand up and turn around halfway through the service and shake a bunch of people's hands. I just *hate* all that and my husband *despises* it." For another, she is under pressure to become involved in one of Bryan Memorial's women's circles. "I just don't want to be in a circle—and my mother would just be horrified at that! I *have* a Bible study group," she explains. Marcia's mother might also be horrified to learn that this Bible study group is not affiliated with any church and accepts members from all denominations. In matters of religion, Marcia picks and chooses in a way her mother never did.

Still, Marcia's faith is based largely on that of her parents and her church in Masonville. When she was very young she angered her mother by saying that she wanted to join the Episcopal church because that was where most of her friends went. Her mother made it clear to Marcia that one does not choose a church for that sort of reason. This response convinced Marcia that a decision to affiliate with a church must be spiritually based, a conviction that reinforced her decision not to join the fashionable Oak Park Presbyterian Church in San Antonio. "I felt like a lot of the people I know that go there, go because it's real convenient, which doesn't seem like a particularly compelling reason to go to a church." It is neither convenient nor fashionable to attend Bryan Memorial. The church building, though imposing in appearance, is old and is located in a decaying section of the city four miles away, and most of the members are elderly.

Now that her daughters are in preschool and she has more time on her hands, Marcia has found a new way to be of service. When school starts in the fall she and some of the women in her Bible study group will begin working in a soup kitchen. "It's kind of coming full circle to that thing that my mother instilled in me," she explains: " 'To whom much is given, much is required,' helping other people and being interested in social work."

Wayne Sanders

Wayne Sanders divides his life into two chapters. The first, which lasted until he was thirty, is "a pre-Christ chapter that included a lot of intentional sin and one-track mindedness toward sin." The second, his "after Christ" chapter, began one night about ten years ago when he accepted "the simple message of the gospel" while watching Billy Graham on television. His life underwent an immediate change. He gave up alcohol, marijuana, and extramarital sex, and began searching for an appropriate church to attend. His life since then has involved a "growing process of being more selfless and willing to see the needs of others and hear God and what He wants."

Wayne had not been attending church regularly when he accepted Christ. He and Vicki, his second wife, had occasionally visited a Presbyterian church in their rapidly growing community in the greater Washington, D.C., area, but after his conversion Wayne realized that this church did not call people to Christ. "Once I *knew* in my heart what the *truth* was, I never thought twice about leaving the Presbyterian church, because I never heard that there." After a period of shopping around, he and Vicki joined Wildwood Christian Fellowship, a nondenominational church he describes as "very fundamental and evangelical in nature." It is also "a friendly, inviting place. It's not austere and it doesn't look like a place that you have to be 'somebody different' to go to." Wayne, Vicki, and their two children are faithful attenders.

Wildwood was growing quickly when they joined and it is still growing. Today it has 2,000 members, operates a fleet of buses to bring children to Sunday school, and holds three services on Sunday. At most services there is standing room only, for many people attend who have not yet joined. The church is housed in a large, plain concrete block building adjacent to a 300-car parking lot. Two huge flags, one American and the other Christian, tower above the entrance to the building.

For a number of years now, much of Wayne's busy life has centered about his church. In addition to his long-term job as manager of a firm that repairs photocopy machines, he serves as one of Wildwood's four paid lay ministers. Each minister is assigned a sector of the community and responsibility for 200 families. On Mondays they receive computer printouts identifying the people to be visited that week. Wayne is very happy with his church and thrilled with the spiritual progress he has made over the last decade. "I'm just trying to be *obedient*," he explains, "and I think that if somebody is, they will experience the same joys and pleasures and blessings that I have."

Before his conversion, Wayne's life was neither joyous nor blessed. Shortly before graduating from junior college, he married his first wife, a woman with no religious interests. Their relationship was shaky almost from the beginning and lasted only three years. At twenty-eight, divorced and childless, he married Vicki, who had been raised a Baptist but seldom attended church. Wayne had high hopes for his new marriage, but within a year he realized that it was not going well, and he began reflecting on the course of his life. "After one marriage of making certain mistakes, here's the second marriage and I'm going through the same cycles, finding myself at the same dead-end spots that were basically caused by *me*. Did I want to go through life making these same mistakes over and over?" Any talk of having children was especially disturbing. "What kind of dad would I be?" he wondered. "I decided that it was going to be really bad if something didn't happen."

After several months of private anguish, an acquaintance at work began talking to Wayne "about spiritual things," and he was ready to listen. He had already identified his major shortcomings, but he had not found the answer to "Where do you go from here?" He "sensed down deep" that what his friend told him "was probably more truth than anything I had ever heard in my life." A week later he accepted Christ as his savior. "Vicki thought I was crazy," he remembers with amusement. "All she pictured were these religious fanatics and she didn't want to become one of them. She had a real problem for about a month or two." Before long, however, Vicki also found the Lord.

Looking back, Wayne believes his desire to make his new marriage work made it easy for him "to hear that somebody else gave himself for me and died on the cross. That whole story made a lot of sense because of my own willingness to see what selflessness was all about." When he accepted Christ he found it surprisingly easy to give up his selfish ways. Earlier, despite his sense that his life was in disarray, he had not really wanted to change, but in converting, "all of a sudden you just have this *willingness* to do it where before it's a grudging thing." The "hardness of heart that comes from sin" vanished. "Sin seems fun for a season, but it didn't do anything but *ruin* my life." Sexual sin had a special appeal for Wayne and he is still tempted to take a "second look" at an attractive woman. He believes that sex is a "*huge issue*, probably the *bottom line* in most people's hearts and minds when you talk about religion—and I'm not talking about 'the Lord,' I'm just talking about church in general." But for Wayne the pleasures of sexual sin pale in comparison to the joy of knowing that his "name is written in the Lamb's book of life. You know what your future is, and it's a hope that transcends *any* difficulty down here."

Since accepting Christ and joining Wildwood Fellowship, Wayne has become more conservative than he used to be. In addition to opposing drug use and extramarital sex, he now opposes abortion. He and Vicki send their children to a Christian school. They would immediately leave a church that "condoned homosexuality or had a pastor that's homosexual." Although financial pressures make it necessary for Vicki to continue working at her job as a program analyst, he believes it best for mothers with small children to stay at home. He does not know what stands on social issues the Presbyterian Church (U.S.A.) has taken or whether the denomination is affiliated with the National Council of Churches, but his pastor has said enough about the Council to convince Wayne that it promotes "a more liberal view than I'm ready to accept."

Now that he has a new perspective on his life, Wayne knows why things had gone wrong for him. He had believed in God and even "prayed to Him at times of real trouble," but his faith "wasn't an internal thing" and had actually grown weaker over the years. As for the way he was brought up, "I think it was wrong. I think a lot of areas were neglected and left undone." His mother attended a Presbyterian church and saw to it that Wayne went to Sunday school and church, but "I think it hurt that my dad wasn't involved, wasn't excited about spiritual issues. He wouldn't talk openly about the Lord." Moreover, even his mother seemed lukewarm and confused about religion. "I can remember I asked my mother, 'What's life all about?' and she didn't have any *answers* for me and I had a hard time accepting all that because she'd gone to church all these years, sang in the choir." To complicate matters, she was an alcoholic and she and his father often quarreled in front of Wayne and his sisters. "I lived through a lot more arguing than I would ever like to see my child go through. Open cussing. The Lord's name was used in vain around the house many times. Faith has to be lived out every day or it doesn't make any sense to a kid. It was all so contradictory." Wayne does not entirely condemn his parents, however. "I'd be pretty naive to think they didn't have their own problems in a deeper fashion than I'll ever know."

He does not entirely condemn his boyhood Presbyterian church either. Located in a prestigious neighborhood in the Washington area, it had a large congregation and a friendly pastor. "I'm sure this pastor tried to be effective in ministering to people," Wayne recalls, but "all I can remember is a very structured, dry, lifeless kind of service" that never "really approached the *issues of life*, the whole deep-seated needs and sins of people. I mean, how can my mom go to a church and be an alcoholic for so many years and never feel much guilt about that? The pastor has to be willing to say, 'If you've got an alcohol problem, meet me after church.'" Wayne's Presbyterian pastor never said such things from the pulpit.

Jim McCray is Wayne's pastor now, and Wayne admires Jim very much. Jim founded Wildwood Fellowship and has put his stamp on every aspect of its ministry. Wayne describes him as "a very pulling, drawing type personality, just an open, honest guy with a certain charisma." Jim has built a friendly, "nurturing, caring church" in an area with many rootless government and corporate employees who are subject to transfer with little notice. Jim's sermons are "Word-oriented, down-to-earth," with a lot of practical advice for everyday living. Wayne especially appreciates Jim's nonjudgmental but life-changing approach to the sins and failures of people's lives. "We have a very *forgiving* congregation. Most of the time people walk in there and they don't feel judged. Jim doesn't constantly beat someone on the head and say, 'You're a sinner, you're a sinner, you're a sinner.' Instead, Jim says, 'If you're here, this is where you need to get and this is how we need to get there.' We'll hear a message that says, 'Look, you have this problem, you come to me and I'll get you some help. We'll work this thing out.'" Wildwood employs a full-time Christian psychologist to help people resolve their personal problems.

No one in Wayne's family was admirable enough in his estimation to serve as a model for his own life, and nothing he experienced at his Presbyterian church provided him with the resources to be an effective adult. Wildwood Christian Fellowship has "something really going on to help people know God and to make a difference in their lives." What Wayne has found in his very conservative brand of Christianity is both a model for living and the power to follow it, and he is seeing to it that his children will follow it as well. Although he has abandoned Presbyterianism, Wayne's break with his past is actually a return to a revitalized version of that past as conveyed to him dimly at Sunday school and from the pulpit when he was a boy. Wayne knew enough about God and Jesus, selflessness and self-control to be dissatisfied with his life and to be receptive to a Christian diagnosis of the source of his dissatisfaction. What his new faith showed him was *how* to change his life.

Ann Brooks

When it comes to religion, Ann Brooks is not sure what she believes. "I don't know if I have ever sat down and analyzed my religious thoughts that deeply," she confesses. "I've never really been compelled to say to myself, 'Well, this is it, this is what I believe.'" Ann has always thought that God exists, but she has no conception of what God is like and no opinion on which religion comes closest to having a true understanding of God. Over the years, her interest in religion has waxed and waned. During her teens she prayed a lot and went to church regularly. Since then she has dropped out of church twice, once when she went away to college and again soon after the birth of her second child six years ago. Now thirty-seven and unchurched, Ann describes herself as a "nominal Presbyterian who's married to a disaffected Catholic."

Ann and her husband have not entirely rejected what they were taught as children. Ann considers herself "spiritual, not anti-religious," but she and Dave are too busy to participate actively in church life. Dave's career as a high school principal takes him away from home several nights a week and sometimes on Saturdays. Sunday is the only day he can count on spending with Ann and their two children. Ann's career as special education teacher at Cass Elementary School leaves her little time for outside activities. In fact, one reason she dropped out of church six years ago was to have more time to be with Stephanie, her infant daughter.

As she makes coffee in the kitchen of her two-story house in Saginaw, Michigan, Ann thinks back to her Presbyterian girlhood in Kalamazoo. Both her parents taught Sunday school and her father was a deacon. "We enjoyed going to church and having Sundays together as a family," she recalls. Ann's mother, who was brought up in a strict Baptist family in Cleveland, "was very, very well studied in the Bible" and read books about religion as well. "That need for going to church has always been a part of my mom." Whenever Ann had a question about religion she asked her mother, not her father. Although he was as active in church as her mother, Ann cannot recall his ever saying anything about his faith. "I honestly don't know if I could tell you what my dad is like religiously," she remarks with a puzzled frown. Ann thinks he was brought up as a Methodist, but other than that, "I don't know anything about his religious background at all." Nor does she know when and why he and her mother became Presbyterians or why they stopped attending church on a regular basis after her youngest sister left home.

Although Ann liked Sunday school, when she was very young the worship services bored her. As she grew older, she came to appreciate the sermons preached by her minister, Marshall Palmer, a man of great serenity who seemed to radiate an air of comfort and assurance. At fourteen she joined the choir and learned to love the melodious anthems they sang at Sunday worship. To this day her ideal church service would feature stately music, a dignified liturgy, and a sermon by someone like Marshall Palmer.

Despite the quickening of her religious interest during adolescence, Ann felt no need for organized religion while attending Bynum College, a small, high-quality liberal arts school that was once affiliated with the Presbyterian Church. "I wasn't involved in religious activities at all in college," she says with a wry smile. For one thing, her college friends did not seem interested in religion. For another, she found the college chaplain a poor substitute for her own minister. She took a course in Asian religions because she was "curious to see if their God was the same as our God," but she remembers very little of what she learned.

Ann has had two experiences in her life that she identifies as spiritual. The first took place at seventeen in a funeral home as she stood alone beside the coffin of her grandfather. She sensed that his soul had left his body and she heard a choir of angels singing a majestic anthem just above the coffin. It was a vivid experience, but she is reluctant to draw any firm conclusions from it. "It just happened," she says with a shrug, "and I don't know what it meant."

Ann's second experience occurred many years later while she was teaching school. It, too, involved a death. A pet dove, which her third grade class was caring for, died as she was feeding it at school one Saturday morning when no one was around. "It was really weird. I thought I could feel something being lifted right up out of that bird. It was like its soul went 'just like that.' " The following Monday, with the schoolchildren present, Ann conducted a funeral service for the dove and buried it in a shallow grave outside the classroom.

These two experiences reinforced her surmise that body and soul are separate and that when life ends "the soul goes somewhere." On the rare occasions when she thinks about the fate of the soul, "just the word 'peace' comes to my mind, and it always has." As for where the soul might go, she is certain that hell does not exist, but she is not certain about heaven and she suspects that even in the afterlife she may never learn what God is like. "Sometimes I think maybe we're not meant to know."

To Ann, religious truth is what seems subjectively plausible and agreeable rather than what can be demonstrated objectively. "You get into a discussion about religion with some people and they think they're right, and that bothers me," she complains. "My gut feeling is that religion is an individual thing. I don't think another person can tell somebody else how to feel." One thing that irritated her about the church she left six years ago was the way the pastor and his wife associated their pet projects with God's will. Ann sometimes volunteered to do things for her church, but she resented being told that " 'God wants you to do this.' I just think that's terrible. I'm not baking cookies for God. I'm baking cookies for the church. And the other thing that turns me off," she says with rising irritation, "is when people come to your house and try to peddle their religion. I tell 'em, 'Go back to your church. Let people come to you instead of you coming to them!' Maybe it's the pushiness that bugs me."

Ann gives more thought to the moral teachings of religion than she gives to questions about God or the ultimate meaning of life. In her opinion, "Whatever religion you have there's always a striving there for good, to be as good a person as you can be." She is very sensitive to anything about organized religion that smacks of hypocrisy. The one vivid, and negative, memory she has of her college chaplain is that he "dated this wild-looking blonde." She liked the minister at Parkview Presbyterian Church in Grand Rapids, which she and Dave joined not long after they were married, but she did not like his successors. It was bad enough that one of them interpreted the Bible more literally than she preferred, but it was even worse that he seduced a church secretary. Her tone turns cynical as she remembers that "this was the same pastor whose wife used to call me and say, 'Why aren't you doing this or that thing for God?' " With bitter amusement she recalls two more incidents of moral failure. One minister stole money from the church, and his successor, a woman, was divorced less than a year after the church had staged an elaborate wedding for her. In view of the church's emphasis on morality, "the degree of hypocrisy just doesn't seem to fit." Disgust with hypocrisy is the second reason she quit the church six years ago.

Despite Ann's jaded view of ministers, she and Dave have recently begun shopping around for a church to join in Saginaw, where they have lived for four and a half years. On Sundays whenever their busy schedule permits, they drop in for worship somewhere. Ann is looking for a minister like Marshall Palmer and for an atmosphere in which she can "feel real comfortable and not pressured." "We like to go for a while to one church," she reports, "to just kind of feel it out, to see what feels comfortable to us." One reason Ann and Dave are visiting churches is that they have always agreed the children should have a religious education. Kevin is now nine and Stephanie is six. What precipitated the present search, however, is that Kevin has recently been asking Ann pointed questions about religion, thanks to the influence of Audrey, a girl his age who has firm opinions about Christianity. Ann wishes she could refer Kevin's questions to her mother, because Ann does not know the Bible well, but her mother has moved to Minnesota. She wants her children exposed to a broader range of opinions than those Audrey has.

Audrey is the oldest daughter of a couple with whom the Brooks jointly hired a child-care worker last year to sit with their children on weekday afternoons after school. Ann knew Audrey's parents were members of the Church of God, but she had no idea that Audrey would try to impose her religious views on the other two children. "I've started calling her 'mini-missionary,'" Ann says with exasperation. "I think all last year she tried to convert Kevin." Audrey even tried to persuade him not to go trick-or-treating because she believes Halloween is the work of the devil. Ann respects Audrey's right to believe anything she wants, but she does object to Audrey's imposing her beliefs on Kevin and Stephanie. When Kevin asks her about Audrey's views on a subject, Ann replies, "Well, some people do believe that, you know, and that's fine for them to believe that," but she never tells him that Audrey's beliefs are wrong. She lets the children know what her own views are, but she does not claim that they are the right views. Ann wants the children "to have whatever perspective fits them."

Audrey's perspective might have fit Kevin and Stephanie very well if Ann had found the Church of God congenial. A few months ago, the Brookses accepted an invitation to attend Audrey's church on its annual Welcome Neighbor Sunday. "The kids loved it there," Ann admits. "They did all sorts of art projects and coloring things and they were really wowed by the whole experience." But Ann soon discovered that Audrey's church expects adults with young children to participate in a Bible study group during the Sunday school hour. Since she has always resisted being "hauled in" to activities at church, she and her family did not return to the Church of God. Ann will never actively impose her own religious perspective on the children, but she will not help them find a perspective that fits them unless it fits her as well.

Meanwhile, Ann has not had much luck finding a congenial church. Among the ones she and Dave have visited to date, Elmira Street United

Church of Christ appeals to her the most. Ann liked the music and the sermon the Sunday they attended, but she was put off when the minister announced their presence to the congregation. "We sort of came in and sat in the back and were real quiet. And then the minister says, 'Oh, I see the Brooks are here,' and everybody turns around and looks. It's like, 'Oh boy, now they're going to come to our church and let's see what we can get them to do.' And that's not what we wanted." Dave's job makes him too well known in Saginaw for the Brookses to escape notice when they visit a church. Ann is so afraid of being put under pressure to get involved in church work that she is reluctant to return to the church she likes best.

Ann may soon overcome her reluctance. A few weeks ago, while the family was attending the funeral of Dave's grandfather, she discovered that Audrey had convinced Kevin and Stephanie that heaven and hell are real places. The children wanted to see the corpse and wanted to know why it was in the casket instead of in heaven. Ann responded as well as she could, but she did so with no real conviction or persuasive power. As she struggled for words, the thought struck her once again that the children needed to go to Sunday school. "So we'd better get going!" she exclaims with an air of determination.

Calvin Caletti

Calvin's mother was the Presbyterian in the family. It was she who named him Calvin and took him and his sister to Sunday school and church every week when they were small, and it was she who persuaded his father to go with them now and then. Calvin's father came from a family of lapsed Catholics and had grown up unchurched, but his mother descended from old Presbyterian stock. Her own mother had come out to California from Virginia as a young bride in the 1920s and settled near Paso Robles, where Calvin grew up. He remembers his grandmother as "a Presbyterian Mother Teresa. She was always doing special things for people, like taking meals to sick people. She even fed stray cats." Calvin himself takes after his father. He goes to church as seldom as possible.

In the Caletti family a perfunctory kind of grace was said at meals, but religion was rarely discussed. Calvin suspects that his father, now deceased, viewed religion as skeptically as he himself now does. As for his mother, "I've always thought of her as actually being reasonably religious, not just taking us to church because she felt that we should have that exposure." "I didn't *hate* going to church," Calvin remembers, "but I didn't have particularly positive feelings about it either." On Sunday mornings he would sometimes try to avoid going by pretending to fall asleep again after his mother told him it was time to get up and get dressed. His most vivid early recollection of Sunday school was having to "wear pants that itched." As for worship services, "I sat through a lot of sermons from Reverend Clark and he was pretty boring." Although no particular Sunday school teachers, lessons, or sermons stand out in his memory, he did acquire "some religious background, some basic things about Jesus and God." The real highlight of Sundays, however, was the horseback rides he took with his grandfather, a man he remembers as "sort of a nature worshiper, just a person who really was in awe of the trees and the rocks" and who never went to church.

As Calvin moved into his teens his interest in religion increased a bit. In high school he dated the minister's daughter and participated occasionally in the evening programs and social activities of the youth group. But Calvin's new interest was that of an observer and a skeptic rather than that of a believer or a seeker of truth. "It wasn't an extremely important part of my life," he recalls, "but I was curious why other people were so taken by religion and I wanted to know more about it." By the time Calvin left home for college he was a confirmed agnostic. "I'm not an atheist," he explains; "I'm not convinced that God doesn't exist, but I'm not totally convinced that he does." At college he enjoyed arguing about religion with his roommates and his girlfriends and even with the devout Jehovah's Witness who cleaned his dormitory room and worried about the state of his soul. "I remember people would say things like, 'The sun rises in the morning and sets at night. How could all this just happen?' Well, I'm a science and engineering major and this doesn't appeal to me very much. It really isn't an argument for anything. I don't know what would prove to me that there is or isn't a God."

Calvin has just turned forty. He, his wife, Joyce, and their two young sons live in a one-story ranch-style house in Buchanan, a fast-growing city on the edge of California's Silicon Valley. Joyce is a clinical pharmacist and Calvin is a mechanical engineer. She was raised a Catholic and whenever she is not on call at St. Joseph's General Hospital she takes the children to Sunday mass and to CCD, a weekly Catholic instructional class for children. Calvin, whose work sometimes takes him away on weekends as well, attends church with them four or five times a year, but only reluctantly.

Calvin would have preferred not having to promise to raise his children as Catholics. To him, CCD is really "CCI—Catholic Christian Indoctrination." It also irritated him that Joyce's parish priest refused to perform their wedding ceremony on a hillside overlooking the ocean and that they had to sign a "ludicrous" statement assuring the church authorities of their intention never to divorce. But religion has not been a major bone of contention in his marriage. For one thing, Calvin doubts that his children will become devout, traditional Catholics. "I think they're not necessarily going to believe everything they hear at CCD," he explains. He laughs as he observes that "they're feeling, I think, the same way that I felt about church when I was that age, and I think the fact that their father isn't going with them regularly is helping this feeling along. They're already asking why Dad isn't there." Calvin is playing the same role of passive resistance his own father played.

Another reason religion is not a serious issue in Calvin's marriage is that he is convinced that Joyce's real views on religion are remarkably similar to his own. "I used to tease her about that all the time. I thought she was a terrible Catholic. I think she would have made a much better Presbyterian. She didn't feel the way they do about birth control or abortion or anything else." In short, Calvin is convinced that the division in his family on the subject of religion is more apparent than real. He has also noticed that Joyce's church attendance increases when her mother comes to visit. "Among the Catholics I've known," he reports, "there's a fair amount more pressure to be religious than I saw in my family." He has concluded that Joyce's conformity is mainly motivated by a desire to satisfy her parents. "For lack of a better word, it's sort of a charade. I don't think she essentially disagrees with the way I feel." The only real difference between them, he suspects, is that Joyce "thinks there *probably* is a God."

In Calvin's opinion, children should know something about religion. He is glad Joyce is in charge of their religious education, however, for he would feel uneasy taking them to Sunday school and church himself. Having to recite prayers and confessions at worship would make him feel like a hypocrite. If both he and Joyce were unchurched he might consider teaching them about religion at home. He would tell them about the religions of the world, including the great religious figures of history and the claims they made, but he would also impart his own skepticism. He is not sure he would be able to take enough time to put "this ideal scenario" into effect, however, for his job makes heavy demands on his time. "I don't even spend enough time playing *catch* with my kids for them to be as good at baseball or football as I'd like them to be." Under the circumstances, Calvin considers CCD to be an acceptable way for his sons to learn about religion.

For Calvin, the really valuable part of religion is not its doctrine or its ritual but its moral teaching. "I try to think that part of what my mother sees in religion is the part that I think is most positive, which is some of the values that the church has in terms of how you treat other people and how you live your life." The most positive thing churches do, he argues, is to teach people to be "reasonably honest and fair and kind and whatever." Even the Mormons, whose beliefs he considers "a bunch of seagull poop," encourage these virtues.

Although Calvin acknowledges that his exposure to Presbyterianism may have contributed to his moral education, he believes he really acquired his values from his family. He would be troubled to see churches disappear if they were the sole promoters of these values, but in his opinion moral standards do not need religious justification because they "sort of stand up on their own." Moreover, he considers it "almost more admirable to do the right things because there's just some inherent good in you or you think those are the things to do rather than because you think you might go to hell or that believing is a ticket to a second life." Calvin thinks the church's emphasis on belief and forgiveness actually works against its moral teaching. He allows that the true believer would "probably not want to really do terrible things," but it offends his ethical sense that churches seem to teach that "it's *believing* that's most important, that you can be forgiven for the bad things you do, but you have to *believe*." As a moralist, he is stricter than many orthodox Christians.

For Calvin, "the inherent good in you" is identified subjectively. "It's what I can feel good about. It's what I wouldn't be embarrassed that my kids knew about. It's something my family would agree with, my mother would approve." For him, moral values also have a pragmatic justification. "You can be a lot happier by living an honest, good life," he claims, "than you can by living dishonestly and screwing people all the time." His standards, however, are a bit less altruistic than those of the Sermon on the Mount or of his Presbyterian grandmother. He thinks that church people "carry some of these good principles a little too far. You know, it's a cruel world out there. You can't be absolutely wonderful with everybody or you're not going to last very long in a lot of environments." His mother scolds him for being cynical, but Calvin insists that "you don't have to love your neighbor if he's a jerk."

Despite his skeptical, scientific worldview, Calvin sometimes verges on prayer when life is not going well for him. "I would be stretching it a bit to say that I pray to God," he insists. He never prays formally "in a verbal way," but "I come close in terms of at least wishing that something would happen. Just in a thought type of way, like, 'If you're up there, would you take care of this one for me?'" Now and then, while scanning television channels for something interesting to watch, he encounters an evangelist who is "worked up about something" and he will pause to watch for a few minutes. "I'll go, 'This guy's really good, on a roll here, I mean really yelling and screaming pretty good.'" Calvin is fascinated by such displays of religious fervor.

A few years ago Calvin's mother left the Presbyterians for another church, one "that she feels to be a little more dynamic, one of these that gets a little evangelical." Now and then he asks her about her new church "just to make sure it's not quite as dynamic as some of these things I see on TV and that she's not giving away my inheritance to these people."

With the Calettis a long Presbyterian lineage has finally come to an end. Calvin's sister stopped attending church when she went off to college, and has rarely attended since. Calvin hopes and suspects that with his sons a long Catholic lineage will come to an end as well. Their childhood conformity, like his own, is a thin shell that will shatter when they come of age. He has not entirely forsaken his heritage, of course. Family and morality mean a great deal to him, but his moral code has a hard edge to it. Calvin admires his grandmother's feeding stray cats and taking meals to the sick, but he speaks of her as if she were a relic from another time.

Marcia Wilson, Wayne Sanders, Ann Brooks, and Calvin Caletti were all confirmed in Presbyterian churches during the 1960s, but only Marcia is an active Presbyterian today, and even she has no special loyalty to the denomination. Calvin and Ann are no longer members of a church and Wayne has become a fundamentalist. Despite their distinct perspectives on religion, Marcia, Calvin, and Wayne have clear opinions about it. Only Ann is uncertain and confused. All four have complaints of one kind or another about churches, but none, not even agnostic Calvin, is entirely hostile toward them. Both he and Ann strongly support the churches' moral teachings, and both want their children to receive instruction about religion. All four had mothers who were active Presbyterians but only Marcia came from a family in which church and religion were regular topics of household discussion. Wayne's parents quarreled and cursed and, in his view, set a poor example for him. Neither his father nor Calvin's was active in church and neither of them shared with his son his own views about religion. Calvin could only surmise that his father was an agnostic. Even Ann's father, who was a regular churchgoer, kept his religious views to himself.

We have begun this book with these four very different voices because their stories are broadly representative of the major patterns of spiritual development we have encountered among the many individuals we studied who were confirmed in Presbyterian churches across the United States in the years following World War II. In the chapters to come we will present more descriptive and statistical information on these patterns, illustrate them with additional material from our personal interviews, and attempt to discover the reasons why some Presbyterian confirmands have remained within the denominational fold and why so many others have taken different paths.

Chapter 2

Who Are These
Young Adults?

Several research strategies were available to us in investigating why so
many young adults are absent from the mainline Protestant churches.
After weighing the advantages and disadvantages of each strategy, we decided to interview a sample of young adults who were confirmed as adolescents in a single mainline denomination.

A Focus on Former Confirmands

Confirmation involves admission to membership on formal profession
of faith. By focusing our attention on that group, which is largely responsible for recent membership losses, we would gain insights into why the
losses have occurred. We would be able to understand better the personal
and social factors influencing these persons' decisions regarding church
membership and participation. We focused on a single denomination for
reasons of convenience and economy, and we chose the Presbyterian
Church (U.S.A.) because of our extensive contacts with that body.

We decided to undertake two levels of interviewing. First, we would
locate a sample of the confirmands and conduct telephone surveys with
them. Then, with a subgroup of these respondents, we would carry out a
series of in-depth, person-to-person interviews following up on themes
that came up in the telephone conversations. At the outset we did not
know what problems might be encountered with this research strategy.

Could such a study be done in a way that would keep biases at acceptable levels? Could we even find enough of the confirmands to constitute a reasonably representative sample? Would respondents talk freely on such sensitive topics as their religious beliefs and personal life experiences? To the best of our knowledge, a study using this research design had never been done.

With the support of the Lilly Endowment, during 1988 we undertook a pilot study of four Presbyterian churches in various regions of the country. We experimented with a variety of approaches to the churches, estimated the difficulties in finding confirmands, and developed a telephone questionnaire. Each interview took about twenty minutes.

In this pilot phase we learned that Presbyterian churches generally have good confirmation records and are willing to share them with us. We also learned that people were available in most churches who were willing to help locate the former confirmands. These were typically older members who served as the "collective memories" of their congregations; they seemed to be intrigued by the task of tracking down the children of their churches. We discovered that the confirmands would talk freely if guaranteed anonymity. We located about 70 percent of the confirmands we wanted, and about 80 percent of these completed the interviews. On the strength of our pilot study, the Lilly Endowment funded the full study, which began in March 1989.

Ages of the Young Adult Sample

Exactly what age group should we study? We decided that people in their twenties were too young. We reasoned that middle-class, mainline Protestant individuals in their twenties tended to be in an unsettled phase of their lives, which made it difficult to predict what their lives would be like in the future. Furthermore, researchers in recent years have agreed that many young adults "come back" to church life after a period of absence, generally returning when they enter into adult roles, such as marriage, parenthood, home ownership, and (in the upper middle class) career commitment.[1] Until these life-cycle transitions are completed, young adults are still in flux, hence limiting their usefulness to our study.

When do these transitions occur? The age seems to be growing later and later, to judge from such indicators as the age of first marriage in the United States. For women, this age has risen steadily, from 20.8 in 1970 to 23.8 in 1989; for men the comparable change has been from 23.2 in 1970 to 26.2 in 1989.[2] In addition, while 74 percent of women aged 20 to 24 were married in 1970, only 37 percent of the same age group were married in 1989. The figures for men aged 25 to 29 are equally remarkable: among this group, 81 percent were married in 1970 but only 50 percent in 1989.[3]

The average number of children per family also plummeted during this period. In 1970, households had an average of 1.34 youngsters under 18; by 1989 this figure had dropped by almost half to 0.69.[4] Smaller families, later marriages, and delayed childbearing were all indicators of the unsettled lives of people in their twenties. One knowledgeable person told us, "It's a waste of money to look at anybody under 35, since they haven't settled down." In the end, we elected to use the age of 33—those born as late as 1956—as the lower age limit of our main sample.

Another consideration was the current age of the so-called Baby Boomers. The Baby Boom in the United States began immediately after World War II and lasted well over a decade, after which it gradually abated. It had no clear end point, but certainly it was over by the middle 1960s. In order to study an identifiable portion of the Baby Boom, we elected to begin our sample with those born in 1947 (aged 42 in 1989). People born between 1947 and 1956 are roughly the first half of the Baby Boom. Thus the population from which we drew our main sample consisted of persons who were 33 to 42 years old in 1989 and who had been confirmed as adolescents in the Presbyterian Church.

An avalanche of attention has been showered on the Baby Boomers as a unique cohort experiencing life in new ways.[5] While many observers seem to believe that Boomers are passing through the stages of life in entirely unprecedented *fashion*, we wondered whether this group are really different from their predecessors or whether it is merely going through the usual life-cycle experiences in unprecedented *numbers*. Accordingly, we decided to create a second sample with which to compare the Baby Boomers. We drew this sample from Presbyterian confirmands who had been born a decade before the Baby Boomers, people who would be between 43 and 52 years old in 1989. This older sample of "pre-Boomers" would provide a base of comparison with the main sample.

In sum, the main sample (the Baby Boomers) would include persons 33 to 42 years old (born between 1947 and 1956), and the older sample (the pre-Boomers) would include persons 43 to 52 (born between 1937 and 1946). We decided that the main sample should have 500 respondents and the older sample should have 100. (Later the older sample was increased to 125.)

Sampling Churches

Because the research method we chose required a great deal of personal contact with individual churches, it would have been too costly and time-consuming to select these churches randomly throughout the United States. Instead, we used a form of cluster sampling. We first divided the nation into four regions: Northeast, Midwest, South, and West.[6] Then, on the basis of 1964[7] Presbyterian membership statistics, we calculated church membership for each of the four regions. This figure told us how many confirmands should be chosen from each. The 1964 statistics also reported the number of members in each region belonging to congregations of varying sizes. On the basis of these two pieces of information, we divided the churches from each region into four size categories: 249 or fewer members, 250 to 499, 500 to 999, and 1,000 or more members. The result was a four-by-four grid telling us how many interviews were needed from each church size in each region.[8]

During the summer of 1989 we met with presbytery executives in all four regions, asking them to help us select representative churches of the proper size. The sizes needed to be correct for the mid-1960s, not for today. Any church organized after the mid-1950s could not be included because it would not have had confirmands in both the age brackets we were studying. Churches that had dissolved or left the denomination since the 1960s were also not included. Using suggestions from the executives, we selected 23 churches.

Finding the Confirmands

In each church we assembled the confirmation lists from the 1950s and 1960s. From these lists of names, random samples were chosen. In a typical middle-sized church, we needed about twenty-five names for the Boomer sample and five for the pre-Boomer sample; we chose a somewhat larger number to provide backup names for those we might not be able to contact. Using veteran members from within the congregations to do the tracking, we sought addresses and phone numbers for the individuals in our samples.

The task of finding the confirmands proved to be an exacting one. Since we knew this would be the case, we kept careful records to assess any resulting biases and enable us to make statistical adjustments to help correct them. Our veteran church helpers were able to find addresses and phone numbers for almost three-quarters (73 percent) of the names we had drawn. Of these, we successfully interviewed four out of five (79 percent); 8 percent were contacted but refused to participate; and 13 percent could not be reached or scheduled for interviews.

Are those who could not be found—one-fourth of the names we had drawn—different in any important respects from those we did find? Are those who refused to participate different from those who did participate? If they are different, what might be done to reduce the bias in our data resulting from their exclusion from the study? We concluded that there were two biases, one that required some adjustments in our data and one that was too trivial to correct for.

In rural churches a high proportion (over 90 percent) of the sampled individuals could be found; thus there was little bias in these congregations. However, in several large urban churches our inability to locate many confirmands was more serious. We tried to discern why. It became apparent that we were much more successful in finding persons with ongoing kinship or friendship ties in the churches than those who had drifted away. This was related in part to the distance that the people now live from the churches in which they were confirmed; those living nearby were more likely to have maintained their ties—and therefore to be found—than those living farther away. We decided that we needed to make adjustments for this bias.

A second, less serious bias became evident during the interview process. People who refused to respond to our interview requests seemed to be conflicted about religious matters or to be worried about exposing their true religious sensibilities. By contrast, the people most eager to be interviewed tended to be those who felt strongly about their faiths and were at home in the church. Apparently some people perceived our study to be an effort by the church to "check up" on them. Those who felt acceptably religious were more cooperative and forthcoming than those who were not self-assured in religious matters. In sum, we sensed greater reluctance to respond among secular or undecided respondents than among fundamentalist or religiously conservative respondents. However, since the total number of refusals was low, and since the refusals were not concentrated in any one region or in any one church size, we decided not to compensate for them statistically.

In the end, we weighted the data from four large urban churches that had the lowest rates of located confirmands. The weighting increased the importance of the responses from the people who lived farthest from their original home church. Even after this adjustment, there is probably a slight conservative bias in the data. That is, the more conventional respondents may have been overrepresented while the unconventional people were underrepresented.

We are confident, however, that the sample of respondents we reached is broadly representative of the Presbyterian population they were chosen to reflect. One set of comparative figures helps to support this confidence. The Presbyterian Panel, a research program administered by the Office of Research Services, Presbyterian Church (U.S.A.), used several questions identical to ours in a 1990 study of its lay members. To get its sample the Panel researchers drew a random sample of congregations from the entire denomination, then requested pastors to draw a random sample of parishioners from each congregation.[9]

In the entire Panel of 1,685, there were 332 persons between the ages of 33 and 42. We compared this subgroup of the Panel with our 145 respondents who were now active members of Presbyterian churches. Are the two groups similar? In rates of church attendance they are the same: 76 percent of the Panel members attended two or three times a month or oftener, compared with 77 percent of our sample. In level of education they are also similar: 68 percent of the Panel members and 66 percent of our sample had finished college. In political self-definition they are also very much alike: 19 percent of the Panel said they were liberal or very liberal, compared with 17 percent of our sample; 39 percent of the Panel said they were conservative or very conservative, compared with 48 percent of our respondents. The rates of interfaith marriage were also close: 30 percent of the Panel members had married Presbyterians and 19 percent had married Catholics, compared with 27 percent and 13 percent in our sample.

When it came to religious beliefs, however, there were some differences. A comparison of six items indicates that the members of our sample are probably a trifle more universalistic and less convinced that truth is to be found through Christ alone. Moreover, the persons in our sample were more likely to agree with belief questions regardless of their wording. This tendency to answer "yes," known to social scientists as "response set," may have been an artifact of our telephone interview process in contrast with the mailed questionnaires used in the Panel. For example, on the statement "The only absolute truth for humankind is Jesus Christ," 66 percent of the Panel members agreed versus 83 percent of our sample. Yet on the item, "All the different religions are equally good ways of helping persons find ultimate truth," 31 percent of the Panel members agreed compared to 59 percent of our sample. Perhaps those who were interviewed personally were more reluctant to offer negative opinions than those who had the greater anonymity of the surveys. Normally the two research methods do not produce divergent results. Why it happened here is not fully clear.

Another comparison was also useful. Are active Presbyterians in the 1990 Panel who were confirmed as Presbyterians different from others who came in as adults? On nine attitude and self-report items, the Panel found that the two groups did not differ. This result indicates that, among today's Presbyterians, those who were raised Presbyterians are not discernibly different from those who have switched in. The active Presbyterians in our sample are probably representative of all present-day Presbyterian members of the Baby Boom generation.

A Patchwork Portrait of the Confirmands

Who are the Baby Boomers of our sample, and what are they like? To begin with, our confirmands are preponderantly of upper-middle-class status. As Table 2.1 shows, six out of ten (63 percent) have completed at least four years of college, and almost half of these have additional degrees beyond the bachelor's level. For comparison, in 1988 only 28 percent of all white Americans between the ages of 35 and 44 had finished college.[10] The Boomers in our study are much more educated than the national average.

Furthermore, this high educational attainment among our Baby Boomers is reflected in comparably high occupational status. Among males, almost a third (31 percent) are managers and supervisors; a fifth (20 percent) are employed in a variety of professional contexts, from CPA to college teaching to social work; and another seventh (14 percent) are involved in technical professions, from computer systems to engineering. By contrast, in 1988 26 percent of the male workforce in the United States

TABLE 2.1

Background Characteristics of the Baby Boomer Sample

	Men %	Women %	Total %
Highest formal education completed			
High school or less	9	12	10
High school plus some college or trade school	24	30	27
College degree	42	36	39
More than college	26	22	24
Current occupation			
Managerial, supervisory	31	9★	19
Professional	20	29	25
Manual, skilled labor	15	8	12
Technical, engineering	14	4	9
Sales	12	7	9
Clerical	4	16	9
Homemaker	0	22	12
Other	6	4	5
Current marital status			
Currently married	84	75	79
Never married	10	10	10
Currently divorced	6	14	10
Widowed	0	1	1
Number of children			
None	26	23	24
1–2	57	60	59
3 or more	17	17	17

★ *These occupational percentages are for all women, including homemakers. See text for non-homemaker percentages.*

were in managerial or professional ranks and only 3 percent were in technical positions.[11]

Among the women, over a fifth (22 percent) are homemakers. When they are eliminated from the tally, high proportions of employed women are involved in upper status occupations: 38 percent of the non-homemakers are engaged in various professions, 10 percent in management, and 6 percent in technical services. Comparable figures for the female workforce throughout the country in 1988 were 25 percent managerial and professional and 3 percent technical.[12]

In sum, roughly two-thirds of the men and over half of the full-time employed women in our sample are working in professional, managerial, and technical positions. These figures are *double* the national norms for each gender.

But not all our Baby Boomers are so well situated in socioeconomic status. More than a third of the sample (37 percent) are not college graduates. Although many of these have completed some college work (a quarter of the whole sample), few are still pursuing degrees. Furthermore, a fifth of the sample (21 percent) are employed in relatively lower status clerical or manual labor positions. Among men, 15 percent are in manual or skilled labor jobs, while among women, 16 percent are secretaries, bank tellers, or other clerical personnel.[13]

Our young adult sample is overwhelmingly family-oriented. Four out of five (79 percent) of the Boomers are currently married. Three out of four (76 percent) have children living with them; more than half have more than one child.[14] Among the quarter of the sample who have no children, there is still a strong strand of hope for children to come; this is true even though the youngest Boomer was already thirty-three years old at the time of the survey. Roughly half of the childless respondents told us they would like to have or to adopt children.

Despite these family-oriented tendencies, not all of our Boomer sample are currently in families or raising families. Of the 21 percent who are not currently married, half have been divorced and the other half have never been married. In all, roughly 24 percent of the Boomers have been divorced, and 14 percent are in their second or third marriages.[15]

Many Boomers show signs of being quite peripatetic (see Table 2.2). Six out of ten (60 percent) have moved at least once in the last five years, and 15 percent have done so three or more times. In addition, another six out of ten (58 percent) have experienced at least one major change in occupation since leaving school or college. A quarter (24 percent) have changed occupations at least three times in those few years, and 50 percent live more than 100 miles away from the neighborhoods in which they attended high school. But mobility is only part of the story. Many other Boomers are not very mobile. Forty percent have not moved in the past five years, 42 percent have stayed in the same line of work since the end of

TABLE 2.2

Mobility Patterns of Baby Boomer Sample

	Men %	Women %	Total %
How many residence changes in the past five years?			
None	42	39	40
1	30	31	31
2	14	14	14
3 or more	14	16	15
How many occupation changes since the end of formal education?			
0	46	39	42
1–2	28	39	34
3 or more	26	22	24
How far do you live from your high school home?			
Under 20 miles	37	36	37
20–100 miles	14	14	14
Over 100 miles	50	50	50

their formal education, and 37 percent live within 20 miles of their high school homes.

As expected, in matters of church life we found much variation among our Baby Boom confirmands (see Table 2.3). Although 62 percent claim church membership, fewer than half (47 percent) attend worship services twice a month or more. Almost a fifth (17 percent) never attend church at all. A large majority (75 percent; see Table 2.5) dropped out of active involvement in the church at one time or another. Men were more likely to drop out than were women (83 percent vs. 69 percent). The mean age for dropping out was 21 years.

The principal reasons our respondents gave for dropping out had to do with matters of personal convenience and lifestyle changes. Thirty-two percent told us they became inactive because they had left home and family; another 31 percent dropped out because of time constraints or "laziness." The final third left because of disagreement with religious doctrine, perceptions of hypocrisy among church members, or loss of faith. Of the Boomers who dropped out of the church, half had returned by the time of our survey. Fifty percent of the female dropouts and 47 percent of the males had resumed attending church at least six times a year. Only half of

TABLE 2.3

Church Affiliation and Ideological Orientation Among Boomers

	Men %	Women %	Total %
Are you now a member of a church?			
Yes	58	65	62
In the last year, how often have you attended church, on the average?			
Once a week or more	20	32	26
Two or three times a month	21	20	21
Six to twelve times a year	17	15	16
At least once a year	24	17	20
Never	19	16	17
If you are now a church member, with what denomination is your church affiliated?			
Presbyterian Church (U.S.A.)	63	60	61
Other mainline Protestant	20	17	18
Conservative or evangelical	15	9	12
Other	3	14	10
In general, how would you identify yourself?			
Religious liberal	28	31	29
Religious conservative	29	22	25
Between the two	28	35	32
Not religious at all	11	8	9
Don't know	5	5	5
In general, how would you identify yourself?			
Political liberal	21	28	25
Political conservative	46	37	41
Neither of the two	32	31	31
Don't know	1	5	3

the returnees, however, had rejoined Presbyterian churches. The mean age for returning was 29 years; 32 percent had returned by age 26, and 37 percent did not resume attending until they were over 31.

We asked them why they returned to the church. A sizable group, about 38 percent, returned because they had "settled down" and felt that a religious experience for themselves or religious education for their children was important. Another 32 percent experienced some spiritual need or reawakening that encouraged them to seek church participation. Others were influenced by friends or family (16 percent) or by return to their childhood communities (4 percent). Fewer than 10 percent returned to church because of outreach efforts by local parishes, such as warm fellowships or inspiring pastors. While these local institutional factors may have been important in the selection of particular congregations, the decision to attend church was a prior one that had largely to do with family or spiritual needs.

While half of the Baby Boomer dropouts were involved in some church at the time of our survey, not all who returned stayed. Twenty-two respondents (4 percent of the entire Boomer sample) became inactive twice. Most of them first dropped out during their teens, returned to church by their mid-twenties, then dropped out again. Of these, a handful had rejoined a church by the time we interviewed them.

The Baby Boomers are currently members of a wide range of denominations. Of those who claim church membership, six out of ten (61 percent) are members of Presbyterian congregations. Another fifth (18 percent) are members of other mainline Protestant denominations, an additional 12 percent are affiliated with conservative and evangelical congregations, and the balance are a mixture of other groups. See chapter 3 for a full listing.

As is apparent from Table 2.3, switching denominations was quite common among these confirmands. Thirty-three percent of the Boomers have switched denominations at one time or another, and 9 percent have switched twice or more. When we asked about the reasons for their switching, one reason stood out by far: influence of a spouse or relative. This switching occurred most often in mixed marriages. Among current churchgoers, only a fifth (20 percent) of those who married Presbyterians switched to other denominations; however, almost half (48 percent) of those who married non-Presbyterians did change. In particular, the Boomers who married spouses from other mainline denominations were most likely to have switched (57 percent did so).

Two other reasons were also commonly cited for switching denominations: (1) moving to a new community and finding a suitable church that happened not to be Presbyterian; and (2) changing to a church that more strongly emphasized "gospel" teaching.[16]

One notable finding is that only 17 percent of those who are currently inactive in a church had switched to some other denomination before dropping out. The vast majority who are not active now have never been active in another religious group. Most of today's dropouts went directly from being Presbyterians to being nothing at all. They did not experiment with other religions along the way. On the other hand, fully 42 percent of those who *are* currently active in a church *have* switched denominations.

Neither the experiences of recent family mobility nor those of divorce were important factors in predicting denominational switching. Among those who have moved in the past five years, 35 percent have switched denominations, a figure only marginally higher than the 28 percent of non-movers who switched. Twenty-seven percent of those who have been divorced have switched denominations, but a *higher* proportion—34 percent—of those who have not been divorced have also switched. Among current church members this discrepancy is even more marked: 32 percent of divorced members, but 44 percent of undivorced members, have switched denominations.[17]

The Baby Boomers have diverse theological and political self-definitions (see Table 2.3). Three out of ten (29 percent) describe themselves as religious liberals; another fourth (25 percent) as religious conservatives; and a third (32 percent) as "between the two." One-fourth of the Baby Boom sample (25 percent) consider themselves political liberals, 41 percent consider themselves political conservatives, and 31 percent consider themselves "neither of the two." On basic matters of religion and politics, the confirmands are a heterogeneous lot.[18]

In the telephone interview we asked two questions: "Do you consider yourself in any way to be a religious person?" and "Do you consider yourself in any way to be a spiritual person?" The possible responses were simply *yes* or *no*. Among the Boomers, 86 percent said they were religious persons and 81 percent said they were spiritual persons. When we crosscut the two, we found that 74 percent said yes to both, 12 percent said they were religious but not spiritual persons, 7 percent said they were spiritual but not religious persons, and 7 percent said they were neither. We thought of looking at these types in more depth, but our interviewing experience made us cautious about making much of them. Numerous respondents were unclear what the words "religious" and "spiritual" meant in the questions. The word "spiritual" was especially vague.

If no overarching generalizations can describe these Baby Boomers, is it possible to point to significant ways in which they differ from their immediate elders? Do their backgrounds, personal characteristics, or cultural experiences help explain why so many of them have left the Protestant mainline? A comparison of Boomers and pre-Boomers yields some clues.

Religious Histories of Baby Boomers and Pre-Boomers

Why do Baby Boomers participate in mainline Protestantism at a lower rate than their predecessors? The answer is *not* that their childhood backgrounds were noticeably different. In fact, the childhoods of Boomers and pre-Boomers had much in common. The vast majority of both groups (92 percent of Boomers and 93 percent of their predecessors) were raised in conventional, two-parent families. The two groups had very similar, and high, levels of participation in church-related events during their youth. As Table 2.4 shows, overwhelming proportions of both groups (over 90

TABLE 2.4

Family Church Participation Patterns, Boomers and Pre-Boomers

	Boomers %	Pre-Boomers %
When you were in high school, were you involved in the Presbyterian church services, Sunday school, or youth programs?		
Yes	94	95
When you were in high school, how often did you attend Sunday school or church?		
Every week	62	69
2 or 3 times a month	26	25
When you were in high school, how often did you take part in Presbyterian youth programs such as fellowship, outings, or camps?		
Often	54	56
During your high school years, what religious preference did:		
your mother have?		
Presbyterian	94	94
your father have?		
Presbyterian	87	81
At that time, how often did:		
your mother attend church services on the average?		
Every week	64	64
2 or 3 times a month	21	20
your father attend church services on the average?		
Every week	51	50
2 or 3 times a month	19	20

percent) participated in church activities of one kind or another when they were youngsters. Of those who did so, 94 percent of the pre-Boomers and 88 percent of the Boomers attended church at least twice a month. In addition, there was little disparity between their levels of participation in other church-related activities: 54 percent of the Boomers and 56 percent of the pre-Boomers "often" attended youth fellowship, outings, and camps.

The Boomers and their predecessors came from families with very similar parental church participation. Ninety-four percent of both groups had mothers who were Presbyterians; 87 percent of the Boomers and 81 percent of the pre-Boomers had Presbyterian fathers. In addition, for both groups 64 percent of the mothers and about half the fathers attended church weekly, with another 20 percent of both mothers and fathers attending two or three times a month. In church attendance, the Boomers' parents were no less loyal than the pre-Boomers' parents.

Furthermore, as Table 2.5 suggests, Baby Boomers differed little from pre-Boomers on a number of other religious dimensions. For instance, Baby Boomers were no less likely than pre-Boomers to have been Presbyterian at the time of their first marriages (81 percent and 82 percent). In addition, Boomers and pre-Boomers were equally likely to choose Presbyterians for

TABLE 2.5

Religious and Other Lifestyle Patterns, Boomers and Pre-Boomers

	Boomers %	Pre-Boomers %
What was your religious preference at the time of your first marriage?		
Presbyterian	81	82
Have you ever had a religious experience? [pre-33]*		
Yes	36	36
If you went to college, did you attend a Presbyterian or other religious college?		
Yes	22	25
During your high school or college years were you ever active in Youth for Christ, Campus Crusade for Christ, Inter-Varsity Christian Fellowship, or a similar student group?		
Yes	12	7

	Boomers %	Pre-Boomers %
Was there ever a time in your life when you became inactive in church life? [pre-33]		
Yes	75	63
If "Yes," what was the main reason you became inactive?		
Left home	32	31
Too busy, not interested	31	31
Conflict with church	15	7
Doubt, lost faith	13	14
Conflict with spouse	3	8
Other	7	10
Since you were about 14, have you ever doubted most religious teachings? [pre-33]		
Yes	40	33
When you were in high school, did your parents force you to go to church?		
Yes	26	16
Was there a time in your junior high or high school years when you rebelled against your religious training?		
Yes	17	6
Were you married in a church or in another setting?		
Nonchurch	17	8

---

* The older group has had an additional 10 years compared to the Baby Boomers. Accordingly, on a number of items we limited our analysis to events that took place before members reached age 33. For these items, the phrase "pre-33" is used.

their first spouses (19 percent and 18 percent). Even at this crucial juncture in their personal lives, Boomers did not show a greater rejection of Presbyterianism.

Baby Boomers are as likely as pre-Boomers to have had "a religious experience—that is, a particularly powerful religious insight or awakening"—prior to age 33 (36 percent for both groups). Boomers who attended college were just as likely to have attended Presbyterian or other religious colleges (22 percent and 25 percent), and they were slightly more likely to have been involved in a Christian student group in high school or college (12 percent and 7 percent). In all these measures of youthful participation, Boomers and their predecessors do not differ markedly. Indeed, it is remarkable how alike they are.

When we compare the average ages at which the confirmands experienced significant life-cycle events (see Table 2.6), the pattern of similarity

TABLE 2.6

Average Ages of Significant Life-Cycle Events, Baby Boomers and Pre-Boomers

Age at which you	Boomers Years	Pre-Boomers Years
rebelled against religious training	15.1	14.9
doubted most religious teachings [pre-33]★	17.9	19.1
moved out of home [pre-33]	18.6	18.6
became inactive in church [pre-33]	20.4	20.8
first married [pre-33]	23.5	22.5
had a religious experience [pre-33]	22.7	19.4
became active in church again [pre-33]	27.1	26.3

★ *The older group has had an additional 10 years compared to the Baby Boomers. Accordingly, on a number of items we limited our analysis to events that took place before members reached age 33. For these items, the phrase "pre-33" is used.*

between the Baby Boomers and the pre-Boomers continues. Among those who rebelled against their religious training, the rejection took place at about the same age (on the average, at age 15.1 for the Boomers and age 14.9 for the pre-Boomers). Moreover, those Boomers and pre-Boomers who dropped out of church life did so for the first time at about the same age (20.4 for the former and 20.8 for the latter). And the reasons Baby Boomers gave for dropping out of church at least once before the age of 33 were not appreciably different from the reasons pre-Boomers gave for doing so. The proportions reporting that they dropped out because they left home, were too busy, had lost interest, or had lost their faith were virtually identical for the two groups. Finally, Boomers who returned to the church prior to age 33 did so on the average only slightly later (age 27.1) than did the pre-Boomers (age 26.3). The average age of return for the Boomers may, of course, rise as time passes, for fully one-quarter of the pre-Boomers who returned to church did so *after* their thirty-third birthdays.

Although the religious histories of Boomers and pre-Boomers are similar in many respects, they also differ in others. Where differences occur, the Boomers are consistently more likely than their predecessors to have rejected church life. For instance, Boomers are more likely to have dropped out of church (75 percent vs. 63 percent; see Table 2.5 above) at some point in their lives. A higher proportion of Boomers than pre-Boomers complain that they were "forced" by their parents to attend church when they were young (26 percent vs. 16 percent), a higher proportion report that they have "doubted most religious teachings" (40 percent vs. 33 percent), more admit that they rebelled against their early religious training (17 percent vs. 6 percent), and more report that they were married in a nonchurch setting (17 percent vs. 8 percent). In each of these differences the Baby Boomers were more negative toward religion than the pre-Boomers.

The generations also differ as to when in the life cycle they first had doubts about religion, and when they had the first experience they identified as religious. Serious doubts about religious teachings tended to hit the Baby Boom generation a year earlier in the life cycle than they hit the pre-Boomers (age 17.9 vs. 19.1). An equal proportion of Boomers and pre-Boomers (36 percent) had religious experiences before age 33, but the Boomers had theirs on an average of three years later than did the pre-Boomers (age 22.7 vs. 19.4). In sum, while the Boomers and pre-Boomers share many religious and familial background characteristics, their personal religious histories are different. Boomers are more likely to have doubted their faith, to have experienced doubt earlier, to have rebelled against religion, and to have dropped out of church.

Other Background Characteristics

On most personal background measures, Baby Boomers and their predecessors resemble each other closely (see Table 2.7). Very similar proportions (39 percent of Boomers and 38 percent of pre-Boomers) have completed a college education; another quarter of each group has gone on for further education beyond the bachelor's level. Four out of five members of each group are currently married. Of the fifth who are not currently married, the older group has a higher proportion now divorced (10 percent of the Boomers and 12 percent of the pre-Boomers), while the younger group has more persons who never married (10 percent and 6 percent).

As Table 2.7 shows, respondents' spouses also have much in common. For instance, they have almost identical educational backgrounds; more than half of the spouses have completed at least bachelor-level education. In addition, roughly three-fourths (74 percent of the Boomers and 77 percent of the pre-Boomers) of each group's spouses are employed full-time

TABLE 2.7

Personal and Spouse Backgrounds, Boomers and Pre-Boomers

	Boomers %	Pre-Boomers %
How much formal education have you completed?		
Less than college	37	37
College degree	39	38
More than college	24	26
Are you currently married?		
Yes	79	81
If No: Currently divorced	10	12
If No: Never married	10	6
Spouse's highest formal education:		
Less than college	47	46
College degree	34	34
More than college	20	21
Spouse employed full-time outside home?		
Yes	74	77
What was your first spouse's religious preference when you were married?		
Presbyterian	19	18
Other mainline Protestant	29	48
Non-mainline Protestant	13	6
Other Christian	25	16
Agnostic/None	14	11

outside the home. As noted above, the groups chose Presbyterians as their first spouses at similar rates (19 percent and 18 percent). Also, comparable proportions married agnostics or those without religious preference (14 percent and 11 percent). However, pre-Boomers were much more likely to find their first spouses from among other mainline Protestant denominations (48 percent vs. 29 percent), while Boomers were more likely to marry Catholics or members of non-mainline Protestant churches (38 percent vs. 22 percent).

The counterculture of the 1960s and early 1970s was much more a part of the lives of the Baby Boomers than of their predecessors. While 71 percent of the Boomers have attended rock concerts, only 23 percent of the pre-Boomers have done so. Furthermore, fully half (51 percent) of the Boomers have experimented with marijuana at some time in their lives, but barely 10 percent of the older group have done so. Finally, a quarter (25 percent) of the Boomers but only a tenth (10 percent) of the pre-Boomers have been involved in demonstrations or marches.

To sum up, Baby Boomers and their predecessors have a number of background characteristics in common. Among them are various parental and spousal attributes, childhood religious practices, and educational attainment. These factors seem unlikely to explain the differences in current church involvement between Boomers and pre-Boomers. However, Baby Boomers were far more likely to have participated in the youth culture of the 1960s, and this may have helped erode their commitment to religion and the church.

Current Religious Practices

We have seen that the personal histories of Baby Boomers and their predecessors are similar in some respects and different in others. Table 2.5 shows that 75 percent of Baby Boomers, as opposed to 63 percent of pre-Boomers, dropped out of church at least once before they were 33 years old. Table 2.8 indicates that virtually identical proportions of the dropouts of both groups (49 percent and 48 percent) are currently active in a church. Because a greater proportion of Boomers dropped out to begin with, their rate of return would have had to exceed that of the pre-Boomer dropouts for the two generations to have identical proportions of active church members today. In fact, the proportion who are now active in a church is 12 percentage points lower among Baby Boomers than among the preceding generation (61 percent vs. 73 percent). The higher *initial* dropout rate for Baby Boomers appears to have had an impact on their *current* church membership rate. More Boomers than pre-Boomers dropped out of church, but the same proportions returned. So the current difference reflects the different initial dropout rates rather than the rate of returning.

The two groups have other similarities. Of the persons now church members, three-fifths of both the Boomers and pre-Boomers continue to be in the Presbyterian Church. An additional fifth of each group are members of other mainline Protestant denominations, and the remaining fifth are affiliated with non-mainline Protestant bodies or with the Roman Catholic Church. Of those who are religiously active today, the Boomers are no more likely than their predecessors to have switched to churches outside the Protestant mainline. Moreover, their rate of church attendance is only a little lower than that of the pre-Boomers. Sixty-nine percent of religiously active Boomers and 72 percent of active pre-Boomers attend church at least twice a month. Of course, since fewer Boomers are religiously active, their overall rate of church attendance is 11 percentage

TABLE 2.8

Current Religious Practices of Boomers and Pre-Boomers

	Boomers %	Pre-Boomers %
Was there ever a time in your life [before you were 33 years old] when you became inactive in church life?		
Yes	75	63
If "Yes," are you active now?		
Pre-33 Yes	43	42
Current age Yes	49	48
Are you a member of a church and did you become active by age 33?		
Yes	61	73
In what denomination are you a member?		
Presbyterian	61	61
Other mainline Protestant	18	20
Non-mainline Protestant	17	17
Roman Catholic	5	3
In the last year, how often have you attended church, on the average?		
Of church members only		
2 or 3 times a month or more	69	72
Of the entire sample		
2 or 3 times a month or more	47	58
Do you ever pray to God?		
Yes	91	95
Once or more a day	49	49

points lower than that of the preceding generation: 47 percent of the Boomers and 58 percent of the pre-Boomers attend twice or more a month.

The vast majority of both groups pray, at least occasionally; 91 percent of the Boomers and 95 percent of the pre-Boomers do so. Roughly half of each group pray at least once a day. The two groups are equally desirous of providing their children with religious education; 96 percent of the

Boomers and 97 percent of the pre-Boomers would want their children to have it. In both groups, three-quarters of those with children at home have enrolled them in Sunday school. Seventy-four percent of the Boomers and 78 percent of the pre-Boomers report that all of their children have been baptized.

To sum up, Boomers were more likely than pre-Boomers to become inactive in the church as young adults. This more frequent dropping out—roughly a 12 percent difference—continues to separate the two groups; the Boomers today are about 12 percent less involved than pre-Boomers. But for the persons who are now church-involved, the levels of involvement by Boomers and pre-Boomers are about the same.

A Comparison of Beliefs

In order to assay the beliefs of the members of our samples, we created seven religious and morality indexes. We were interested in respondents' opinions about basic Protestant beliefs, whether salvation is available only through Jesus Christ, and whether individuals should make their own decisions on matters of faith, and their positions (liberal or conservative) on current controversial moral issues. The questions used in these indexes are presented in Table 2.9.

Traditional Protestant doctrine centers on the divinity of Christ, the inspiration of scripture, and the promise of life after death. As is evident from their responses to three items concerning these doctrines, both Boomers and pre-Boomers can be considered quite orthodox. Well over 90 percent of each sample assert that the Bible is divinely inspired. Furthermore, eight out of ten respondents from each group affirm the divinity of Christ, and even higher proportions (83 percent of the Boomers and 90 percent of pre-Boomers) reject the notion that there is no life after death. When these items are combined into a Core Belief Index (see Table 2.10), it becomes apparent that traditional beliefs are widely held within these groups. In order to score high on this scale, respondents had to give orthodox answers to all three questions. Even by this exacting standard of traditionalism, 72 percent of the Boomers and 79 percent of pre-Boomers hold orthodox theological views.

Almost all Boomers and pre-Boomers believe in life after death; however, many fewer accept traditional teachings concerning the next life. As the responses to the items comprising the Otherworldly Index items suggest, there is considerable reluctance in both groups to accept the notion that this life is primarily a preparation for life to come (see Table 2.9). Forty-six percent of the Boomers and 45 percent of the pre-Boomers accept it, but equal numbers (45 percent and 48 percent respectively) do not. Furthermore, while there is significant belief in a divine judgment after death (56 percent of the Boomers and 61 percent of the pre-Boomers

TABLE 2.9

Items Used in Indexes: Responses from Boomers and Pre-Boomers

	Boomers %	Pre-Boomers %

Core Belief Index Items

Here are four statements about the Bible. Which is the closest to your own views?

	Boomers %	Pre-Boomers %
★ The Bible is God's Word and all it says is true.	23	36
★ The Bible was written by men inspired by God, but it contains some human errors.	69	61
The Bible is a good book because it was written by wise men, but God had nothing to do with it.	6	2
The Bible was written by men who lived so long ago that it is worth very little today.	1	1

What do you believe about Jesus Christ?

	Boomers %	Pre-Boomers %
★ He was God or the son of God.	78	84
He was another religious leader like Mohammed or Buddha.	15	14
He never actually lived.	1	0
Other (volunteered answer)	2	1
I don't know.	4	2

Humans should live with the assumption that there is no life after death.

	Boomers %	Pre-Boomers %
Strongly Agree or Agree	10	7
★ Disagree or Strongly Disagree	83	90

Otherworldly Index Items

The primary purpose of the human being in this life is preparation for the next life.

	Boomers %	Pre-Boomers %
★ Strongly Agree or Agree	46	45
Disagree or Strongly Disagree	45	48

I believe in a divine judgment after death
where some shall be rewarded and others
punished.

	Boomers %	Pre-Boomers %
★ Strongly Agree or Agree	56	61
Disagree or Strongly Disagree	32	29

Christ Only Index Items

The only absolute Truth for humankind
is in Jesus Christ.

★ Strongly Agree or Agree	60	68
Disagree or Strongly Disagree	32	28

Only followers of Jesus Christ and members of His church can be saved.

★ Strongly Agree or Agree	29	35
Disagree or Strongly Disagree	61	55

Universalism Index Items

All the different religions are equally good
ways of helping a person find ultimate
truth.

★ Strongly Agree or Agree	55	55
Disagree or Strongly Disagree	37	35

All the great religions of the world are
equally true and good.

★ Strongly Agree or Agree	39	43
Disagree or Strongly Disagree	49	46

Individualism Index Items

In the realm of values, the final authority
about good and bad is the individual's
conscience.

★ Strongly Agree or Agree	53	47
Disagree or Strongly Disagree	43	50

(Continued on next page)

	Boomers %	Pre-Boomers %
Individual persons should seek out religious truth for themselves and not conform to any church's doctrines.		
★ Strongly Agree or Agree	54	53
Disagree or Strongly Disagree	37	36

Morality Index Items

	Boomers %	Pre-Boomers %
In general, premarital sexual relations between persons committed to each other are morally appropriate.		
# Agree	56	32
+ Disagree	32	52
Laws making abortion legal should be repealed.		
+ Agree	20	31
# Disagree	69	61
Should a man who admits he is a homosexual be allowed to be ordained as a Protestant minister?		
# Yes	50	37
+ No	34	46

Note: "Don't know" responses are omitted here.

★ Respondents who gave all these answers were deemed "High" on the respective indexes.

 # Respondents who gave all these answers were deemed "Liberal" on the Morality Index.

+ Respondents who gave all these answers were deemed "Conservative" on the Morality Index.

believe this), sizable groups in each sample reject this teaching (32 percent and 29 percent respectively). As a result of this variation, fewer than four out of ten in either group scored high on the Otherworldly Index (see Table 2.10).

Although most respondents from both samples have traditional theological beliefs, the Christ Only Index items tell us that both Boomers and pre-Boomers have mixed views about the unique nature of Christ. A majority of each group (60 percent of the Boomers and 68 percent of the pre-Boomers) believe that Jesus Christ is "the only absolute Truth for humankind." Yet

TABLE 2.10

Belief Indexes of Boomers and Pre-Boomers

	Boomers %	Pre-Boomers %
Core Belief Index	72	79
Otherworldly Index	37	35
Christ Only Index	28	34
Universalism Index	32	38
Individualism Index	36	28
Morality Index: Liberal	35	13
Morality Index: Conservative	14	18

many are reluctant to say that Christ is the *exclusive* pathway to salvation. No more than 29 percent of the Boomers and 35 percent of the pre-Boomers believe that only Christians will be saved. When these two items are combined in a Christ Only Index, barely a third in either sample say Christianity is the only road to salvation (28 percent of the Boomers and 34 percent of the pre-Boomers).

This reluctance to be exclusive is also seen in the two samples' responses to the items in the Universalism Index. Fifty-five percent in each age group believe that "all the different religions are equally good ways of helping a person find ultimate truth." A lower number in each group (39 percent of Boomers and 43 percent of pre-Boomers) believe that these other religions "are equally true and good." Evidently, many believe that the world religions are equally useful in guiding the *search* for truth, but that all of them do not *possess* the truth.

When combined in a Universalism Index, these two items suggest that roughly a third of each group (32 percent of the Boomers and 38 percent of the pre-Boomers) can be considered "universalist" in matters of religious faith. That is, only minorities in each group would be inclined to see truth as available through a broad range of religious avenues. Interestingly, the Baby Boomers are slightly *less* universalistic than their elders.

Since many of our confirmands reject the doctrinal claims of the major religious traditions of the world, perhaps they locate religious authority within the individual. We asked two questions to see to what extent people believe that individuals should rely on their own personal resources in finding religious truth. Opinions varied widely. But once again the principal differences are within each sample rather than between the two samples. The Boomers are not noticeably more individualistic on religious matters than the pre-Boomers. When the individualism items are combined in an Individualism Index, they show that the number of people who take an individualistic position on both items is much smaller than the number who do so on just one. Only 36 percent of the Boomers and 28 percent of the pre-Boomers agree with both items and thus score high on the Individualism Index. Majorities of both groups have reservations about whether the individual should be the final arbiter of right and wrong.

In all four indexes of theological beliefs, Boomers and pre-Boomers made similar responses. Boomers tend to be slightly less traditional on the Core Belief, Christ Only, and Individualism Indexes, but a bit more traditional on the Universalism Index. Yet we see that both groups are largely traditionalist in their beliefs.

Some important differences between the Boomers and the pre-Boomers appear, however, on controversial moral issues. Issues such as abortion, homosexuality, and gender equality have been contentious topics for at least two decades and are at the center of well-known factional disputes within the mainline Protestant denominations.[19] Respondents who agreed that premarital sexual relations can be appropriate, that a homosexual should be allowed ordination to the Protestant ministry, and that abortion should be legal were scored as liberal on the Morality Index. Conversely, those who rejected premarital sexual relations, who rejected ordination of homosexuals, and who favored anti-abortion laws were scored as conservative.

The majority of each sample did not answer all three items consistently in either a liberal or a conservative way, and they were scored in a middle category. For example, many respondents took a liberal position on abortion rights and a conservative position on the ordination of homosexuals. In all, 51 percent of the Boomers and 69 percent of the pre-Boomers scored in this middle category.

On the Morality Index the Boomers are more liberal than the pre-Boomers. In Table 2.9 the difference between the two groups ranges from 8 percent on the issue of abortion to 24 percent on the issue of premarital sex. Thirty-five percent of the Boomers, as opposed to 13 percent of the pre-Boomers, scored as liberals. Fewer than 20 percent of either group scored as conservatives, with very little difference between the groups.

Two additional measures attest to the more liberal perspective of the Boomers and to their broad acceptance of the "middle ground" on theological and political issues (see Table 2.11). In these two realms, respondents were asked whether they considered themselves liberal, conservative, a combination of the two, or something else entirely. On both measures Boomers were more likely than pre-Boomers to say that they are liberals, and pre-Boomers were more likely to say that they are conservatives. A great many in each group see themselves as neither of the two.

The "liberalism" of the Baby Boom generation, as suggested by this

Table 2.11

Religious and Political Self-Identification Items, Boomers and Pre-Boomers

	Boomers %	Pre-Boomers %
In general, how would you identify yourself?		
Religious liberal	29	15
Religious conservative	25	29
Between the two	32	43
Not religious at all	9	5
Don't know	5	8
In general, how would you identify yourself?		
Political liberal	25	14
Political conservative	41	50
Neither of the two	31	34
Don't know	3	2

evidence, is principally related to matters of morality that are currently controversial rather than to alienation from institutions or rejection of theological orthodoxy. Although the experiences of the counterculture were uniquely felt by this generation, the residual effect seems to have been only a more liberal position on such morality issues. We found only marginal differences on other measures.

Landon Jones[20] portrays the Baby Boom generation as a pig swallowed by a demographic snake. As it makes its way through the snake's digestive tract, it creates a visible moving bulge. Its sheer size changes things. However, the evidence presented here suggests that the Boomers are not much different from the smaller rodents that the demographic snake has swallowed in the past. They make up a larger mass but do not differ dramatically from their predecessors. Their lifestyle is not vastly altered. While they have promoted a few innovations in behavior and attitudes, they are making their way through the stages of life in much the same manner as their predecessors did. Although they are less likely than their predecessors to be active church members, few of them are harsh critics of Christianity or of religion in general. They are more liberal than their predecessors on theological, moral, and political issues, but they are not inclined to reject moral constraints out of hand. And, although they have fewer children per family, they are as ready as the pre-Boomers to seek religious training for their young.

The search for the reason why the mainline Protestant churches have lost members must focus on subgroups within the Baby Boom generation, and not on the generation as a whole. Since no single explanation can encompass all members of this generation, and since so many Boomers are as conventional as their elders, explaining mainline church decline requires special attention to certain groups *within* the sample. In particular, attention must be paid to those Baby Boomers who, at greater rates and earlier ages than their predecessors, dropped out and stayed out.

Chapter 3

Where Are They?
Eight Religious Types

Where are these young adults today in terms of Christian belief and the church? The answer to this question is best given in the form of a map with a category scheme for describing them. Category schemes can be made in numerous ways. For example, we could have divided the confirmands into biblical literalists and non-literalists, into current Presbyterians and others, or in other ways. We chose a method that centered on *church-relatedness*, and we used it to describe the Boomer sample, those 33 to 42 years old.

Churched and Unchurched

We began by dividing the confirmands into *churched* and *unchurched,* that is, whether each person is "in" or "out" of church life. To be categorized as churched, a person must (1) be a member of a religious body now, and (2) have attended a religious service at least six times during the past year. To some people this seems like a minimal level of church involvement, but in defining the types we preferred to err in the direction of inclusiveness.

Most of the confirmands could easily be classified as churched or unchurched according to these two criteria. A small number of people, however, were hard to classify, and it was necessary to devise special rules for deciding in which category they belonged. A few religious groups, for example certain nondenominational Bible churches and a few Unitarian-Universalist fellowships, have no membership rolls. Several persons in the sample participated in such groups, and we decided to regard them as unchurched. Also a handful of confirmands who had moved away from their hometowns told us that they are still a member of the church they attended in high school and that they have never joined a church where they now live. In the interview we asked these persons how often they travel to their hometowns, how often they attend church there, and how far away the hometown is from their current place of residence. We decided to classify such people as churched only if they currently reside no more than twenty miles from their hometown and also attend church there six times a year or more. We reasoned that people who live farther away are not churched in any real sense because they have not transferred their membership to a church in their community.

Another complication was that a few of the confirmands (2 percent of the sample) attend one church but belong to another. These situations arose from influences pulling people in different directions, causing a change in attendance but not membership. For example, four persons have started going to different churches without shifting membership from their former churches, and three are married to spouses of different denominations and now go to their spouses' churches. We decided to classify them as churched and to regard them as belonging to the denomination in which they held membership.

Under our two basic criteria, 52 percent of the sample of confirmands were classified as churched and 48 percent as unchurched. Since we have reason to believe that our data suffer from a mild conservative bias, even after we applied weighting procedures (see chapter 2), the true figure of churched persons may be as low as 47 percent. In all subsequent discussions of our findings the reader should keep in mind the high likelihood of a conservative bias in the data.

What would have happened if we had set more stringent criteria for being churched? If we had required both membership and attendance at least monthly, 49 percent of the sample would have been classified as churched. If we had required both membership and attendance at least two or three times a month, 43 percent would have been churched.

Four Types of Churched Persons

We divided the 52 percent churched into four types: *Presbyterian, other mainline Protestant, fundamentalist,* and *other.* The first type consists of those who are now members of the Presbyterian Church (U.S.A.). It makes up 29 percent of the sample; it does not include members of smaller Presbyterian bodies such as the Presbyterian Church in America or the Orthodox Presbyterian Church.

The second type of churched persons are those who currently belong to other mainline denominations. The churches in this category include the United Methodist Church, United Church of Christ, Christian Church (Disciples of Christ), Episcopal Church, Evangelical Lutheran Church in America, and Reformed Church in America.

The third type of churched persons are those we have labeled "fundamentalist." Although we never doubted that such a category is real and recognizable, identifying who belongs in it proved difficult in many cases. Such people cannot be identified by denomination, since many of them are members of nondenominational churches or of denominations that contain both fundamentalists and nonfundamentalists, such as several of the Baptist denominations or the Church of the Nazarene. After the pilot study we decided to ask the persons in the final study to help us by identifying themselves. We asked all current church members two questions about their churches: "Is that a fundamentalist church?" and "Is that an evangelical church?" Many respondents readily understood what these two terms meant and how to define themselves, but others did not, and they asked us to define the terms or give examples. As a help, one interviewer mentioned Jerry Falwell and identified him as a fundamentalist, then asked the interviewee to decide whether his or her church was also fundamentalist. To help define "evangelical" we sometimes referred to Billy Graham. On the whole, the term "evangelical" was more confusing to respondents than was the term "fundamentalist."

We decided to classify as fundamentalist all those who described their church as fundamentalist and who did not belong to a religious body that we had decided to classify in a different way. Several members of the Presbyterian Church (U.S.A.) told us that their congregations were fundamentalist, but after consulting with our advisors we decided to keep all members of this denomination in the Presbyterian category. We also decided not to classify as fundamentalist anyone belonging to a denomination outside the broad religious community in which the fundamentalist and the conservative-evangelical movements had their origins. Thus, Mormons or Jehovah's Witnesses were not classified as fundamentalist, even if they used that term to describe their churches. But self-identified fundamentalists who were members of charismatic, holiness, independent Baptist, or pentecostal bodies were so classified.[1]

Applying the above criteria, we ended up with 6 percent of the total sample in the fundamentalist category, one-third of whom attend nondenominational churches. A small number of these persons could probably be better described as evangelicals, not fundamentalists, even though they called their churches fundamentalist. We did not have enough information to be precise. Our word "fundamentalist" should not be understood in a narrow sense.

After identifying the fundamentalists, we were left with 7 percent in a residual category we labeled "other churched." This group is made up of persons who are active members in churches other than the Presbyterian Church (U.S.A.), other mainline Protestant churches, or churches we classified as fundamentalist. The largest number of this residual category are Roman Catholics, who make up 3 percent of the total sample. One percent are Baptists, and there are several Church of the Brethren, two Jehovah's Witnesses, one Mormon, and one Unitarian-Universalist.

Four Types of Unchurched Persons

We classed everyone not meeting the above criteria as "unchurched," and we divided this group as well into four types. Three of the four are easily described. They are (1) persons meeting the attendance criterion but not the membership criterion; (2) persons meeting the membership criterion but not the attendance criterion; and (3) persons meeting neither. (For details see chapter 5.) We found that 10 percent met the attendance criterion only; we called these "unchurched attenders." Another 9 percent met the membership criterion only; we called them "unchurched members." The remainder of our confirmands, 29 percent, neither belonged to a church nor attended one as often as six times a year. We decided it would be useful to subdivide this important category of respondents into two groups on the basis of whether they consider themselves religious in any way. We were able to identify a subgroup of persons who told us they were not religious. It was made up of everyone who did not meet either criterion for being churched and also answered "not religious at all" to the question, "In general, would you identify yourself as a religious liberal, a religious conservative, between the two, or not religious at all?" Eight percent of the total sample fell into this category.

Thus we have four types of unchurched persons in the sample—unchurched attenders, unchurched members, uninvolved but religious, and nonreligious. They comprise 10 percent, 9 percent, 21 percent, and 8 percent of the total sample, respectively. These four and the four categories of churched persons constitute the eight types of confirmands today. Figure 3.1 shows the scheme for deriving the eight types. The two main criteria are at the top and the left side. The four types of churched persons are all in the upper left section, and all eight types are drawn in proportionate size.

Overview of the Eight Types

These types describe the religious affiliation, participation, and self-description of our confirmands. In the chapters to come we will describe each of these eight types in detail and will attempt to identify the factors that help explain how the individuals in our study "ended up" in each of them. When referring to the types, we will use the numbers 1 to 8.

FIGURE 3.1. Outline of the Eight Types

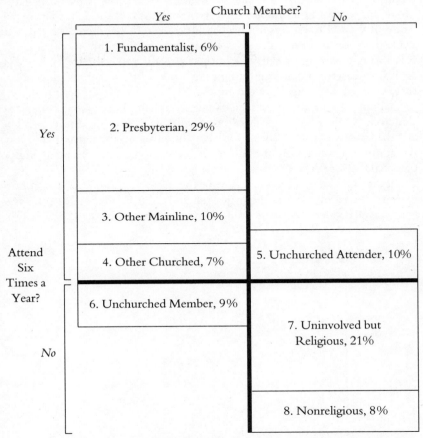

NOTE: The upper left portion includes the four types of churched persons. All other types are unchurched.

Figure 3.1 shows that only 39 percent of our sample currently belong to and participate actively in a Presbyterian or mainline Protestant church (Types 2 and 3). Fully 61 percent have fallen away at least to some extent. Nineteen percent can be described as partly involved (Types 5 and 6), and 21 percent—the second largest type—are uninvolved in church life but still consider themselves to be religious (Type 7). Seven percent have become members of other nonfundamentalist Christian bodies (Type 4), 6 percent have become fundamentalists (Type 1), and 8 percent are neither involved in church life nor personally religious (Type 8). As we will see, the fundamentalists and the nonreligious are the extremes of a continuum on many matters pertaining to theology, lifestyle, and moral attitudes. For this reason we have called them Type 1 and Type 8.

One of the more noteworthy findings of the study is how few of our interviewees have become Catholics (3 percent) or Baptists (1 percent). Since these two religious communities comprise almost half the Christian population of the United States, on probabilistic grounds one might predict that many defectors from mainline Protestantism would end up in one of them. It is also noteworthy that no one in the sample is a member of a New Age group, an Eastern religious group, or any other of the religious movements that achieved wide publicity during the 1970s and were thought to have a special appeal to Baby Boomers. Finally, our sample contained only one Unitarian-Universalist, one Mormon, and two Jehovah's Witnesses. The fact that so few of our confirmands have joined any of these groups suggests the continuing operation of traditional constraints against joining a religion perceived as very different from one's original faith.

Figure 3.2 is a graphic depiction of the religious history of our confirmands. The paths indicate the major religious directions these interviewees have traveled since they were confirmed as Presbyterians. At the top of the

FIGURE 3.2. The Eight Types

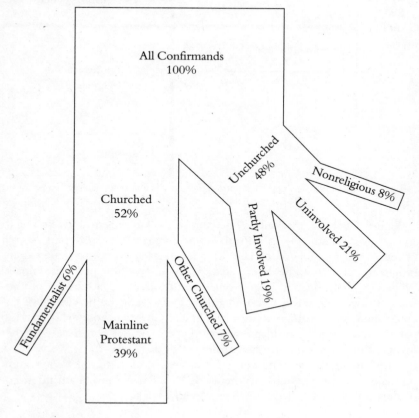

figure they all began as Presbyterians, but farther down they branched out in various directions. For the sake of simplicity, Types 2 and 3 have been combined and designated "Mainline Protestant," and Types 5 and 6 have been combined and designated "Partly Involved."

A Demographic Overview of the Eight Types

The people in the eight types differ in their life experiences. The confirmands with college degrees are more likely to be churched than the sample as a whole, and those raised in cities with populations of 100,000 or more are more likely to be unchurched. In both cases, however, the differences are rather small. Fundamentalists are no less likely than the other confirmands to have earned a college degree. The proportions in each type differ appreciably, however, according to the region of the United States in which the confirmands resided when they were in high school. All prior research has shown that the West is the least churched region of the country, and our own data agree. In our sample, confirmands brought up in the West have a much higher church dropout rate than those raised elsewhere. Seventy percent of our westerners are now unchurched, and only 17 percent remain Presbyterians. They are also quite a bit more likely to be unchurched attenders (Type 5) or uninvolved but religious (Type 7). On the other hand, westerners are no more likely than easterners or midwesterners to be nonreligious (Type 8). Confirmands who live in the South are the most likely to have remained Presbyterians.

Table 3.1 presents the gender, marital status, and fertility of each of the eight types as well as their residential mobility and involvement in community life. The percentage female is lower than the overall average in Types 7 and 8. The fundamentalists are the most likely to have ever married, and Types 7 and 8 are the least likely to have done so. The proportion currently in their first marriage varies from 94 percent among the fundamentalists to 43 percent among the unchurched attenders (Type 5). The four churched types are considerably more likely than the unchurched types to have children, either natural or adopted, with the fundamentalists the most likely of all to have them. The fundamentalists are also the most fertile of the eight types, having produced an average of 2.4 children each; least fertile are Types 7 and 8, with an average of 1.1 for Type 7 and 1.2 for Type 8.

As for geographical mobility, the unchurched members (Type 6) are the least likely of all the types to have changed residences within the past five years or to have moved more than 100 miles from their hometowns, and the unchurched attenders (Type 5) are the most likely to have done so. This is a first hint that residential mobility is an important influence on

TABLE 3.1

Gender, Family Life, and Community Life of the Eight Types

	All	1	2	3	4	5	6	7	8
Gender and Family Life									
Percent female	54	55	58	51	68	62	56	46	44
Percent never married	10	0	9	6	11	6	9	19	16
Percent currently in first marriage	65	94	70	84	63	43	68	51	59
Percent ever divorced	24	6	20	7	23	52	21	31	27
Percent who have children, natural or adopted (regardless of marital status)	76	94	83	84	86	65	73	62	68
Average number of children (regardless of marital status)	1.5	2.4	1.6	1.9	1.9	1.3	1.5	1.1	1.2
Residential Mobility and Community Life									
Percent with one or more changes of residence in the last five years	60	58	54	57	60	79	48	67	55
Percent now living more than 100 miles away from their hometown during their junior high and high school years	49	44	34	49	60	77	24	62	64
Percent participating in a committee or organization aimed at improving their community or changing government policies—such as civic associations, PTA committees, service clubs, or political committees, and who attended a meeting in the last month	35	16	38	44	23	49	32	29	32

Key:
1. *Fundamentalist*
2. *Presbyterian*
3. *Other Mainline Protestant*
4. *Other Churched*
5. *Unchurched Attender*
6. *Unchurched Member*
7. *Uninvolved but Religious*
8. *Nonreligious*

current religious status. Persons who remain Presbyterians (Type 2) and unchurched members (Type 6) are the groups who have moved least from their hometowns during high school. Table 3.1 also shows that fundamentalists are by far the least involved in community life of all the eight types, with only 16 percent having participated in a service club or community group within the preceding month.

We asked our interviewees whether they had been involved in countercultural activities when they were growing up. We asked whether they had ever attended a rock concert, smoked marijuana, or taken part in a demonstration or march on a current issue. In all, 71 percent had attended a rock concert, 51 percent had smoked marijuana, and 25 percent had been in demonstrations. To our surprise, these experiences were not very strongly associated with the persons' church involvement today. The types with highest countercultural involvement were 7 and 8, but the differences were small. Apparently these earlier experiences did not have a lasting effect.[2]

Church Involvement

Table 3.2 compares the church involvement of the eight types. Beginning with the first item in the table, we learn that most of the interviewees, including those who are currently churched, reported that there was at least one period in their lives when they were not active in a church. Those who have remained Presbyterians are the least likely to have once been inactive. A third of all the confirmands have switched from one denomination to another since high school years. (A few currently active Presbyterians joined another denomination and then returned to the Presbyterian fold.) Moreover, very few of those who are no longer involved in church life joined some other church before finally dropping out. The vast majority of the uninvolved are not religious seekers who are now searching for a suitable spiritual home; they are simply lapsed Presbyterians.

Moving down the table, we see that virtually all the fundamentalists and those classified as "other churched" have attended church at least two or three times a month during the preceding year. By contrast, 77 percent of mainline Protestants and only 37 percent of those who attend but are not members have done so. Of the eight types, the fundamentalists are by far the most likely to be involved in other church activities, for example, as members of committees or governing bodies. They are also the most likely to participate in Bible study groups, spiritual growth seminars, charismatic prayer services, and healing groups.

The confirmands consider the religious instruction of children to be of great importance, for 96 percent of them would want a child of theirs to receive a religious education, and more than four-fifths of church attenders

TABLE 3.2

Church Involvement of the Eight Types (in Percentages)

	All	1	2	3	4	5	6	7	8
Was there ever a time in your life when you became inactive in church life, that is, did not attend church as often as six times a year?									
Yes	75	67	52	65	57	79	100	100	100
Did you switch from one denomination to another at any time since your high school years?									
Yes	33	100	8	100	100	36	15	12	3
In the last year, how often have you attended church, on the average?									
2–3 times a month or more.	47	97	77	77	94	37	0	0	0
(If attended at all:) In the last six months, have you been active in any group or committee in the church, such as the Sunday school, governing committees, a Bible study group, or any other?									
Yes	38	91	53	59	63	15	–	–	–
(Ask everyone:) Would you want a child of yours to receive any religious instruction?									
Yes	96	100	99	100	97	98	98	96	71
(If children living with you now:) Do you have any children attending Sunday school now, either regularly or occasionally?									
Yes	65	90	80	78	83	81	37	28	29
(Ask everyone:) In the past five years, have you attended any Bible study groups?									
Yes	33	97	41	48	57	34	15	5	3

	All	1	2	3	4	5	6	7	8
Any spiritual growth seminars?									
Yes	24	72	21	35	43	29	11	9	10
Any charismatic prayer services?									
Yes	9	47	5	6	20	17	2	4	0
Participated in any healing groups?									
Yes	8	26	1	8	20	19	4	5	10

Key:
1. *Fundamentalist*
2. *Presbyterian*
3. *Other Mainline Protestant*
4. *Other Churched*

5. *Unchurched Attender*
6. *Unchurched Member*
7. *Uninvolved but Religious*
8. *Nonreligious*

(Types 1–5) with children at home are sending them to Sunday school. Although Types 6, 7, and 8 are not active in church life and only a handful have participated in Bible study groups or spiritual growth seminars, a surprisingly high proportion desire a religious education for their children. In fact, fully 71 percent of those who say they are not religious at all (Type 8) want their children to know something about religion, and 29 percent of the nonreligious with children living at home have actually enrolled them in Sunday school. These last two findings, together with other findings to be presented later, suggest that few of the nonreligious are actively hostile to religion or to churches in general.

Table 3.3 contains three items concerning attitudes toward the church. The first two are criticisms of churches today—that they have lost a clear sense of the real spiritual nature of religion and that they are not concerned enough with social justice. Regarding spiritual focus, 81 percent of the fundamentalists believe that most churches have lost it. Presbyterians are the least critical of all the types on this item, with only 33 percent agreeing that the churches are in spiritual decline. Fewer than a third of the sample believe that the churches pay too little attention to social justice, and there is little variation from type to type.[3]

The last item concerns the teaching authority of the church. It asked whether respondents consider "long-standing church doctrines" to be "the surest guide for knowing ultimate religious truth." Thirty percent of the sample agreed, with the mainliners and "other churched" most likely to do so. Those who have left the mainline churches to become fundamentalists or to join the ranks of the religious dropouts now have much less trust in long-standing church doctrines than those who have remained.

TABLE 3.3

Attitudes Toward the Church (in Percentages)

	All	1	2	3	4	5	6	7	8
Percentage saying "Strongly Agree"or "Moderately Agree":									
Most churches today have lost a clear sense of the real spiritual nature of religion.	45	81	33	39	43	54	45	44	53
Most churches today are not concerned enough with social justice.	31	31	31	29	29	42	18	35	31
Long-standing church doctrines are the surest guide for knowing ultimate religious truth.	30	22	41	37	37	25	29	20	11

Key:
1. *Fundamentalist*
2. *Presbyterian*
3. *Other Mainline Protestant*
4. *Other Churched*
5. *Unchurched Attender*
6. *Unchurched Member*
7. *Uninvolved but Religious*
8. *Nonreligious*

Core Religious Beliefs

In chapter 2 we described a Core Belief Index and an Otherworldly Index, each constructed from several questions about specific beliefs. As a reminder (see Tables 2.9 and 2.10), to score as a "believer" on the Core Belief Index, a person must affirm that the Bible is inspired by God, that Jesus Christ was God or the son of God, and that people should live with an expectation of life after death. A total of 72 percent of the total sample were believers, and the percentage in each of the eight types is shown in Figure 3.3.[4] The proportion of believers ranged from 100 percent of the fundamentalists to only 6 percent of the nonreligious. What is striking about Figure 3.3, however, is the high level of Christian belief among the other three unchurched types. Seventy-six percent of the unchurched attenders, 72 percent of the unchurched members, and even 51 percent of the uninvolved but religious are believers. Very few of the nonreligious are believers, but we have also seen preliminary evidence that few of them are actively hostile toward religion. Now we see evidence that a considerable proportion of the other unchurched types respond in seemingly traditional ways to items about the Bible, Jesus, and the afterlife.

FIGURE 3.3

Core Belief Index

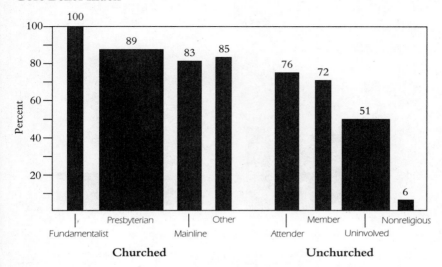

As mentioned in chapter 2, to score high on the Otherworldly Index respondents had to say that they believed in a divine judgment after death where some shall be rewarded and others punished, and to agree that the primary purpose of this life is preparation for the next life.

This second question caused difficulties for some respondents during the interviews. The root of the difficulty seems to have been the perception by many believers in an afterlife that agreeing with the item as worded implies a devaluing of life in this world. Many respondents said that living morally in this life is no different from preparing for the next life. Others believed in a last judgment but told us they also believe in stressing this life. As Figure 3.4 shows, only 37 percent of the sample scored high on the Otherworldly Index and only among the fundamentalists did as many as 72 percent score high. For reasons that are not clear, the level of otherworldliness is higher among the unchurched members (Type 5) than among the unchurched attenders (Type 6).

The interview included several other questions about Christian beliefs that were not included in the Core Belief Index and Otherworldly Index. All the questions are shown in Table 3.4. The first three items in the table are those forming the Core Belief Index, and the responses to all three have a similar pattern. The fourth and fifth items make up the Otherworldly Index. The sixth asked respondents to identify themselves as religious liberals, religious conservatives, "between the two," or not religious at all. (As you inspect the table it is important to remember that self-identification as nonreligious was the basis of distinguishing Type 8 from

FIGURE 3.4

Otherworldly Index

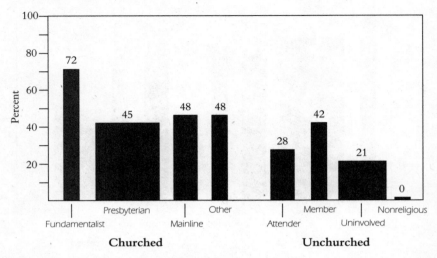

Type 7, which is why 100 percent of the former but none of the latter are listed as nonreligious.) Among the other types, only a handful regard themselves as nonreligious. The vast majority of the people in our sample see themselves as religious in some way. The only type with a preponderance of religious conservatives are the fundamentalists. Among Presbyterians, there are almost an equal number of conservatives and liberals, with almost half responding that their own religious position is "between the two." By far the most liberal type are the uninvolved but religious (Type 7).

The final question in Table 3.4 was asked because in the pilot study we found a surprising number of persons who believed in reincarnation. In the total sample the proportion was 19 percent, and except for the fundamentalist group all the groups include a noticeable number who believe in reincarnation. Even among Presbyterians and other mainline Protestants, about 15 percent held such beliefs.[5] Apparently beliefs about reincarnation have made inroads into mainline Protestant circles. On the other hand, it is possible that many respondents were not entirely clear what reincarnation refers to and may have confused that doctrine with the Christian belief in the incarnation or with Christian expectations concerning the afterlife.

Many contemporary believers in reincarnation also espouse New Age beliefs such as spirit channeling, astral projection, or the healing effect of crystals. We encountered no such beliefs among our confirmands.

TABLE 3.4

Beliefs of the Eight Types (in Percentages)

	All	1	2	3	4	5	6	7	8
Core Beliefs									
Your view of the Bible: "The Bible is God's Word and all it says is true" or "The Bible was written by men inspired by God, but it contains some human errors."	93	100	99	97	96	98	98	89	47
What do you believe about Jesus Christ? He was God or the son of God.	78	100	94	93	94	82	85	58	11
Human beings should live with the assumption that there is no life after death.									
Strongly Agree or Moderately Agree	10	0	4	11	9	10	11	10	41
Strongly Disagree or Moderately Disagree	84	100	94	83	85	86	81	82	28
Otherworldly Beliefs									
The primary purpose of the human being in this life is preparation for the next life.									
Strongly Agree or Moderately Agree	47	72	55	52	63	46	55	31	8
I believe in a divine judgment after death where some shall be rewarded and others punished.									
Strongly Agree or Moderately Agree	56	100	64	66	65	62	58	38	5

(Continued on next page)

	All	1	2	3	4	5	6	7	8
Other									

In general, would you identify yourself as:

	All	1	2	3	4	5	6	7	8
A religious liberal	29	10	25	19	35	33	30	54	0
A religious conservative	25	71	24	35	28	30	26	12	0
Between the two	32	19	46	40	37	24	31	26	0
Not religious at all	9	0	1	3	0	4	9	0	100

Do you believe that souls of individual persons are reborn or reincarnated in another life?

	All	1	2	3	4	5	6	7	8
Yes	19	3	14	18	21	32	22	28	11

Key:
1. *Fundamentalist*
2. *Presbyterian*
3. *Other Mainline Protestant*
4. *Other Churched*

5. *Unchurched Attender*
6. *Unchurched Member*
7. *Uninvolved but Religious*
8. *Nonreligious*

Universalism and Individualism

From the beginning of the study we expected that individualism and religious universalism would be influences on these young adults, and possibly even the most important intellectual factors pulling many away from mainline Protestantism. As defined in chapter 2, individualism in matters of religion refers to the view that a person should make theological choices without authoritative guidance from religious communities. Universalism refers to the belief that no religion is truer than any other. To score high on the Universalism Index a respondent had to agree that all religions are equally true and good, and that all the different religions are equally good ways to find truth. We constructed the Christ Only Index to measure what we considered to be the obverse of religious universalism, namely Christian exclusivism. To score high on that index a respondent had to agree that the only absolute truth is in Jesus Christ and that only followers of Christ and members of his church can be saved. The findings are presented in Figures 3.5, 3.6, and 3.7.

Figure 3.5 shows the percentage of people in each type scoring high on the Universalism Index. In none of our eight types were even a majority of persons universalist in their beliefs. Not surprisingly, there were no universalists at all among the fundamentalists. The unchurched types were only slightly higher on universalism than the churched types. Universalism as measured by this index is not strongly associated with church involvement.

FIGURE 3.5

Universalism Index

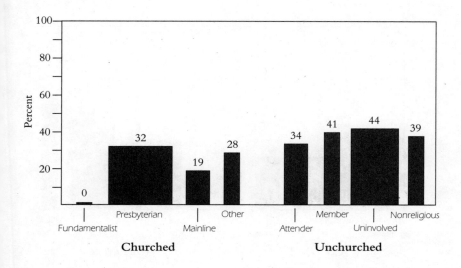

FIGURE 3.6

Christ Only Index

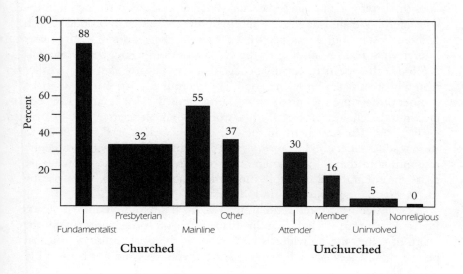

Figure 3.7

Individualism Index

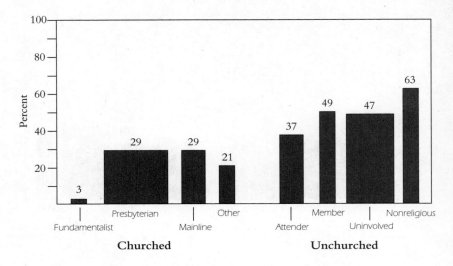

The index score of Presbyterians, for example, is only 7 percentage points lower than that of the nonreligious.

Figure 3.6 shows the percentage of each type scoring high on the Christ Only Index. We had expected that this index and the Universalism Index would be mirror images of each other, but this turned out not to be the case. The Christ Only Index varies much more from type to type than does the latter and appears to be more strongly associated with church involvement. We are not entirely sure why the two indexes produced such different results, but we suspect that the answer lies in the difficulty many interviewees had responding to the two items comprising the Universalism Index. It appears that many believe that *some* but not *all* religions other than Christianity are "true and good." Numerous persons wanted to make distinctions among the different world religions. Evidently, in many people's minds religious universalism is not the only alternative to Christian exclusivism. The statements in the Christ Only Index, on the other hand, were readily understood by most of our confirmands and few had difficulty responding to them. In our opinion, scores on the Christ Only Index are more meaningful and therefore more theoretically pertinent in our study than scores on the Universalism Index.

As reported in chapter 2, the Individualism Index was composed of two items. To score as a religious individualist a person had to agree that in the realm of values the individual's conscience is the final authority and that people should seek out religious truth for themselves and not conform to any church's teachings. Figure 3.7 shows the index scores for the eight groups. In general, the level of individualism varies inversely with the level of church involvement. As we have seen in several other instances, the largest differences in scores are between the fundamentalists and the non-religious (Types 1 and 8), with 63 percent of the latter but only 3 percent of the former scoring high on the Individualism Index. Individualism seems to be a factor in the departure of many young adults from the church.

Table 3.5 shows the percentage of confirmands in each type who agreed with each item making up the three indexes. It is worth noting that the third item in the list, "The only absolute Truth for humankind today is in Jesus Christ," produced the greatest variation from type to type of any item as well as the strongest association with church involvement. One hundred percent of the fundamentalists agreed with it and all of the nonreligious disagreed.

The last two items in Table 3.5 were not used in any of the three indexes, but were included because they have been asked repeatedly in nationwide polls and hence allow us to compare the responses of our confirmands with the responses of adult Americans within the same age range. The item, "An individual should arrive at his or her own religious beliefs independent of any churches or synagogues," was included in a 1988 nationwide Gallup poll, and 82 percent of those thirty to forty-nine years old agreed with it strongly or moderately.[6] This figure is higher than the 63 percent agreement of our confirmands. The final item, "Do you think a person can be a good Christian or Jew if he or she doesn't attend church or synagogue?" was also included in the 1988 Gallup poll, and 79 percent of those thirty to forty-nine years old answered "yes."[7] This figure is slightly lower than the 82 percent who did so in our sample. We conclude that our sample as a whole is no more individualistic religiously than the average young adult American, and probably less so.

On all four items at the bottom of Table 3.5 the unchurched are more individualistic than the churched, and the nonreligious are the most individualistic of all. But even among the churched groups (other than the fundamentalists), between 40 percent and 60 percent agree with most of the items, which shows how widespread the belief is that final religious authority resides with the individual rather than with the church or its teachings. For example, about half of the churched types agree that the individual should make decisions about religious beliefs independent of churches, and three-fourths of them (except for the fundamentalists) agree that a person need not attend church to be a good Christian. In popular theology the church does not have the ultimate authority to define truth or form Christian character.

The spirit of religious individualism may be more prevalent in the mainline denominations now than it was a generation or more ago, and it may have assumed new forms, but it is important to remember that one

TABLE 3.5

Universalism and Individualism Among the Eight Types (in Percentages)

	All	1	2	3	4	5	6	7	8
Universalism									
All the different religions are equally good ways of helping a person find ultimate truth.									
Strongly Agree or Moderately Agree	56	3	59	40	48	63	65	70	53
All the great religions of the world are equally true and good.									
Strongly Agree or Moderately Agree	39	0	38	31	35	37	44	50	52
Christ Only									
The only absolute Truth for humankind is in Jesus Christ.									
Strongly Agree or Moderately Agree	60	100	83	68	74	61	56	32	0
Only followers of Jesus Christ and members of His church can be saved.									
Strongly Agree or Moderately Agree	29	88	33	55	40	30	16	5	0
Individualism									
In the realm of values, the final authority about good and bad is the individual's conscience.									
Strongly Agree or Moderately Agree	53	6	55	47	38	45	69	60	79

	All	1	2	3	4	5	6	7	8

Individual persons should seek out religious truth for themselves and not conform to any church's doctrines.

	All	1	2	3	4	5	6	7	8
Strongly Agree or Moderately Agree	54	28	36	42	43	66	65	74	82

An individual should arrive at his or her own religious beliefs independent of any churches or synagogues.

	All	1	2	3	4	5	6	7	8
Strongly Agree or Moderately Agree	63	49	50	49	54	66	66	82	92

Do you think a person can be a good Christian or Jew if he or she doesn't attend church or synagogue?

	All	1	2	3	4	5	6	7	8
Yes	82	45	80	72	71	83	94	95	92

Key:
1. Fundamentalist
2. Presbyterian
3. Other Mainline Protestant
4. Other Churched
5. Unchurched Attender
6. Unchurched Member
7. Uninvolved but Religious
8. Nonreligious

aspect of this spirit has deep roots in the Protestant teaching that salvation is not mediated through priests or the institutional church. Eighty-three percent of Presbyterians in our sample agreed that ultimate truth is only in Jesus Christ, but only 33 percent agreed that "Only followers of Jesus Christ and members of His church can be saved." Many of our interviewees told us that they could not agree with the latter statement because it includes the phrase "and members of His church."

Issues of Sexuality and Gender

The Morality Index, which we described in chapter 2, was designed to help identify liberal and conservative factions on controversial issues of sexuality and gender. To score as a moral liberal, a person must say that premarital sexual relations between persons committed to each other are morally appropriate, abortion should be legal, and an avowed homosexual man should be allowed to be ordained as a Protestant minister. Figure 3.8 shows the percentages of our eight types scoring liberal, conservative, or "mixed" on this index.

The figure reveals a diversity of viewpoints on these controversial moral issues, but it indicates that the churches are not, as some observers have alleged, divided into two large camps with opposing views. Rather, the majority of all the churched types except the fundamentalists have mixed, or moderate, attitudes. Sixty-three percent of the Presbyterians, for example, scored in the mixed category on the index and only 8 percent scored as conservatives. Moreover, among these young adult Presbyterians, moral liberals outnumber moral conservatives by more than three to one. The real polarization in this sample of confirmands is not among active mainline Protestants but between fundamentalists and those who are not involved in church life. Among the former, 89 percent are moral conservatives, and among respondents who are Type 7s or Type 8s there are virtually no moral conservatives at all. Sixty-six percent of the Type 8s, and only 3 percent of the fundamentalists, are moral liberals. Attitudes on these

FIGURE 3.8

Moral Liberals and Conservatives

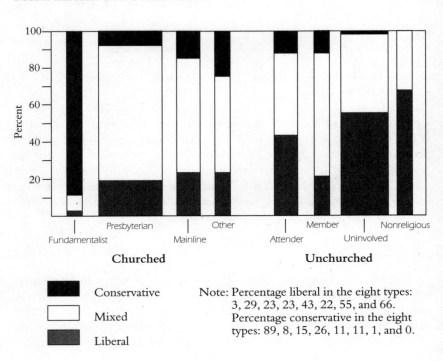

Churched   Unchurched

■ Conservative

□ Mixed

▨ Liberal

Note: Percentage liberal in the eight types: 3, 29, 23, 23, 43, 22, 55, and 66. Percentage conservative in the eight types: 89, 8, 15, 26, 11, 11, 1, and 0.

moral issues are as accurate a way of identifying the eight types of confirmands as are beliefs about the Christian creed.

Table 3.6 shows responses to nine questions on feminist and sexuality issues. (The three items in the Morality Index are the third, sixth, and ninth in the table.) Overall, the majority of respondents agreed with feminist and liberal views on these topics. The second item in the table, about whether churches emphasize a too-masculine view of God, was asked in order to determine whether feminist critiques of the church are widely accepted by young adults. To judge from their responses, these critiques are not widely shared. Only a fourth agreed with the item, and except for the fundamentalists the level of agreement differed little from type to type.[8]

Table 3.6 also shows that on all nine of these moral issues the active Presbyterians are far closer to the religiously uninvolved than they are to the fundamentalists. The difference between Presbyterians and unchurched nonreligious (Type 8) averages only 17 percentage points, whereas the difference between Presbyterians and fundamentalists averages 51 percentage points. On most of the individual items the Presbyterians are surprisingly liberal. Eighty-three percent of them oppose outlawing abortion and 86 percent would approve of a homosexual man teaching high school. Only a quarter oppose the Equal Rights Amendment to the U.S. Constitution and only a third would oppose the ordination of an avowed homosexual man as a Protestant minister.[9] Differences between men's responses and women's responses to the questions in Table 3.6 were small, except for the last two in the table, which are about homosexual men. On those questions the male respondents were about 10 percentage points more conservative than the women.

In general, there is little tension between active Presbyterians and the liberally-minded unchurched types on feminist and sexuality issues, and we conclude that alienation of persons with feminist commitments from mainline Protestantism has not been very great.

Interrelations of Indexes

The six indexes seem conceptually distinct to us, but it is not clear how distinct they are in the minds of our interviewees. Perhaps many of them make fewer distinctions and structure their attitudes along a smaller number of underlying dimensions. If that is so, all six attitude topics may be restatements of one or two basic viewpoints. To check on this possibility we correlated the scale scores with each other.[10] Three of the indexes turned out to be so closely intercorrelated that they are apparently seen as identical by most of the interviewees. They are the Otherworldly Index, the Christ Only Index, and the Morality Index (conservative score). The Otherworldly and Christ Only Indexes correlate at .66; the Christ Only and Morality (conservative) Indexes correlate at .63, and the Otherworldly and

TABLE 3.6

Attitudes on Feminist and Sexuality Issues (in Percentages)

	All	1	2	3	4	5	6	7	8
Feminist Issues									
It is much better for everyone involved if the man is the achiever outside the home and the woman takes care of the home and family.									
Agree	26	78	25	29	34	20	19	15	17
In churches today there is too much emphasis on the masculine aspects of God and not enough on the feminine aspects.									
Agree	25	0	24	17	30	31	22	33	30
Laws making abortion legal should be repealed.									
Agree	21	89	17	23	43	13	18	8	0
Where abortions are legal, the decision about an abortion should be left up to the woman.									
Agree	71	24	77	68	43	74	72	79	87
There has been a proposed amendment, called the Equal Rights Amendment, or ERA for short, to assure women equal rights under the law. Do you favor it, or not?									
Favor	68	24	74	67	62	62	70	77	73
Sexuality Issues									
In general, premarital sexual relations between persons committed to each other are morally appropriate.									
Agree	56	9	52	38	40	63	50	78	91

	All	1	2	3	4	5	6	7	8

All things considered, is society's more widespread acceptance of sexual freedom for people before marriage a change for the better, worse, or do you have mixed feelings?

	All	1	2	3	4	5	6	7	8
For worse	35	94	32	54	51	34	40	15	0

Suppose a man admits that he is a homosexual. Should he be allowed to teach in a high school, or not?

	All	1	2	3	4	5	6	7	8
No	16	48	14	21	12	17	20	13	3

Should such a person (homosexual man) be allowed to be ordained as a Protestant minister?

	All	1	2	3	4	5	6	7	8
No	34	97	33	47	40	31	36	20	3

Key:
1. *Fundamentalist*
2. *Presbyterian*
3. *Other Mainline Protestant*
4. *Other Churched*
5. *Unchurched Attender*
6. *Unchurched Member*
7. *Uninvolved but Religious*
8. *Nonreligious*

Morality (conservative) Indexes correlate at .53. These are fairly strong relationships. All three indexes seem to reflect a single attitude polarity—a dimension having openness, tolerance, and cognitive uncertainty at one end and definiteness, adherence to rules, and exclusiveness at the other. Persons at the liberal end are uncertain about the next life, open to the possibility of truth and morality in all religions, and accepting of diversity and individual choice on matters of sexuality, gender, and human reproduction. Persons at the conservative end are firm believers in the next life, definite in their belief that Christ is the only truth, and decisive in upholding Bible-based moral rules.

This is an important finding. The strong intercorrelation of three of these indexes moves the task of explaining attitude differences from the level of individual issues down to the level of the assumptions underlying them. Something deeper is affecting all of them, and it seems to be the person's basic belief about religious authority and whether Christian teachings are exclusively true.

TABLE 3.7

Political Attitudes of the Eight Types (in Percentages)

	All	1	2	3	4	5	6	7	8
In general, would you identify yourself as a political liberal, a political conservative, or neither of the two?									
Liberal	25	9	17	18	28	27	28	35	42
Conservative	41	63	48	52	40	52	39	23	19
Neither of the two	31	27	30	30	29	21	27	40	39
How much confidence do you have in the following institutions in American society?									
Great Deal or Quite a Lot									
Public schools	52	27	59	56	60	41	45	53	49
Church or organized religion	66	45	91	83	74	56	60	53	18
U.S. Supreme Court	49	27	58	47	45	45	50	51	45
Do you favor or oppose an amendment to the U.S. Constitution that would allow prayer in the public schools?									
Favor	56	73	64	66	54	61	67	41	18

Key:
1. *Fundamentalist*
2. *Presbyterian*
3. *Other Mainline Protestant*
4. *Other Churched*
5. *Unchurched Attender*
6. *Unchurched Member*
7. *Uninvolved but Religious*
8. *Nonreligious*

Political Attitudes

Table 3.7 includes three questions on political self-definition and political attitudes. In political self-definition the fundamentalists are predominantly conservative; the other churched groups are mixed, but still more conservative than liberal. By contrast, the uninvolved and nonreligious unchurched are more liberal than conservative. Even among the Presbyterians, who, as we have just seen, tend to have liberal attitudes on feminist and sexuality issues, only 17 percent identify themselves as politically liberal.

Respondents were asked a question about their confidence in the public schools, the church or organized religion, and the U.S. Supreme Court. The responses to these items form a pattern different from the pattern in all the other tables. Instead of being in the middle of a continuum with the fundamentalists at one end and the nonreligious at the other, the Presbyterians, mainline Protestants, and other churched have the highest levels of confidence and the fundamentalists and the unchurched have the lowest. The fundamentalists have a very low level of confidence in organized religion, and have even less confidence in the public schools and the U.S. Supreme Court.

Our respondents were also asked about their confidence in the military, organized labor, big business, and Congress, but the responses are not included in Table 3.7 because no clear patterns emerged. It should be mentioned, however, that the religiously uninvolved, who tend to be quite liberal on many issues, are not notably more pro-labor, anti-business, or anti-military than members of the other seven types.

The last question in Table 3.7 asks about a constitutional amendment to allow prayer in the public schools.[11] A majority of the respondents favor it, with the fundamentalists most in favor and the nonreligious by far the most opposed. On this issue those who have maintained at least some contact with a church (Types 2 to 6) are much closer to the fundamentalists than they are to the uninvolved or the nonreligious.

To sum up, the eight groups clearly differ on core Christian beliefs, on religious universalism and individualism, and on attitudes about gender and sexuality. They differ less on political measures. The current Presbyterians and other mainline Protestants are situated between the ends of the spectrum, a bit nearer the traditional end than the secular end in theology, but nearer the secular end than the traditional end on gender and sexuality. Of the Presbyterian young adults who have left the church, the main exodus has been in the individualistic, universalistic direction.

We are now ready to take a closer look at each of the eight types. We will examine the four churched types in the next chapter and the four unchurched types in chapter 5.

Four Types
of Churched Persons

In chapter 3 we introduced the eightfold typology for describing the various religious outcomes of the young adults we studied, and we showed that the types differ in many important ways. In this chapter and the next we will look more closely at each of the types, using information from both the telephone survey and the in-depth interviews we conducted with forty confirmands of all types. How do these people approach problems of religion, of life's meaning, of family and community? What were their experiences during youth and early adulthood? Chapter 4 describes the four types of churched persons and chapter 5 the four types of unchurched.

Type One: Fundamentalists

Many Americans think of fundamentalists as hard-edged, brittle fanatics with a hostile attitude toward outsiders and a low level of formal education. We learned in chapter 3, however, that the fundamentalists in our sample are not less well educated than the sample as a whole. Moreover, they have occupations typical for the overall sample and they live, on average, typical distances from their childhood hometowns. As for brittleness and hostility, virtually all the fundamentalists we talked to in our study impressed us as open, generous persons who were trying to live according to Christ's will for them. They were also eager to cooperate in our research project—partly because they wanted their viewpoints heard and they felt that helping us write a book about religion might contribute to that end.

No single denomination predominates in the religious choices made by the thirty-three confirmands in our sample who have become fundamentalists. In fact, thirteen of them have chosen, like Wayne Sanders, to affiliate with an independent, nondenominational church. Four others have become members of one of the fundamentalist Baptist churches, and three each have joined the Assemblies of God, the Church of God, and a Presbyterian splinter body. Two have joined the Christian and Missionary Alliance, and the rest are scattered in five different denominations.

The fundamentalists are different in a wide variety of ways from the rest of the sample, including those who have remained active Presbyterians. Most fundamentalists in the sample are strongly committed to marriage and family. A lower percent have been divorced (6 percent of those ever married, compared with 24 percent for the entire sample), more are currently married (97 percent vs. 79 percent), more of the currently married are in their first marriages (97 percent vs. 82 percent), and more have children (94 percent vs. 76 percent). Furthermore, their families are larger. Forty-one percent of the fundamentalists, as opposed to only 17 percent of the sample as a whole, have three or more children.

A thirty-nine-year-old fundamentalist engineer was typical in his commitment to family life:

> I'm very excited about any social issue that has to do with the family. My church is very much involved in pro-life. I'm excited about that; I can really get excited about giving my money and my time to an organization that I think will make a big difference in the next generation. Our church is excited about the way God has called man and woman to be together and to raise families.

The fundamentalists in the sample are also strongly committed to their churches. Ninety-one percent attend once a week or more, compared with only 33 percent of the active Presbyterians and 26 percent of the total sample. Ninety-one percent are active in some group or committee in the church, compared with 53 percent of the active Presbyterians. On the question, "Do you think a person can be a good Christian or Jew if he or she doesn't attend church or synagogue?" only 45 percent of the fundamentalists, but 80 percent of the Presbyterians, answered yes. Fundamentalists are also far more likely than any of the other seven types to have recently participated in Bible study groups, charismatic prayer services, spiritual growth seminars, and healing groups. They are also more likely to have participated in nationwide evangelical Christian groups during high school or college (26 percent vs. 12 percent overall). In short, the church and its activities are more central to the lives of fundamentalists than they are to those active in other churches. Figure 4.1 contrasts the fundamentalists with all others in the sample.

FIGURE 4.1

Comparison of Fundamentalists with All Others (percentages)

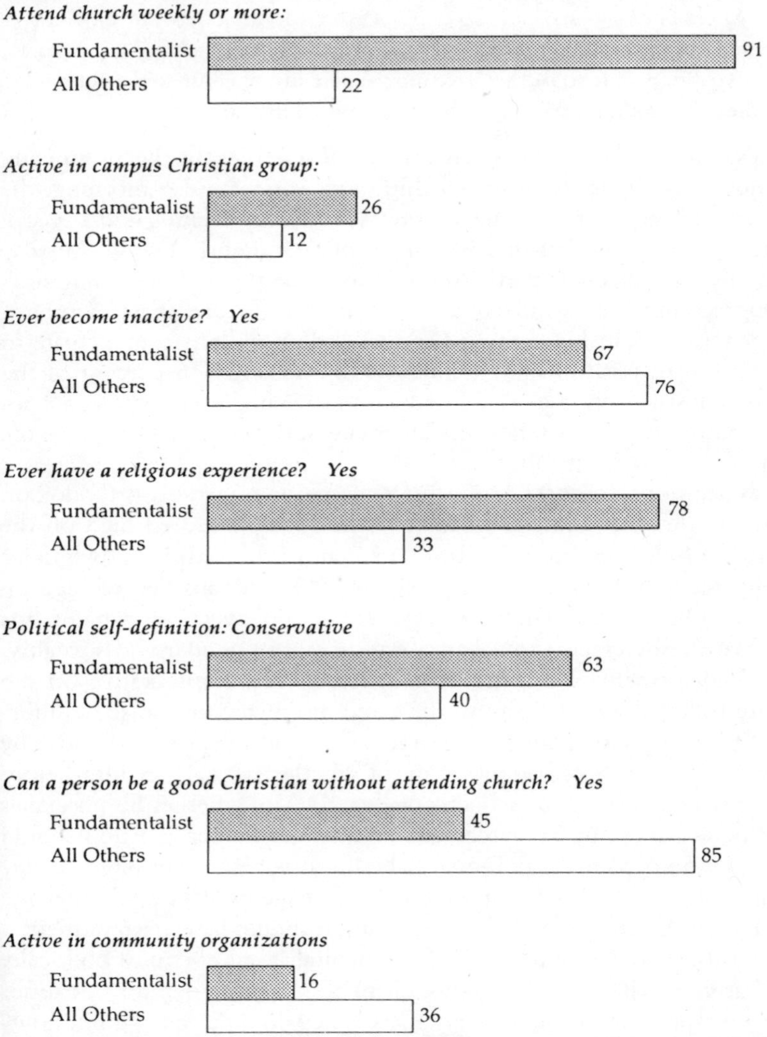

Attend church weekly or more:

Fundamentalist	91
All Others	22

Active in campus Christian group:

Fundamentalist	26
All Others	12

Ever become inactive? Yes

Fundamentalist	67
All Others	76

Ever have a religious experience? Yes

Fundamentalist	78
All Others	33

Political self-definition: Conservative

Fundamentalist	63
All Others	40

Can a person be a good Christian without attending church? Yes

Fundamentalist	45
All Others	85

Active in community organizations

Fundamentalist	16
All Others	36

The fundamentalists who attended college are less likely than college attenders of other types to have concentrated in the social sciences or humanities (9 percent vs. 20 percent overall). A great many of them received training in technical subjects.

In chapter 1 we saw that much of Wayne Sanders's life revolves around the church. To Dan Fuller, a forty-two-year-old fundamentalist who works as an engineer for RCA in Pennsylvania, his church is more important to him than his job:

> If it came to choosing between my job and my church I think I would choose my church. I would say that unless the Lord led me to a ministry somewhere else, I would not leave. If RCA said I would have to move or lose my job, I would look for another job. That's pretty much my priorities. We have four people so far that have moved here just to come to the church, and then they found work. That's how committed they are.

Dan's church, like Wayne's, has a round of activities that keeps him and his family busy. In addition to worship services on Sunday morning, the family attends regular prayer meeting on Wednesday evening and a special prayer meeting on the fourth Friday night of each month. Every Thursday evening Dan and his wife participate in one of the three "house churches" his congregation has organized for the spiritual nurture of its members. Absorbed as he is in his church, Dan has little time left to participate in community organizations. As Figure 4.1 shows, only 16 percent of the fundamentalists, as opposed to 35 percent of the sample as a whole, are active in community groups. For fundamentalists, the church tends to be the principal community of concern.

As we learned in chapter 3, our fundamentalists are strictly orthodox on matters of Christian faith. All of them in the sample scored high on the Core Belief Index, compared with 89 percent of the active Presbyterians; and 88 percent, as opposed to 32 percent of Presbyterians, scored high on the Christ Only Index. The sharpest differences between fundamentalists and active Presbyterians, however, are on issues of gender and sexuality. Whereas 89 percent of the fundamentalists scored Conservative on the Morality Index, only 8 percent of the active Presbyterians did so, a difference of 81 percentage points. Fundamentalists and Presbyterians differ by 62 percentage points on the question of whether sexual freedom before marriage is a good thing, by 64 percentage points on whether homosexuals should be ordained, by 72 percentage points on whether abortion should be legal, by 53 percentage points on whether it is best for mothers to stay at home with their children, and by 50 percentage points on whether the Equal Rights Amendment to the Constitution should have been ratified.

As we also saw in chapter 3, the fundamentalists are the most politically conservative of all eight types, though in this regard they do not differ quite so sharply from active Presbyterians. They do differ quite a bit, however, in the confidence they have in major social institutions. The greatest contrast between the two is the degree of confidence they have in organized religion, with 91 percent of Presbyterians, but only 45 percent of fundamentalists, having trust in it. Fundamentalists have little confidence in the public schools. Wayne Sanders sends his children to a private Christian school. We found that several other fundamentalist families are doing likewise or are educating their children at home.

Why did 6 percent of our sample leave the Presbyterian Church and become fundamentalists? Our data show that in a great many cases their ties to Presbyterianism had weakened long before they joined a fundamentalist church. Sixty-seven percent of them, as opposed to only 52 percent of those who remain Presbyterians, had been religiously inactive at one time, and a high proportion had once doubted most religious teachings. Moreover, only 3 percent, as opposed to 27 percent of loyal Presbyterians, married spouses who were Presbyterians. In most cases these marriages took place before the conversion to fundamentalism. About two-thirds of the switches to fundamentalism can be described as two-step in nature. There was first a decision to stop Presbyterian church involvement, and then a few years later a second decision to become involved in a fundamentalist church.

About two-thirds of those who became fundamentalists did so as a result of a profound religious experience. In fact, fundamentalists were far more likely than any of the other types to report having had "a particularly powerful religious insight or awakening" at some time in their lives. Fully 78 percent of them, but only 33 percent of current Presbyterians, told us about such an experience. For the fundamentalists, these experiences conveyed a distinct theological message that led them to change their lives. Wayne Sanders's salvation experience saved his second marriage and turned him into a vibrant, happy man devoted to church and family.

Dan Fuller also had a salvation experience, and he, too, underwent a profound change. Dan speaks of his new life as if a great burden had been lifted from his shoulders:

> My outlook on life is different. It's the freedom! I am not shackled by the way you feel about me or by whether you hurt me. I'll come to you and say I'm sorry. If you don't want to forgive me, that's your shackle. I'm free! *You* can suffer if you want. It doesn't bother me.

Like Wayne Sanders, Dan Fuller attends a nondenominational church. He is fed up with denominations in general. "Denominations have a lot of overhead and bureaucracy," he complains. "Power corrupts! Look at the hierarchy in the Catholic Church, and you wonder what has created that. God didn't put that in place the way it is today!" Dan has not, however, abandoned his Presbyterian heritage entirely. His Covenant Bible Church takes a Calvinist position on theological issues. His pastor graduated from a Presbyterian seminary and, like many Presbyterian clergy of past generations, makes teaching and scholarship a central part of his ministry. "He has written some books," Dan told us with admiration. "He does a lot of personal teaching, one-on-one, and the people discuss a lot and challenge him. We want a thinking church." There is another way in which Dan's new religious life resembles the lives of Presbyterians of several generations ago. At one time, Presbyterians placed great emphasis on family worship and on religious instruction in the home. Dan and his wife study and pray together with their children. For them, the Sunday school only supplements what parents should do. When Dan was a boy, his mother would sometimes urge the family to sit down together and read the Bible, but she got no support from his father.

For about a third of the fundamentalists, the initial influence to become involved appears not to have been either theological or moral in character. Some became fundamentalists after following a parent, spouse, or friend into a fundamentalist church. Two persons went along with the decisions of their mainline congregations, under fundamentalist leadership, to leave the parent denomination. A few others simply found a local fundamentalist church more congenial than their mainline congregation.

The reason most frequently given for leaving the Presbyterian Church was that it was not preaching the full plan of salvation. As Wayne Sanders put it,

> I said to my wife, "We can't go to the Presbyterian church any more." And the main reason was that there was no call to the gospel of Christ. I mean, Paul says this is the call that you get called to, this is the hope. I mean, *that wasn't said* at the Presbyterian church!

Time and again the fundamentalists complained that mainline churches fail to preach the gospel, fail to teach the Bible, fail to set standards of Christian conduct, and fail to create a close spiritual fellowship. Dan Fuller's parents were active in the Presbyterian church when he was growing up, but they had no close friends in the church. As for Sunday school, "I don't think the teachers really cared a whole lot about us individually." Before he was saved at a Jesus Festival in 1976, Dan was active in a congregation of the United Church of Christ. Looking back at that church now, he realizes that

> there was no fellowship there. As far as I can remember there were no midweek meetings. Once in a while they had a youth activity, which they tried to make as secular as possible to pull in all the kids. But if you tried to do anything too in-depth, the kids didn't come. We knew people on a personal level, but we didn't talk about spiritual things. If you talked about spiritual things they just tuned you out.

Another fundamentalist who had left the United Church of Christ claimed that the mainline churches are "way too liberal. They will accept anybody, anything, without any explanation. If I did wrong, there is no confession that it was wrong, or that Christ made a difference now, or that he could help me live through this situation and forgive me for what I did." In his experience, "people are asked more questions to get into some civic organizations today than the UCC asks people to get into a church!" His desire for concrete standards of conduct was echoed by several other fundamentalists we interviewed. "I would really want to see from the pulpit an expression of biblical teachings that are pertinent to everyday life," one of them told us. "What does God say about the role of women, the role of men, the role of husbands, mothers, children?"

About one-fifth of our fundamentalists mentioned a desire for a more charismatic or spirit-filled church. "In our old church," a thirty-nine-year-old businessman told us, "the spontaneity in worship was not there. So we felt we really had a need to change, so it could be an experience every Sunday that Christ was alive and real in people's lives." At his Abundant Life Gospel Fellowship "the people get up and sing and clap their hands. They raise their hands and dance like David did. Very joyful. Speaking in tongues. Plus, it's very fundamental in what it teaches from the pulpit." Dan Fuller's new church does not encourage dancing or speaking in tongues, but he, too, criticized his boyhood Presbyterian church for being "much too large and too stiff, with a lot of rich people."

Several of the fundamentalists complained that the Presbyterian and other mainline churches are too liberal politically. Almost all who did so focused on one or more of the controversial moral issues on which the fundamentalists in our sample differ so sharply from those who have remained Presbyterians. The fundamentalists were especially critical of the willingness of some mainline Protestant leaders to ordain practicing homosexuals. Wayne Sanders vehemently opposes such a practice, and so does Dan Fuller, who considers it the worst step the Presbyterian Church (U.S.A.) could take. As one thirty-seven-year-old nurse told us, "I just don't want a pastor being gay. I don't think that's God's calling."

In spite of all the complaints our fundamentalists have against the mainline churches, few have angry or bitter feelings toward them. As we saw in chapter 1, Wayne Sanders believes his boyhood pastor was honest and sincere. Dan Fuller, critical as he was of his "stiff" childhood Presbyterian church, does not accuse it of neglecting the gospel entirely. "I keep thinking back, didn't they preach the gospel at First Church? I'm *sure* they did. I'm sure it was there, as feeble as it might have been. It was there, but the Lord just didn't have me hear it at that point in time." To Dan, everything, including faith itself, is a gift from God. Dan's complaints against the mainline churches are tempered by his knowledge that if God had so ordained, even the "feeble" gospel preached at First Church could have been the vehicle of his salvation.

We interviewed several parents of these fundamentalists and got the impression that some of the persons now in fundamentalist churches were actually reaffirming religious motifs they had been exposed to in their childhood. In these cases, the switch to a fundamentalist church did not involve a radical change of perspective on life. We are unsure how general this pattern is among the fundamentalists in our sample. The parents we talked to did not complain that their children were no longer mainline Protestants. Instead, they told us how happy they were that their children were "back in church again."

Type Two: Active Presbyterians

Type 2, currently active Presbyterians, comprises 29 percent of our confirmands. It is the largest type in our study. In order to be classified as Type 2, respondents had to tell us that they belong to a Presbyterian Church (U.S.A.) and have attended it at least six times in the past year.

Although 52 percent of the active Presbyterians dropped out of church at some time in the past, only 9 percent of them ever joined a church of another denomination. (Those 9 percent returned later.) In this respect they resemble the religious but uninvolved (Type 7), only 12 percent of whom ever belonged to another denomination. Neither category has had much exposure to any church but the Presbyterian.

In several respects the active Presbyterians have had more stable lives than the average confirmand we interviewed. Twenty-seven percent of those who married chose Presbyterian spouses, as opposed to only 3 percent of the fundamentalists and 19 percent of the sample as a whole. The active Presbyterians are also more likely than the others to have remained close to their home communities. Fifty-one percent of them, versus 37 percent of the overall sample, now live less than 20 miles from the church they attended during high school. They are also somewhat less likely than the sample as a whole to have doubted most religious teachings at some time since they were 14 years old.

In many respects, however, the active Presbyterians are typical of the entire sample. For example, 66 percent, compared with 62 percent of the total sample, completed a bachelor's degree; and 80 percent, compared with 79 percent, are currently married. They were a little more likely than the other seven types to have attended Sunday school or church weekly when they were in high school, and to have gone to a church-related college; and their parents were a little more likely to have been weekly church attenders. But the differences in each case amount to only a few percentage points.

A Moderate Level of Commitment

In view of their upbringing it is noteworthy that the current level of church involvement of active Presbyterians is far *below* the average of that of the three other "churched" types in the study. Sixty-five percent of the other three churched types, but only 33 percent of the Presbyterians, told us they attend church weekly. Sixty-eight percent of the other churched types, but only 53 percent of the loyal Presbyterians, are active in a group or committee in their church. Moreover, Presbyterians are the least likely of all the churched types to have participated in Bible study groups, charismatic prayer services, healing groups, and spiritual growth seminars during the past five years. In short, the overall level of commitment to the church among the active Presbyterians in our sample is lower than that of the other churched types.

Some we interviewed told us they were simply too busy to invest large amounts of time in church activities. They were like Ann Brooks, whom we met in chapter 1, who has children and works full-time; or like her husband, whose job takes him away from home many weeknights and Saturdays. Among the men we interviewed, none of the active Presbyterians were like Dan Fuller, the fundamentalist whose career takes second place to his church and family. A few let us know that church involvement was low on their list of priorities in life. A thirty-six-year-old dentist confessed, with only a slight expression of guilt, that remodeling his house is more important to him and his family than going to church frequently or participating in its activities:

> I have weakened spiritually, and the reason is, I'm caught up in putting this house in shape. I find myself more preoccupied than I should be with having an income of a certain amount and using that money to do the things I want. For me, life isn't directed at religious things, to say the least. My life is directed towards relating to my family, bringing in an income, and playing tennis, playing golf, and that kind of stuff.

Some, of course, put a far higher priority on church and spiritual life than this dentist does. They are like Marcia Wilson, whom we met in chapter 1. Marcia is strongly committed to Christian service and is deeply interested in the Bible. Or they are like Betty Taylor, a thirty-six-year-old full-time homemaker who lives with her husband and their two young sons in a suburb outside a large Michigan city. "I'm doing *too much* at the church," she chuckles, "that's what I'm doing."

> I'm doing vacation Bible school—I'm the director of that for the third year in a row. I'm on the Christian Education Committee. I just got off the Sunday Scheduling Committee, when we decided to go to two services. I also teach Sunday school. What else? [she pauses to think] I was circle leader for three years and I just stepped down from that last year.

Like Marcia Wilson, Betty was brought up in a family of active, committed Presbyterians who paid close attention to her religious education and did everything they could to guide her life in directions they considered wholesome. Despite some religious doubts during her adolescence and a period of absence from church during the two years she attended a large public university, Betty has lived up to the example her parents set for her. She is seeing to it as best she can that her own children have the same exposure to the church that she had.

> My older boy is just like me. He loves to be the good kid. He's almost eleven, and he loves to go to church, because everyone tells him how cute he is. He loves to dress up, and he believes in everything he's taught. And then I have the seven-year-old. He absolutely hates Sunday school, which is why I have taught it, because he would only go if I was there. They both hate Bible school, but they don't have a choice because I'm the director and they have to go!

Betty is trying hard to give her boys a religious education. But, as we shall see below, the probability is not very great that her boys, or the children of others like Betty, will be highly committed Presbyterians themselves when they become adults.

A Wide Range of Beliefs

Although most of the active Presbyterians we interviewed have orthodox views on at least some aspects of Christian faith, in matters of belief they are far more heterogeneous than the fundamentalists.

A few of the active Presbyterians we interviewed are as orthodox on our measures of religious belief as most of the fundamentalists of Type 1. Marcia Wilson believes "that Christianity is the answer and that the acceptance of Jesus Christ means eternal life, and that a relationship with him means being wrapped in a blanket of love that is truth and light." She and those like her among the active Presbyterians make living a Christian life as they understand it a top priority. Like so many of the fundamentalists we interviewed, Marcia has had a personal experience, a "quiet Nicodemus rebirth," as she puts it, that convinced her that God exists and that Jesus is His son. "My primary argument for God," a thirty-eight-year-old lawyer explained, "is that I felt his presence right at my elbow, and it changed my life." Compared with many active Presbyterians today, Marcia and the lawyer are highly committed orthodox Christians, but they are not orthodox in a historically Presbyterian sense. Neither cares much for creeds and confessions. Marcia learned the catechism by heart when she was a girl, but it had little impact on her. Beyond the bare foundations of the Christian faith, both she and the lawyer are open to a variety of interpretations. In fact, the lawyer is "skeptical about *everything else*, including churches and their interpretations." "I question authority," he told us, "more than I follow it." Dan Fuller, the fundamentalist, is closer to orthodox Calvinism than any of the active Presbyterians we interviewed.

Betty Taylor, the Michigan homemaker, is more typical of active

Presbyterian Baby Boomers than Marcia Wilson is. What Betty likes about the Presbyterian Church is not its teachings but the fact that it allows "so much leeway" in matters of belief. She remembers with gratitude that in her communicants' class "the minister had encouraged questioning and arriving at your own conclusions about beliefs." As a teenager, she was pleased that he did not ridicule the doctrine of reincarnation when she went to him in grief over the suicide of a cousin.

> My big thing was that I didn't want to believe that his life had "just ended," and I thought reincarnation sounded like a pretty good deal. The minister just said, "Look, that's not what the church teaches, but I haven't been there, and I can't say you're really wrong." And he said, "If it makes you feel better right now, I'm not going to tell you that you're a terrible person for thinking that." And he was very comforting.

Betty continues to wonder about what happens after death. She believes in an afterlife and that God is "very loving and very forgiving," and she firmly disbelieves in hell. ("I guess I believe more in a hell on earth than I do hell after death.") She remains unclear about the exact nature of the afterlife, however. "There don't seem to be any clear-cut answers." In a recent Lenten series on death, she was happy to learn that "not only am *I* grappling with this, but the ministers are too. They were quite open in saying, 'Well, this is tough. This is tough for us too.'" To Betty, being a Presbyterian means being able to tackle hard issues in an undogmatic way. She would agree with the factory manager who told us that "I never considered the Presbyterian religion to be the one that says 'This is the way it is.' We basically believe in Christ and that's about it. Maybe that's what pulled me to the Presbyterian religion as compared to some other ones."

Betty was one of many Presbyterians we interviewed who rejects the idea of hell, and she was not the only one who found reincarnation an attractive alternative to the doctrine of eternal punishment. "I think maybe God sends us back to try again," another homemaker told us. "Maybe we didn't learn everything we were supposed to learn the first time." She has serious difficulties, too, with the notion that our bodies will be resurrected. "I just can't picture that kind of thing." Quite a few brought up the issue of whether non-Christians living, let us say, in some corner of Africa who had never heard about Jesus Christ would go to hell because they had not accepted Him. Everyone rejected the view that such a person was doomed; it seemed too unfair.

Asked whether he believed in heaven or hell, a forty-year-old active Presbyterian replied, "No, that's where I back away from religion. After you die you go into the ground, you deteriorate, and that's it." A few we talked to had not given the subject of the afterlife much thought. A Presbyterian contractor told us:

I don't know what I think about a heaven or hell. It doesn't seem to be that important. I think my life right now is important, not what's going to happen to me if I die. I believe in *one's own* enjoyment of the Christian life while we're on earth—apart from any last judgment later.

This man's view was not common among the active Presbyterians we interviewed, but his focus on "my life right now" instead of on the next life was characteristic of everyone we talked to. No one, not even the theological conservatives, told us that they longed to escape from the troubles and temptations of this world or that they were deeply concerned about the fate of their souls. Few told us that they were seriously grappling with the meaning of life or the purpose of human existence. In fact, some Presbyterians seemed quite unprepared for questions about meaning and purpose, as if they had never given them much thought. The theological conservatives are convinced that they are going to heaven, but their main interest is in living a Christian life on earth. The others have various opinions on God and the afterlife, but none of them seem driven by a need to clarify spiritual issues or discover religious truth. Like Ann Brooks, many doubt they will ever know for sure about the afterlife. For most, getting on with their lives "right now" is their main priority.

Growing Up

All research on the religious development of young people highlights the influence exerted by parents, ministers, youth leaders, Sunday school teachers, and peers.[1] Most of the active Presbyterians we talked to had some pleasant memories of their experiences with the church when they were growing up. A thirty-eight-year-old man we interviewed uses his father as a model for his own life. "I had a highly committed father who did everything around the church, taught Sunday school, and so forth. He set a positive example." Marcia Wilson is glad, in retrospect, that her mother made her play the piano against her will at the weekly Sunday school assembly.

A great many of the Presbyterians in the sample had fond memories of ministers, Sunday school teachers, or church-sponsored activities. Time and again we heard compliments about ministers. Marcia Wilson adored hers—"and he loved me, and I know that he did, and still does." A man from Pennsylvania remembered his minister as "*a regular person,* and that's the way he always wanted to be treated, not wanting to put himself above everyone else." His sermons "were always related to everyday activities. I really respected the man." Several singled out younger, less tradition-bound ministers for special praise. A forty-two-year-old homemaker recalls that

our minister when I was in high school was very, very good. And he could relate to our group very well. He wasn't well liked by a lot of the older members of the congregation. He was probably in his late 20s. And I think he kept a lot of the students out of trouble where they might very well have gone the other way. And he was always available if you wanted to go in and just talk.

Many also singled out church staff and Sunday school teachers for special praise. "John Meeks, the choir director, was a big influence—and still is—for me," a businessman told us. "I respect the man. That's what kept me involved in the church services." A computer programmer told of her memories of Sunday school:

> I remember very early years of Sunday school and Sunday morning being an exciting time. I dressed up. It was a fun place to go. You went to Sunday school and then everyone told you that you had goodie shoes on. I remember two teachers who always noticed how nice I looked: "You've got new shoes on," or "Look at the flowers on your little socks," and that kind of stuff. So I always thought, "Oh wow, I like coming here!"

Marcia Wilson was also made to feel special at her home church. "Whatever I did at school, if my name was in the paper I'd come to church on Sunday morning and they'd all read it and they'd pull me over and say, 'Great going, great going!'"

Not all the reports on experiences at church were positive, however. Some people could not remember anything specific about church or Sunday school, and a few were critical. Marcia Wilson complained to her pastor that a new religious education curriculum did not focus on the Bible. One man, looking back on his religious education, could not recall "any particular plan to the Sunday school."

> My recollection of it is, they took whoever was available to teach and were grateful that they volunteered. The materials they used didn't have any consistent focus to them, and I didn't see a lot of commitment in terms of a unified, overall Christian education program. It was just something that they did to occupy the children, and I think a better program could have been developed.

Ann Brooks's complaints about hypocrisy among churchgoers were echoed by several people we interviewed. When she was in her teens, Betty Taylor told her mother, "I'm not going to church anymore, because it's just a big fashion show! That's all anybody cares about—what everybody wears, and the big social scene." A thirty-six-year-old dentist from the Middle West recalled the trip he took as a teenager to a religious conference in southern California. "Kids from all over the country were there and they were extremely religious. If you looked at a good-looking woman with lustful intent, they called it 'carnal.'" All expenses for the trip had been paid by a wealthy member of the dentist's home church who had a reputation for piety. A few months after the trip, the member was indicted on a federal charge of securities fraud. He left the state soon afterward.

Dropping Out

As we noted earlier, 52 percent of those who are now active Presbyterians dropped out of church for one or more periods of time after they were confirmed. Many more reduced their church attendance without dropping out. Even Marcia Wilson, who never dropped out, stopped attending every Sunday in the early stages of her career as a paralegal.

A small handful of people we interviewed dropped out for reasons of conscience. They had previously participated fully in the life of their church, but had been repelled by something that took place, or failed to take place, there. A forty-year-old woman told us how disillusioned she was during the Vietnam War, when her Presbyterian church refused to raise its voice against the war.

> I didn't see the session at Antioch Church standing up and taking a stand. I didn't even see anything other than some letters in the paper. The churches didn't do anything with Vietnam, and I was pretty mad. I thought, "You cowards. You have no guts. You're not ready to put your money where your mouth is." So I pretty much threw all away during that time. I was angry at the government and I was angry at the church. I ended up with just no use for the church for a while after that. It had very little to offer me.

The vast majority who dropped out, however, did so for less high-minded reasons. For many people, especially the males, cutting down on church attendance seems to have been the normal thing to do in high school. Postponing male dropout was one of the principal objectives of a "dynamo" minister of music a forty-year-old technician told us about.

> He realized that you can't get twenty to thirty boys together without giving them some way to vent off their steam. So every Saturday morning he'd have you play basketball for a half hour, and then you'd go upstairs and you'd do voice training for a half hour. It went by just like a snap.

This minister of music, the technician told us, "was one of the big influences in keeping my interest up in the church." But despite his best efforts many of the boys in the group had lost interest in the church by the time they entered the ninth grade, and most had stopped attending regularly or dropped out altogether by the time they graduated from high school.

Parents sometimes intervened to prevent or forestall dropping out while their children were in high school and still living at home. Betty Taylor, who complained that churchgoing "was just a big fashion show," would have dropped out in her teens if her parents had not prevented her from doing so. The parents of a thirty-seven-year-old executive from North

Carolina, however, voiced no objection when he dropped out for a less principled reason shortly after he was confirmed. "I just didn't *care*" about church, he told us. Sports and girls were his main interests. One reason he may not have cared about church is that his parents seldom attended themselves because they felt snubbed by the "socialites" who controlled it. From our interviews, we formed the impression that parents were an important factor in determining whether a confirmand dropped out in high school.

For many who did not drop out in high school, going away to college was the beginning of a period of little or no church participation. The great majority who went to college lived away from home and were not supervised directly by their parents. Ann Brooks stopped attending church when she was in college. When Betty Taylor went to the state university she became briefly interested in Campus Crusade for Christ, but "I found there were lots of other things to do at college on Sunday than go to church." A salesman recalled that he, too, dropped out during college. "I thought perhaps the way a lot of the people of that age do, that we can smoke and drink and do whatever we want to. You just think when you're twenty years old you'll never die. Religion just didn't *matter.*"

Coming Back

Why did the dropouts who are now active Presbyterians return to the church? According to our interviews, the single most important reason is their belief that children need a religious education and that they should be exposed to church life. In their opinion, churchgoing and Sunday school are a necessary ingredient of successful child-rearing. A forty-year-old woman was typical in her attitudes toward church after becoming a parent:

> Having a child is what brought us back. Partly it was because of the happy association I had as a child with the church and partly because of that bigger-than-myself responsibility now for another human being—that you'd better get this right! [laugh] It is a big responsibility, something we wanted to do right. So we started going to church.

Our confirmands also gave other reasons for returning to church. Some spoke of a need for community with a group of like-minded, supportive people, others mentioned a desire for inspiration and spiritual nourishment, and still others told us they wanted to improve their relations with spouses, parents, or other family members who were already committed to the church. Many who returned to church for their children's sake discovered unexpected benefits for themselves. The forty-year-old woman quoted above told of her own discovery:

> There was a whole community of young married couples with young babies that I'd run into every Sunday in the nursery. And then there was an every

Wednesday morning group of moms that would meet at the church, and it was a support group. It was a group made of people in the church who also had little kids, who also were going nuts at home with peanut butter and diapers and all of that, who needed a lift once a week and who would look forward to it. It was a great thing once a week. I loved that.

One man, who became a Presbyterian again mainly for the sake of his small son, discovered that churchgoing strengthened his own faith. "I got very clearly and very firmly rooted back into that church," he told us. "Very quickly it became a home. There just were some terrific people in there. And they're real family. We've gone through an awful lot together." Some who returned found fulfillment in projects of service to people in need. A thirty-seven-year-old Pennsylvanian regained a clear conscience by returning to church:

> I feel very comfortable. I feel happy now that I have a church life again. Because I have to say that there were times when I felt guilty that I wasn't going to church. It was like, you wake up on a Sunday morning and say, "I should have went to church today." But you just didn't. It's just because I felt sometimes that my parents were a little disappointed in me that I didn't go a little more often.

Few of the dropouts who came back to the Presbyterian Church did so because they had had a conversion experience and accepted Jesus Christ as their personal savior. Almost no one who returned reported experiences like those of Marcia Wilson, Wayne Sanders, or Dan Fuller. No one returned for the primary purpose of learning more about the Christian faith or serving God or humanity more fully. Many who came back welcomed the opportunity to learn or to serve, but these were not their main motives for returning. The people we interviewed came back because they wished once again to be part of a community whose values and outlook on life they endorsed. Most had families now, and they were affirming, or reaffirming, the church's way of life.

A few returnees had strayed far from the way of life of the churchgoing community. The thirty-seven-year-old executive from North Carolina who dropped out of church shortly after confirmation had strayed much farther than most. At college he partied, smoked marijuana, grew his hair long, "streaked," and was sexually active with his girlfriends. "I really didn't take a long-term approach to my life," he remembers. In his early thirties, deeply depressed by the failure of his first marriage, he began taking stock of himself. Having married for a second time, he threw himself into his new career. The day his son was born he had an experience that led him back to church.

> I think that I truly witnessed a miracle, a spiritual feeling, when Andrew was born. It was a real, definite experience. This was a *life*, it was another person,

and I contributed to that. I honest to goodness didn't know completely what it was like to say that you really *love* something. And it was just that word. "Love makes the world go 'round," you've heard. There's something to it. I was real emotional during that time.

Suddenly, family life seemed much more important to him than it had ever been. "I'd had my blinders on," he realized. Simultaneously, "the church and all the good things that it adds to a person's experience" became very important too. He and his wife soon joined a Presbyterian church. He wants Andrew, now two years old, to "care about the church and have a meaningful spiritual development during that youth period," something he himself did not have.

This man's sudden insight into what is really valuable in life is not typical of those we interviewed who have come back to the Presbyterian Church, but the link between family responsibilities and a way of life that churches represent was made by virtually everyone who returned to the fold. "I read somewhere," a thirty-nine-year-old woman volunteered, "that children make their parents grow up. I think they do. They force them into taking stands where before you've just been kind of saying, 'Well, this is OK and that is OK.' But you can't be like that always, and you've got to take stands." For her, as for so very many others, what the church stands for is "that you're an honest person, that you're a family person—that you love your family—that you look after other people. The church teaches you to care for others."

A Shared Moral Code

This woman's understanding of what the church stands for was voiced in one manner or other by everyone we interviewed in depth. Everyone, regardless of their degree of church involvement, told us of their respect for a code of conduct that stresses honesty, fairness, not hurting others, and generally "leading a good life"; and they identified this code in some way with the churches. This agreement is especially striking because we asked our interviewees no formal questions about this code. They brought it up themselves at some point in the interview. Our confirmands differ greatly among themselves in many ways, but they concur in believing that a valuable aspect of churches is the moral code they inculcate, "the Ten Commandments," or the "Golden Rule," as many called it. The fundamentalists, for whom the most important thing about churches is the proclamation of God's Word, place a heavy emphasis on living in obedience to God's moral commandments. Wayne Sanders turned to God to help resolve the moral problems that were destroying his marriage. Both he and Dan Fuller now feel empowered by divine grace to conduct their family lives in accordance with God's will. Calvin Caletti, the agnostic we met in chapter 1, believes that families can teach morality to their children without sending them to Sunday school, but he respects the church for upholding it. For Calvin and other permanent church dropouts, the most valuable thing about the churches is that they uphold the moral code.

This shared moral code has three important features. First, it consists of a set of value orientations, or guidelines for living, rather than a set of specific rules. Wayne Sanders and Calvin Caletti would heatedly disagree on how these guidelines should be interpreted in certain cases pertaining to sexuality, gender roles, and abortion rights, but they would not disagree on the guidelines themselves. Second, the moral code stresses being mindful of others in social life, a virtue that is essential for social solidarity, or at least for social harmony. In speaking about the "good life" no one mentioned money, success, or personal achievement, even though it seemed clear that many people we talked to were in fact very much interested in these things. Finally, in talking about the moral code, people convey the impression, either explicitly or implicitly, that it is both universally valid and obligatory. Many want their children to choose the *religion* that seems best for them, but no one told us their children should choose the *moral code* that seems best for them. No one said that children should have a choice of whether to be honest, or whether to be mindful of others. The moral code defines the very basis of upright living.

Lay Liberalism

All those we talked to who reported having had an experience of saving grace affirm that Christianity is the only true religion. Most theological conservatives who have not had such an experience also affirm it. "If we had a Buddhist sitting here," one active Presbyterian told us, "I think we would begin by introducing him to our scripture."

> I would try to explain to him *my* belief that on one occasion God sent His son and broke into history and gave people a chance to escape the punishment they deserved. And there is a lot of evidence that this is historically true.

His view, though not distinctively Presbyterian, has been articulated repeatedly by orthodox Protestant leaders both past and present. They have helped frame a standardized discourse concerning religious truth that is shared by a multitude of Christians.

But most of the active Presbyterians we interviewed do not speak this language of orthodoxy when they address the issue of religious truth. Instead, they give voice to a theological perspective that we call "lay liberalism." This perspective is "liberal" because its defining feature is a rejection of the orthodox teaching that Christianity is the only true religion. Lay liberals have a high regard for Jesus, but they do not affirm that He is God's only son and that salvation is available only through Him. We use the modifier "lay" because no one we talked to seemed to know about, or speak the language of, any of the formal systems of thought that might be regarded as theologically liberal or post-orthodox. No one spoke the language of liberation theology, of feminist theology, or of process theology; and we heard nothing of neo-orthodoxy or of the classic liberalism that preceded it. Among the laity, theological conservatives speak the language of an articulate leadership; lay liberals do not. If those we interviewed are typical of Baby Boomers currently active in the Presbyterian Church, then lay liberalism, and not the various theological systems emanating from seminaries, universities, or General Assembly pronouncements, is the popular alternative to evangelical discourse among the rank and file of the Presbyterian laity.

Lay liberals cannot say that they are Christians because Christianity is truer than other religions. Instead, they told us they are Christians because they were brought up that way, or, more commonly, that Christianity meets their needs or is true "for them." When we asked a thirty-seven-year-old factory supervisor whether Christianity is truer than other religions, he replied:

> For *me* it is. That's just the way I feel. I know I could have a Buddhist sitting here and he would feel that *his* religion is more true. But I feel that's not for me—what I know of it. What I have is what I like.

We heard responses of this sort from many people we interviewed. Ann Brooks responded this way when she told us that she wants her children to have a religion with which they feel comfortable. She would like her children exposed to religious teachings, but she will not force her own preferences on them, nor is she able to give strong reasons for her preferences.

Lay liberals acknowledge that an accident of birth or upbringing, or a sense of comfort, may have influenced their religious choice, but most of them we talked to also try to justify their religious preference by associating it with something of universal value or validity. One way they do so is to link religious choice to the shared moral code we have just described. For example, a forty-year-old health care administrator gave the following answer to a question about whether Christianity is preferable to other religions:

> No. It doesn't matter. I don't think God is going to punish anyone because they choose the wrong religion. As long as they live a good moral life with good values, you know, and don't kill people.

This woman is not certain which, if any religion, is exclusively true, but she maintains that what God really cares about is the moral code. By making a religious choice of some kind she has embraced an ethical standard she believes to be universally valid. Betty Taylor, the active Presbyterian homemaker from Michigan, goes one step further. Asked what the "absolutes" of Presbyterianism are, she replied, "I guess, any of the basic things that go with *any* religion—you lead a good life and treat people the way you want to be treated: 'Do unto others,' the basic Ten Commandments." For her, all religions do in fact teach this code. A similar view was expressed by a woman who told us that although religions disagree as to "who or what that [supreme] Being is," they "have pretty much the same basic beliefs" on "what that Being is trying to teach us. I think it comes back to pretty much the Golden Rule." Such a notion may have underlain former President Eisenhower's famous remark that "our government makes no sense unless it is founded in a deeply felt religious faith—and I don't care what it is."[2]

Some lay liberals we interviewed explicitly endorsed a theology of works righteousness—that God's blessings depend on good deeds. One man told us that

> there's an inside feeling you get when you do something that's good. If you do bad things, you feel bad about yourself, you suffer hell while you're alive! It's God inside that makes you feel good. I go quite a bit on what I feel inside.

A handful of the lay liberals are openly skeptical of all theological claims. For them, morality and morality alone is the valuable part of religion. An active Presbyterian told us that he wants his son to know the Bible because it is "a good building block for morals and for giving a basis for everyday life." A businessman who does not believe in an afterlife justified living morally in the following way:

> If you lived your life in an honorable way, those people that knew you will say, "He was a good guy, he did a lot for his community, he did a lot for his kids." What you *leave* is your testament. That's it. If before you close your eyes the last time. you say to yourself, "I did everything I could in the best way I could have done it," that's heaven.

A few lay liberals justify their religious choice by positing that a common *spiritual* truth lies concealed behind the different religions of the world. "We've got Jesus Christ, but there may be common threads in the religions," a thirty-nine-year-old real estate agent told us. Another person conjectured that

> I might believe in Christ but someone else believes in Buddha, and his Buddha is the same person as what I'm calling Christ. A Supreme Being. We might find out someday that the different interpretations weren't so different, and we might all believe in the same thing.

This position combines an acknowledgment that no religion has a monopoly on the truth with the assumption that religious truth does exist and that all religions teach it in some way.

We asked some of those we interviewed whether the churches should send missionaries to foreign lands to convert adherents of other religions. Not surprisingly, lay liberals responded that missionaries should *expose* people to Christianity but should not try to convert persons who are devoted to other faiths. Moreover, missionaries should never criticize other faiths and they should never use pressure to convert people. By contrast, the theological conservatives told us that it is the duty of Christians to go into all the world and preach the gospel.

To sum up, lay liberals reject the view that Christianity is the only true religion. They differ in their views of what religious truth might be, but they agree that morality is an essential part of religion. Most lay liberals would probably endorse the position of the forty-year-old active Presbyterian who declared that

> I don't think it matters what religion you are in as long as you are comfortable with it and following sound principles, you are raising your kids and spending time with your family, and you are moral. Then it doesn't matter.

Talking About the Faith

According to our in-depth interviews, few active Presbyterians spend much time talking or learning about matters pertaining to religion. Dan Fuller, the fundamentalist, is eager to learn more about his faith, and so is Marcia Wilson. But for many active Presbyterians the Sunday sermon is their only regular encounter with religious discourse. A few teach Sunday school, participate in study groups, read books on religion, or consult their ministers about a spiritual problem, but for the most part they neither talk about nor investigate matters of faith. Marcia Wilson's parents discussed religion at home—Marcia even argued with her mother about Sabbath observance—and she discusses the faith with her own stepdaughter, but hers is an exceptional case among the active Presbyterians we talked to. Presbyterians still say grace at meals, but they rarely have family devotions or read the Bible together, and religion is not a frequent topic of family conversation. From all accounts, this is a sharp departure from practices common among Presbyterians a century or more ago.

Some of our active Presbyterians remember asking their parents—usually their mothers—questions about religion, but only a few recall hearing their parents talk about it. Some had only the vaguest idea of what one or both of their parents actually believed. One woman, whose mother and father were deeply involved in the church, was startled when, in response to our question, she realized that they had talked about the church but not about God, theology, or the Bible. "No, they didn't talk about them—and that's funny. Isn't it funny!" she exclaimed. "We don't articulate those kinds of things. I think they articulated the *values* of the church more than maybe their religious feelings." Asked what these values consist of, she described the moral code we have already discussed. If her case is typical, then "religious" discourse in Presbyterian families both now and a generation ago is mainly moral discourse.

Most of the active Presbyterians we talked to also adhere to the unwritten rule of middle-class society that one does not impose one's religious beliefs on other people. Such a rule helps maintain harmonious relationships in an environment that is religiously pluralistic. In practice this unwritten rule bans any talk about religion unless the other person shows an interest in the subject. One middle-class woman told us, "We Presbyterians are a little bit standoffish and reticent about talking to other people about our religious beliefs. And we wouldn't force them on anybody or even try to *persuade* anybody else." Although she would never attempt to convert anyone, "if someone is coming to town and brings up something that would say they were *looking* for a church, I would certainly invite them to my church and say good things about it." A man from Pennsylvania said that people "feel uncomfortable when religion is brought up as a subject. You almost feel like you're overstepping your bounds if you start to talk too much about religion." As for himself, "I can't even tell you the last time I got into a conversation with anybody talking about their religious beliefs."

Active Presbyterians are also reluctant to share their faith with others because they believe that people should make their own religious choices. A forty-two-year-old homemaker confessed that she does not discuss religion with her brother. "I'm not going to try to force my brother to join a church. It's got to be his choice." She does not mind calling on people new to the community in order to tell them about her church, but she dislikes calling on long-term residents, for they know about the church and presumably have chosen not to join it. "I don't feel like we should go out and try to pull them in."

Lay liberals are especially reluctant to share their faith with others because they cannot assert its truth in relation to other forms of religion. Ann Brooks even hesitates to defend her religious views to her own children. Lay liberalism is not the robust faith of a people who debate and elaborate on religious matters as a community. Dan Fuller complained that his former friends at the United Church of Christ "just tuned you out" if you talked about spiritual things. Many lay liberals we spoke with responded to our questions about religious belief in a tentative and hesitant manner, and without strong conviction. Fundamentalists, by contrast, participate in a community that talks about its faith, and they responded to our questions articulately and with confidence.

Much has been written in recent years about the increasing conflict within America's mainline Protestant churches between religious conservatives and religious liberals. Some contend that these denominations are now divided into two hostile camps over a host of issues.

Ever since the late 1960s, Presbyterian General Assemblies have been the scene of stormy debates between liberals and conservatives. There was considerable opposition, for example, within the former United Presbyterian Church U.S.A. to the new creed its General Assembly adopted in 1967. Three years later, the General Assembly refused to adopt a committee recommendation that would have liberalized the church's standards concerning sexuality. Not long afterward, a furor erupted over the contribution of money that a denominational agency had made to the legal defense fund of an admitted Communist. In 1978 the General Assembly rejected a committee recommendation that would have permitted the ordination of homosexuals, and less than a decade later there was widespread indignation in the new Presbyterian Church (U.S.A.) concerning a recommendation of an official committee that Presbyterians resist American preparation for nuclear war by withholding a portion of their income taxes. In 1991 a new proposal to liberalize sexual standards created consternation within the denomination and was rejected by the General Assembly. In the higher reaches of the denomination there has been a polarization between liberals and conservatives in recent times.

Our study leads us to suspect, however, that active Presbyterians of the Baby Boom generation are not divided into two hostile camps over theological, moral, and political issues. In chapter 3 we learned that the majority of active Presbyterians in our sample scored neither liberal nor conservative on the Morality Index but took a liberal position on some issues and a conservative position on others. We also learned that they are not divided into two major factions on issues of religious belief.

Moreover, very few of the active Presbyterians we talked to were concerned about or even familiar with General Assembly pronouncements or with the various recommendations and projects of the national commissions and agencies of the Presbyterian Church (U.S.A.). Most active Presbyterians of the Baby Boom generation, like most Presbyterians in general, identify primarily with their local church and its programs. They think of "church" in terms of the congregations available in their own communities.

We did hear a few criticisms of trends at the national level of the denomination. Marcia Wilson was worried that the 1991 General Assembly might condone the ordination of homosexuals. A thirty-eight-year-old lawyer complained that national leaders have no interest in the opinions of rank-and-file Presbyterians and a forty-year-old real estate agent dislikes the denomination's new creed because "it incorporates many fashions that deal with things that I do not feel have biblical connotations." But we rarely encountered such demonstrations of knowledge about and concern for larger denominational matters. Moreover, the few who did show concern were theological conservatives. Among active Presbyterians, the lay liberals we talked to had almost nothing to say about the national church. The statistical data and our face-to-face interviews lead us to believe that most active Presbyterians of the Baby Boom generation form their opinions about controversial moral issues in the same way they form their opinions about theological issues—largely on their own. Few appear to be influenced substantially by the views of the various caucuses and interest groups in the denomination.

We did not systematically ask people to reveal the moral reasoning behind their stands on controversial issues, but in a handful of cases it seemed clear to us that compassion for the needy influenced some of the decisions they make about how to lead their lives. Such people had been raised in devout families and had participated actively and eagerly in church life when they were growing up. Marcia Wilson is one of this handful. She remembers that her parents were concerned about starving people in her hometown, and her mother's maxim, "To whom much is given, much is required," has governed many of the major decisions Marcia has made about her life, including her recent decision to work in a soup kitchen. Another active Presbyterian recalled that as a boy he was "always amazed at the missionaries—how they could go and survive" in poor countries "and live in these kinds of conditions amongst these people, just to be a minister, to be a pastor to these people." Although he is a social and theological conservative, he is a generous supporter of Habitat for Humanity and he wishes his senator, Jesse Helms, would stop harping on sexual issues and do something for the homeless. This man would have understood why Calvin Caletti's grandmother fed stray cats and took food to the sick.

Boundaries

How loyal are our active Presbyterians to their denomination, and what religious alternatives would they consider acceptable for themselves and others? A bare handful of those we interviewed proclaimed their loyalty to the Presbyterian Church. "We've been Presbyterians since John Knox," one man quipped. "It's in the DNA!" "I've always been pretty much of a big touter of Presbyterianism," another loyalist told us. "My closest friends say I would never have married my wife if she had not been a Presbyterian." Among the things he likes about the denomination are "the meat and substance" of the sermons and "the way the government's set up." He is also intensely loyal to his local church. "I feel like your church is your home. It's like a marriage; you should be there in the good, in the bad, and in the ugly. I will never leave my church."

This man is keenly aware, however, that his views are out of step with the times. Several people, including Marcia Wilson, told us that their mother or father had a strong identification with Presbyterianism, but a principled loyalty to the denomination was all but nonexistent among the Baby Boom Presbyterians we interviewed. Marcia, for example, was a Methodist for a few years and is a Presbyterian again only because she admires Jack Earl's sermons. Wayne Sanders left the Presbyterian Church with no regrets after he was saved. Ann Brooks is looking for a church, but it need not be a Presbyterian church. Moreover, theological position has little if any relationship to denominational loyalty. Marcia is a theological conservative, Wayne is a fundamentalist, and Ann is a lay liberal.

Theology does, however, influence the extent to which our confirmands are making an effort to inculcate their own religious views in their children. Conservatives and fundamentalists are much more concerned than lay liberals that their children's convictions resemble their own. One conservative Presbyterian is doing his best to "instill" his own religious views in his daughter. Dan Fuller is seeing to it that his children will make the same choice he made. However, for lay liberals it is more important that their children make *some* choice than that they make the "right" one. Lay liberals have no conviction that it is possible to be religiously "right." If religious truth is elusive or nonexistent, then it is perfectly sensible for people to make religious choices on purely subjective grounds, provided only that the religion they choose does not violate the shared moral code. It makes sense to be like Ann Brooks, who is reluctant to impose her own religious views on her children, and who wants them to choose what "fits them" or is "comfortable for them." One active Presbyterian whose two daughters are enrolled in Sunday school told us that he would not object if they decided to become Jews or Catholics or to reject organized religion entirely. "It's okay with me," he informed us, "if that's what they felt was best for them."

On the whole, these active Baby Boom Presbyterians seem to be putting less pressure on their children to make the "right" religious choice than their own parents put on them. There were many Jews in Betty Taylor's high school, and her parents were quite alarmed at the prospect of her marrying one. "I think that was probably my mom's biggest concern, that I would find some Jewish boy to marry." Her parents also warned her about dating Catholics. "They said that if Catholics got you in trouble, 'Boy, they would be running!'" Later, her parents were alarmed when they learned that Betty had attended several meetings of Campus Crusade for Christ while at college. "That was the age of the cults. They wanted to know exactly what was going on there, and I'm sure they made a few phone calls to find out." Betty sees to it that her own children attend Presbyterian Sunday school, but given her theological views, she has no arguments in stock that might persuade them to remain Presbyterians, or even Christians, later in life. Betty's parents were more successful in keeping her within the orbit of Presbyterianism than Betty is likely to be with her sons.

Other nationwide studies also show a marked weakening of older religious boundaries in the past several decades. Studies show, for example, that in recent years over 40 percent of young Jews who marry have chosen gentile spouses.[3] Fifteen percent of the active Presbyterians in our Baby Boom sample—including Betty Taylor—have married Catholics, up from 9 percent in the sample of pre-Boomers. For the vast majority of our confirmands the old boundaries that Presbyterians used to draw between themselves and other faiths are vanishing.

But the boundaries have not vanished entirely. The public outcry against "dangerous cults" that emerged during the 1970s and 1980s shows that many people were outraged by practices that seemed contrary to the shared moral code. Moreover, our interviews convinced us that it is important to distinguish between religions that our confirmands consider acceptable for *others* to choose and religions they might consider choosing for *themselves*. The first set of religions defines their *tolerance zone* and the second set defines their *personal comfort zone*. Needless to say, the two sets overlap to some extent, since people's comfort zones are also a part of their tolerance zones. But the two sets are rarely identical. In most cases, the tolerance zone is much broader than the comfort zone. The vanishing of old religious boundaries in recent decades primarily reflects the expansion of tolerance zones. By contrast, the personal comfort zones of the confirmands we interviewed are surprisingly narrow and traditional. For the great majority, the comfort zone extends no farther than mainline Protestantism, and quite a few draw the line at the Episcopal Church.

The fact that most modern Presbyterians would feel comfortable in Methodist, Lutheran, or United Church of Christ churches reflects a breakdown of denominational loyalty and identity, but it also reflects the realistic perception that most aspects of Presbyterian religious culture have become virtually indistinguishable from the culture of Methodism or of the United Church of Christ. The great majority of the active Presbyterians we interviewed would agree with this observation by a forty-one-year-old professional man:

> When I was growing up in the fifties and sixties, I don't think there was a dime's worth of difference among Presbyterians, Methodists, or Episcopalians in terms of the way theology impacted on the people. If you get the ministers and priests together, they could have World War III arguing about issues that nobody cares about. But as far as most people are concerned, they're really interchangeable. And I don't think there is any particular value

in having a Presbyterian heritage or ethos or way of doing things. The only distinguishing characteristics in the church today deal with our form of government. Anything specifically Calvinistic is gone, and most Presbyterians aren't interested.

On the other hand, most of our confirmands do make a distinction between mainline Protestantism and other religious traditions. We encountered, for example, a very traditional distaste for Roman Catholicism. Some confirmands were aware that the Catholic Church had changed in certain respects, and some commented to us that modern Catholics do not accept everything it teaches, but most active Presbyterians do not consider the Catholic Church as being within their comfort zone. Objections to Catholicism center on its highly ritualized worship, its emphasis on dogma, its official ban on birth control, and the authority claimed by the pope. We did encounter a few active Presbyterians who said they might consider joining the Catholic Church. None of them, however, mentioned Catholic teachings on faith or morals as reasons for including it as a religious option.

We also found a considerable amount of distaste for fundamentalism and for the Baptist church. "I could never be a fundamentalist," one active Presbyterian told us, "or those stricter religions that dictate what our beliefs are." "I associate Baptists with hellfire and brimstone," another Presbyterian declared, "and I couldn't go to a hellfire and brimstone-type sermon." Still another remarked, half-seriously, that "Baptists are not a real religion—that's just a group of people that get together and say 'amen' and ask whether you're saved." One woman reported that a distaste for the Baptist style of worship had even caused a friend of hers to leave the Presbyterian Church after moving to Tennessee. The friend, accustomed to the decorous Old School style of North Carolina Presbyterianism, was so put off by the "Baptist" tone of the neighborhood Presbyterian church in her new community that she became an Episcopalian.

In view of what active Baby Boom Presbyterians told us, it seems unlikely that many of them are candidates for conversion to any faith beyond the bounds of mainline Protestantism. They would simply not feel comfortable there. Of the 500 Baby Boomers in our sample, a scant 13 percent are currently active members of a religious body outside the tradition of mainline Protestantism. Six percent, as we have seen, are now fundamentalists; the remainder have joined churches ranging from Catholic to Unitarian-Universalist. The old boundaries are vanishing, but to date the tolerance zone has expanded much farther than the comfort zone.

Looking Ahead

Fundamentalists assign a higher priority to Christian faith and practice than do those belonging to the other three churched types in our study, and among active Presbyterians, theological conservatives assign a higher priority to these things than do lay liberals. Dan Fuller puts his church ahead of his career. But the man who became a Presbyterian again after gazing on his newborn son is too busy with his work to attend church more than twice a month. He would like to be more involved, but making money for his family comes first. He is now doing very well indeed; he has recently paid $38,000 for the luxury car of his dreams.

If our findings can be generalized, lay liberals are more numerous than theological conservatives among active Presbyterians of Baby Boom age. Very few of these liberals, however, seem candidates for conversion to a form of the Christian faith that would motivate them to devote more time and energy to the church and its various missions. As we have just seen, lay liberals are not likely to become fundamentalists. But neither are they likely candidates for conversion to any of the theological options or programs of service that are currently promoted by liberal religious leaders. For one thing, the theological discourse of lay liberals does not connect well with the options that national leaders offer. Many lay liberals take the same stands on issues of gender and sexuality that national leaders take, but very few of them expressed a serious concern for such causes as justice for peoples of the Third World, safeguarding the environment, or alleviating homelessness. For another, lay liberals do not seem eager to support church-sponsored programs that demand much sacrifice of time and energy. They want to "lead good lives," but they do not talk about selfless service. In this respect they seem closer to Calvin Caletti, the agnostic, than to Marcia Wilson or to the conservative Presbyterian whose heart goes out to the homeless. Calvin Caletti respects the basic moral code, but in his opinion some Christians carry it a bit too far. Unlike his Presbyterian grandmother, he does not take food to the sick, and he believes that "you don't have to love your neighbor if he's a jerk."

Most lay liberals will probably produce offspring who are comfortable with a mainline Protestant church, but their reluctance to take a strong stand on religious issues, or even to discuss them, makes it likely that their children will be even less committed to Christianity or to the church than they themselves are. Few of their children will rebel, for there is little to rebel against; they are more likely to be marginally involved in church life or to drift away entirely. As long as people who are brought up in churches believe in the basic moral code we have described, the churches will have children in Sunday school. The role of the church as moral teacher is unique in modern society. In most communities, no institution other than the family itself is in the business of moral teaching. The closest alternatives are such character-building programs as the Scouts or 4-H clubs. But for most people with a church background Sunday schools are the preferred place for moral education, and they want Sunday school for their children.

Type Three: Other Mainline Churched

A total of forty-eight people—10 percent of our sample of confirmands—are active in other mainline Protestant churches. The percentages of the total sample in each were 4 percent Methodist, 2 percent Congregational or United Church of Christ, 1 percent Episcopalian, 1 percent Lutheran, and 1 percent Reformed. All but four of these people have switched denominations only once in their lives; two have switched twice and two others are now in the process of making a second switch.

In the telephone interviews we asked these forty-eight people why they had switched. Given the time constraints of the interviews, it was impossible to explore in detail the brief responses most of them gave. On the basis of what they did tell us, however, we estimate that about half of the switches were motivated wholly or in part by marriage to someone of a different mainline denomination. Fifteen (about 30 percent) apparently switched to their spouse's church without exploring alternatives. Eleven others might have remained Presbyterian if they had found a suitable congregation nearby. For example, three joined their spouse's denomination after moving to a new community that had no Presbyterian church. Three more shopped around for a church in their new community and ended up choosing one affiliated with their spouse's denomination. Two others switched after enrolling their children in a preschool operated by a church of their spouse's denomination.

A second category of persons, ten in all, had no interfaith marriage. They simply moved from one town to another, went church shopping, and chose a church of another denomination. The reasons for their choice were mainly that they liked the minister, the church had good programs, it was convenient, it had a good reputation, or they felt comfortable going there. In two cases the person mentioned that there was no Presbyterian church in the new town.

Some who switched did so after visiting local Presbyterian churches and finding them uncongenial. A thirty-six-year-old dentist described his experiences this way:

> Before our son was born we went to some different churches in town here, "shopping" if you would. We went to Plymouth Presbyterian Church. It was Mother's Day, and the minister there gave a speech on the virtues of the woman at home raising her family. And he really did insinuate that if the woman wasn't at home taking care of her kids but was rather out working or something, that wasn't good. So that kind of blew my wife out of the water. We didn't go back there. Then we went to First Presbyterian Church here, which is the bedrock, foundation Presbyterian church in this area. And we went in there a couple of times, and boy, I don't know if we went during the summer and everybody was up at cottages or what, but there was us and

then the next youngest people in the church were seventy-five practically. So I thought, "Well, bag this!"

Only two of our confirmands switched for theological reasons, one to join a more relevant and liberal church, the other to join a more conservative group. No one else switched for such reasons. People who switch within mainline Protestantism do so to accommodate their spouses or because they prefer a particular congregation that happens to be in another denomination. The dentist we have just quoted found a Lutheran church that suited him and his wife fairly well:

> We ended up at a Lutheran church, where we go now. And to be honest with you, I don't really like the service there that well. There are three pastors in the church and two of them I like real well, and one is okay. But really we go there because they have got an outstanding K through 8 school right there that blows the other schools out of the water as far as test scores and all that. Well, we go because I like to go to church, and we picked that church because it's got a good school, and we'll send our kids there when they are old enough. We know a lot of people who have their kids there, and they rave about it and what have you, so we're going to send ours there too.

When it comes to switching, the major difference between active Presbyterians and Type 3s is that whereas most of the former said they *could* switch, all of the latter *have* switched. Mainline Baby Boomers are like people who prefer cars with an American brand name but who do not insist on any particular American brand. Within these people's comfort zones, factors other than brand loyalty determine the choices they make.

Switchers do, however, differ noticeably from active Presbyterians in several important ways. For one thing, their rates of church attendance are higher. Fifty-one percent attend weekly or more, compared with only 33 percent of the active Presbyterians. This finding agrees with the conventional wisdom that converts make the best church members, a view that sociological research tends to support.[4] Type 3s are also a bit more conservative than active Presbyterians in theology and on controversial moral issues. For example, on the Christ Only Index, 55 percent of the Type 3s scored high, compared with only 32 percent of the active Presbyterians. On the Morality Index 15 percent of the Type 3s scored conservative, compared with 8 percent of the Presbyterians. In addition, these people are less accepting of all religions. On the statement, "All the different religions are equally good ways of helping a person find ultimate truth," 40 percent of the Type 3s agreed, compared with 59 percent of the active Presbyterians. Finally, more Type 3s than active Presbyterians now belong to churches they describe as evangelical. Thirty-two percent of them, but only 17 percent of Presbyterians, label their current churches as "evangelical." On the other hand, Type 3s scored slightly less conservative than the Presbyterians on the Core Belief Index (83 percent vs. 89 percent).

Several pieces of evidence may help us understand why people who have switched to other mainline denominations are a bit different from those who have remained Presbyterian. They tend to live a longer distance from their hometowns than do active Presbyterians. Forty-nine percent now live more than 100 miles away, compared with 34 percent of the Presbyterians. Type 3s are also better educated; 80 percent have a bachelor's degree or equivalent, compared with only 66 percent of active Presbyterians. More Type 3s than Presbyterians married outside the Presbyterian Church. Of those ever married, only 9 percent married other Presbyterians, compared with 27 percent of those who are currently active Presbyterians. Moreover, among those married only once, 82 percent of Type 3s still considered themselves Presbyterians at the time they married, whereas fully 99 percent of active Presbyterians did so. Thus even prior to marriage many of those who later switched to another mainline denomination had ceased to be Presbyterians.

In sum, more Type 3s than active Presbyterians completed college, married outside the Presbyterian community, and moved a long distance from home. We checked the data to see whether these differences, and not denomination itself, explain the theological differences between Type 3s and active Presbyterians. They do not. The reason why the Type 3s are different from Presbyterians in degree of church involvement and in some beliefs remains unclear. Possibly Presbyterians who married theologically conservative spouses were disproportionately persuaded to join their spouses' more evangelical churches. This is speculation only; we do not know.

Type Four: Other Churched

Type 4, the last category of confirmands classified as churched, consists of persons who are active in churches or denominations not included in the first three categories. It is a residual category. Like Type 1, it consists of people who have made religious choices that are outside the comfort zones of most Presbyterians. Type 4 contains thirty-four cases, or 7 percent of the total sample. The largest number of these—3 percent of the total—are Catholics. Four people (1 percent of the total) are now Baptists, two are Jehovah's Witnesses, two belong to Presbyterian splinter denominations, three belong to independent churches, and one each belongs to the Mennonites, Unitarian-Universalists, Church of Christ, Mormons, Evangelical Free Church, Church of the Brethren, and Armenian Martyrs Congregational Church. None belong to the Unification Church or to any of the new nontraditional religious movements sometimes identified as "cults." In a few cases (see chapter 3) we had to use our best judgment as to whether persons should be placed in Type 4 or Type 1 (fundamentalists).

What brought these people to their present denominations? Let us look at the Catholics first. Conversion to Roman Catholicism is strongly associated with marrying a Catholic.[5] Of the sixteen converts to that faith, three-fourths married Catholics. To what extent did theological considerations motivate these switches to Catholicism? Our information on this matter is sketchy, but we estimate that theological factors were probably involved in one-fourth to one-third of the cases.

Of the eighteen people other than Catholics in Type 4, only three are pure cases of interfaith marriage and switching to accommodate the wishes of a spouse. Eleven other cases involved interfaith marriages that led to church shopping and exploring alternatives. A forty-two-year-old Baptist explained that "we moved several times, and we chose churches in each place. When we got to North Carolina we shopped around but found no good Methodist or Presbyterian churches. We liked the Baptist Church." Another Baptist told us that "we wanted to get the family into religion, mainly for the sake of the children. We preferred the Baptist minister here. There was no other reason. He has been a good influence." A forty-one-year-old Church of the Brethren member switched because "we felt our daughter needed a Sunday school. The Brethren church was better than the Presbyterian. Some of my family and friends went to it, and I felt more at home there."

A few switched for spiritual or theological reasons. One person who joined an independent charismatic church after a period of inactivity expressed her reasons this way:

> I realized a lack in my life. Also we had some marital troubles. I heard about this church from friends; it had made them stronger. This church brought us closer to the Lord than the Presbyterian Church had.

At the other end of the theological spectrum was the forty-year-old Unitarian who told us that

> during college I was not relating to traditional churches, and I enjoyed outdoor activities. I became progressively less and less comfortable in the Presbyterian Church, and doubted so much I couldn't even say the Apostles' Creed. I visited a Unitarian church, and it felt like home to me. It expressed my values, but still had a meaningful tradition.

Are these people distinctive in any other way? Perhaps it is pertinent that they have slightly less college education than the active Presbyterians and other mainline Protestants; 55 percent of them have a bachelor's degree, compared with 66 percent of the Presbyterians and 80 percent of the other mainline Protestants. Type 4s also have tended to marry earlier than the active Presbyterians, and they have a higher divorce rate. Moreover, as a group they tend to live farther from their hometowns than do either active Presbyterians or other mainline Protestants. Being very far away from home may embolden those with serious religious interests to try out a faith outside the comfort zone of most mainline Protestants. The overall picture of Type 4s is of persons who have less education and fewer social ties that keep them involved in mainline Protestantism.

Type 4s attend church more frequently than the Presbyterians and other mainline groups (though not the fundamentalists); 63 percent have attended weekly in the past year, compared with 33 percent of the Presbyterians and 51 percent of the other mainline church members. Their religious and moral attitudes are generally similar to those of Presbyterians and other mainline Protestants, and clearly different from those of fundamentalists. To sum up, we know *how* this group is distinctive, but we are not quite sure *why* it is distinctive. The principal explanations probably have to do with marriage, friendships, effectiveness of ministers, and positive or negative experiences in various churches.

Chapter 5

Four Types of Unchurched Persons

A s reported in chapter 3, 48 percent of our main sample were unchurched, and four types can be discerned—unchurched attenders (10 percent), unchurched members (9 percent), uninvolved but religious (21 percent), and nonreligious (8 percent).

Type Five: Unchurched Attenders

Unchurched attenders (Type 5) have attended church at least six times in the last year but are not members of a church. Fifty of our sample of confirmands—10 percent of the total—are of this type. Of these fifty, four (1 percent of the total) attend fundamentalist churches, nineteen (4 percent) attend Presbyterian (U.S.A.) churches, four (1 percent) attend other mainline churches, six (1 percent) attend Catholic churches, and eleven (2 percent) attend other churches, including Baptist, Friends, Christian Science, and Unity. Six people (1 percent) have sampled a variety of churches during the past year.[1]

It seems reasonable to assume that people who attend a church without joining it are less committed to the church or its teachings than are those who both attend and belong. Our data agree. On the whole, people in Type 5 are less committed than are those we classified as churched. Their rate of church attendance is much lower than that of the churched types.

Only 10 percent attended weekly during the past year and only 27 percent attended as often as two or three times a month. The comparable figures for active Presbyterians are 22 percent and 44 percent respectively. A higher proportion of the unchurched attenders have dropped out of church during their lives (79 percent compared with 57 percent), and their level of confidence in "church or organized religion" is lower than that of the churched types. As we saw in chapter 4, unchurched attenders are also somewhat more liberal in their beliefs than active Presbyterians. They scored lower on both the Core Belief and Otherworldly Indexes, slightly higher on the Individualism Index, and more liberal on the Morality Index. Moreover, they are the most liberal of the five types of confirmands (Types 1 through 5) who now attend church at least six times a year.

Compared with the churched types, unchurched attenders are also less likely to be involved in stable marriages that include children. Twenty-six percent are currently unmarried, compared with 16 percent of the churched types. Of those ever married, fewer were married in church (72 percent compared with 92 percent). Fully 52 percent have been divorced, compared with only 16 percent of those who are churched, and a higher proportion have married a second time (34 percent compared with 10 percent). Unchurched attenders are also more likely to be without children (35 percent compared with 15 percent). As a group they live farther from their hometowns and are more geographically transient. Seventy-seven percent, as compared with 42 percent of the churched, now live more than 100 miles away from home. In the past five years, 79 percent of the unchurched attenders, compared with only 56 percent of the churched, have had one or more changes of residence. On the other hand, they have higher rates of involvement in nonchurch community organizations and social movements (49 percent are involved, compared with 34 percent of the churched). They do not differ from churched persons in level of education.

From the interviews we were able to discern several kinds of motivations for attending a church without joining it. About thirteen of the fifty unchurched attenders go to church mainly for the sake of their spouses, parents, or children. In all but three of these cases the churches they attend, but have not joined, are outside the comfort zone of most active Presbyterians. For example, all six of the unchurched attenders who go to Catholic churches are married to Catholic spouses.

Twelve of the persons in Type 5 were in the process of "shopping around" or "trying out a church." About half of these have visited several churches, and the others have gone to one repeatedly to try it out. A few of these people are newly arrived in their communities, but the majority are not; most are experimenting with church involvement or moving to a new church after a bad experience in an earlier one. Several persons told us why they are currently shopping for a church. A thirty-six-year-old divorced homemaker, now married to a Catholic, attends church on holidays and special occasions with her husband and his children by a former marriage, but she does not find the Catholic Church congenial. Now that her own daughter is two years old, she has decided that she wants her daughter brought up as a Protestant, and she has a feeling of urgency to find a church in which she will feel comfortable.

About sixteen of the fifty unchurched attenders are "settled in" at their churches and are no longer shopping around. Some are quite active and teach Sunday school or attend Bible study groups. Two expect to join their church in the near future. Four others participate in churches (Unitarian-Universalist, Friends, Unity) that do not put a great deal of emphasis on formal membership. Many, however, have misgivings of one sort or other that deter them from joining their church. A forty-two-year-old printer with two children who attends a Wesleyan church explained his misgivings this way:

> I am not against being a member in a church. We were members in the last two churches we went to. But now I am hesitant, since lots of the people in this church are different from us. We don't feel a sense of identity here. We have some problems with this church, and we may even be leaving it.

Ann Brooks, whom we met in chapter 1, would readily understand what deters the following thirty-eight-year-old store manager from joining the church she attends:

> I would rather attend a church only, and not join it. Because when you join, you take on an obligation. Then the church is no longer a refuge. It becomes a burden. If you aren't a member, no one asks "Where were your kids last week?" and no one calls you asking you to help with bingo or a youth program or whatever. You have no obligation to donate, and you don't have to ask your company to donate to some local project. You have more freedom. Our life, with my three kids, is already too hectic. There is too much pressure. It's sports, lessons, and this and that. I don't want to have to answer to anyone else. Sometimes I have to take the phone off the hook just to have some time with my kids. I have a few friends who feel the same way.

The question of whether working women attend church less frequently than women who are homemakers has been studied repeatedly in the past. Results have been mixed. Either the studies found no association between working status and church attendance, or they found that working married women attended a bit less than others. In the present study we found no association between working status—homemaker, part-time working, or full-time working—and church attendance. On the other hand, a 1990 nationwide study by Bradley Hertel did find an association.[2]

A forty-one-year-old businesswoman had a different reason for not joining the conservative church she attends. She is in her second marriage, and she would join if the church's membership standards were less exacting. She and her husband attend Sunday school and church weekly. But in that church asking for membership requires going before a board of elders—all men—who might raise questions about her divorce, and she refuses to submit herself to such an ordeal. Similarly, in several cases people seemed hesitant to join their churches because of self-doubts related to recent divorces or to alcoholism or to bad experiences at other churches.

In sum, there are many reasons why people attend church without becoming members. Those who are shopping around are like people who are "playing the field" in an effort to find a mate. They have not joined yet because they have not found the church that suits them. Others have entered into a longer-term relationship with a church, but, like many couples who live together out of wedlock, they have reservations about the relationship and are unwilling to "tie the knot" by formalizing it. Overall, compared with the churched types, the unchurched attenders are more geographically mobile, less involved in conventional family life, less involved in their churches, and more likely to have spouses with religious backgrounds different from their own.

Type Six: Unchurched Members

Unchurched members are the obverse of churched attenders. They maintain church membership but attend fewer than six times a year. Nine percent of the total sample (48 people) are unchurched members. All but eight are members of Presbyterian churches. Two belong to the Church of the Brethren, two are Methodists, one is Baptist, one is Episcopalian, one belongs to the United Church of Christ, and one belongs to a nondenominational church.

Type 6 contains three distinct groups of people. The first group are those who continue to live in or near the community in which they resided as adolescents, but who dropped out of church by the age of twenty-two and have attended seldom if ever since then. This group contains approximately nineteen persons. Why did they drop out, and why did they retain their membership all these years?

We heard a wide range of explanations for why they dropped out. Some of the responses were vague, partly because the event took place years ago. Many simply said they had been too busy to attend. Others told us that they had lost interest, had always doubted the teachings of Christianity, disliked the hypocrisy of organized religion, or rebelled against religion in general. A few said that they left out of a sense of shame for the lives they were leading. We also heard several stories critical of particular churches.

Why have these inactive people not dropped their church membership as well? Although we did not ask them this question directly, we suspect that a desire for religious education for their children is a large part of the answer. All nineteen told us they would want a child of theirs to go to Sunday school, and of the eleven who have children living at home, ten now have them enrolled in Sunday school or expect to do so in the near future. A desire to maintain family traditions or good family relationships may also keep some from dropping their church membership. A few persons mentioned that members of their family have long-standing ties to their church.

The second group within Type 6 is made up of those who dropped out a little later in life. The seven persons in this group dropped out in their late twenties or early thirties, in every case before age thirty-four. None of them have children in Sunday school. The reasons they gave for dropping out were vague. For example, they "just got out of the habit," they were "too busy," or their "work schedule" prevented them from attending. In most cases there was also a loss of interest in the church. For this group, maintaining good family relationships may be the main reason they have not dropped their membership. Six of the seven are still members of their hometown churches.

The third group is composed of thirteen persons who stopped church attendance recently because they were hurt or dissatisfied with something related to their church. For example, one woman stopped attending when she was removed from a job at a social agency sponsored by her church. Another left with her husband after he became upset with the cliques at their church. A few who had remarried dropped out because their new spouses were not made to feel welcome. Others departed because of church conflicts of various kinds, usually involving a change of pastors. One woman was angry about an episode when she transgressed the unwritten rules the "old biddies" in her church had established for using the church kitchen. Because none of these people quit out of boredom or lack of time and interest, we suspect that most of them are candidates for becoming active again in the future. Some may return to their old churches if the conditions that antagonized them are rectified; others will find new churches.

The remainder of the unchurched members, about ten in all, cannot be neatly categorized. Several told us, either explicitly or by implication, that other claims on their time and energy take precedence over church participation. For example, one woman dropped out because she must care for her mother, who is ill. Two women recently withdrew from all church activity because their lives had become too hectic rearing small children. They hinted that they might still be attending if someone at church had not nagged them to become even more involved. Feeling both guilty and put-upon, they responded by dropping out entirely. Both are uneasy with their decision. One woman, a wife and mother of three, who works part-time as a nurse, told us:

For me to give up a whole morning is a lot. I had a friend here from Utah who looked at me and said, "This is crazy, this is crazy here." My job, up until two weeks ago, made my life crazy and busy. My kids walk in here at quarter to four and we have a snack. And it's da, da, da—this, then that. And it's maybe rush one to piano, and it's do homework, and then it's dinner, and then it's clean-up, and it's do the homework, and get them ready to go to bed, or get one to soccer or get one to ballet or get one to piano or violin or wherever you've got to go. And all of a sudden it's Friday and there are certain things you have to do to maintain your home. Or certain things you want to do as a family unit.

Like Ann Brooks and the store manager who sometimes disconnects her telephone "just to have some time with my kids," this woman wants to enjoy the benefits of church without having to contribute a great deal of time and energy to it. Ann is a Type 7 because at the time we interviewed her she neither attended a church nor belonged to one. The store manager is a Type 5 because she has found a church she likes but hesitates to commit herself to it fully. The woman we have just quoted is a Type 6 because she has scaled back her involvement but does not want to cut her church ties completely.

Like Ann Brooks, this woman would also like to attend church unobtrusively. She went to a large Lutheran church with a friend and enjoyed "the anonymity of it." "I'm not going to church to see who has a new outfit on or to see how many hours somebody gave," she declares. "I go to church to reach for a little higher dimension, something a little more intangible." She has even tried out a Catholic church:

> I wouldn't mind going to a Catholic church. I don't know much about the religion. The only thing that attracts me to their church is that I can go to a five o'clock service in a pair of pants.

Type Seven: Uninvolved but Religious Persons

One-fifth of our Baby Boomers (21 percent) fall into the seventh type, "uninvolved but religious." These persons are not church members and do not attend as often as six times a year, yet they think of themselves as religious. All other respondents who are not church members or attenders, and who said they are "not religious at all," were put into the eighth type, the "uninvolved and nonreligious" (8 percent of the sample).

Type 7 is the largest category of unchurched persons and the second largest of the eight types. If the mainline denominations want more Baby Boomers to become involved in church life, they must learn something about Type 7 confirmands.

Those classified as Type 7 are disproportionately men. Fifty-five percent are male, compared with 46 percent of the entire sample and only 42 percent of the active Presbyterians. They tend to come from families that were less likely than the average to have been Presbyterian; 89 percent of their mothers and 77 percent of their fathers were Presbyterian, compared with 94 and 87 percent respectively in the sample as a whole. As high school students, Type 7 confirmands attended Sunday school or church less often than others in our sample (50 percent attended weekly, compared with 62 percent overall), and participated less in church youth programs (39 percent participated "often," compared with 54 percent overall).

Type 7 respondents are slightly less conventional than their peers in other family-related matters. Fewer are currently married (70 percent vs. 79 percent of the whole sample), and fewer have children (62 percent vs. 76 percent) (see Figure 5.1). Nineteen percent were never married, compared with 10 percent overall. Those who married tended to do so later: 40 percent married at age twenty-six or older, versus 31 percent of the entire sample. Only 13 percent of the women are now homemakers, versus 23 percent of the women in the total sample. People in Type 7 tend to live farther from their hometowns now; 62 percent live more than 100 miles away, compared with 50 percent overall. On the other hand, they differ little from the rest of the sample in their educational and occupational histories.

In the realm of religion, Type 7 persons tend to have less orthodox views than do members of the sample as a whole, and a higher proportion take liberal positions on controversial moral issues. For example, only 7 percent, as opposed to 23 percent of all confirmands, believe the Bible is God's Word and all it says is true. Seventy percent, as compared with 56 percent of the entire sample, agree that "all the different religions are equally good ways of helping a person find ultimate truth." A scant 5 percent agree that "only followers of Jesus Christ and members of His church can be saved," compared with 88 percent of the fundamentalists and 33 percent of the active Presbyterians.

In general, Type 7 persons are uncertain about life after death. While 56 percent of the entire sample believe in "a divine judgment after death where some shall be rewarded and others punished," only 38 percent of Type 7 respondents agree. Type 7s also tend to be more individualistic in religious matters than their peers are. Eighty-two percent, compared with only 63 percent of the entire sample, agree that "an individual should arrive at his or her own religious beliefs independent of any churches or synagogues." A higher proportion agree that individuals "should seek out religious truth for themselves and not conform to any church's doctrines."

FIGURE 5.1

Comparison of Type 7 Persons (Uninvolved but Religious) with Others (percentages)

Have children:

Uninvolved	62
All Others	79
All Churched	85

Now live more than 100 miles from hometown:

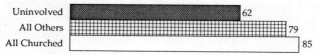

Uninvolved	62
All Others	46
All Churched	42

Changed residences at least once in the past 5 years:

Uninvolved	67
All Others	58
All Churched	56

Religious conservative:

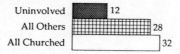

Uninvolved	12
All Others	28
All Churched	32

Political conservative:

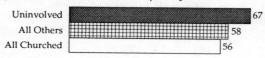

Uninvolved	23
All Others	46
All Churched	49

They are also more likely to consider themselves religious liberals and to score low on the Core Belief Index. Clearly Type 7 contains a high proportion of lay liberals, perhaps as much as two-thirds.

On controversial moral issues, Type 7 respondents are again more liberal than the sample as a whole. For example, 78 percent agree that "in general, premarital sexual relations between persons committed to each other are morally appropriate"; by contrast, 56 percent of the entire sample agreed. They are also more liberal on these issues than are active Presbyterians, though the differences in some cases are very small. They differ most sharply from Presbyterians in their evaluation of today's more permissive sexual standards, with Presbyterians considerably more likely to view them as "a change for the worse."

In chapter 4 we learned that many active Presbyterians grew up in families in which religious matters were rarely talked about. According to our taped interviews, discussions about religion were even less common in the families from which Type 7 respondents came. Most of them were not deeply nourished in the Christian faith at home or at church, and their dropping out did not reflect a radical change of belief. The seeds of their departure were planted years earlier. In some cases one parent was not involved in the Presbyterian church; in others both parents were regular churchgoers but gave few signs that Christian faith was an important part of their lives. Betty Taylor's family prevented her from dropping out; the families of Type 7s were less likely to resist. Few Type 7 respondents grew up in families like Marcia Wilson's.

For example, a thirty-nine-year-old unmarried accountant recalled that her father had taken the children to Sunday school and church every week, but that her mother never attended. The reason her mother stayed at home was not discussed in the family, nor did her father share his own religious views with the children. While she was away at college her parents were divorced and her father soon moved to another state, where he remarried and embarked on a new career. Although he had always been a faithful churchgoer, he dropped out as soon as he moved away and he has never returned. Looking back, his daughter suspects that her father had attended church

> because he saw himself as a good parent, and it was a very small town we lived in. I mean, you know, people "go to church" there. And he was the publisher of a local newspaper, and at one time a candidate for political office. You just *do* those kinds of things. You go to church on Sunday!

In all likelihood her father, like herself, was a lay liberal. Now unmarried, busy with her career, and living in a metropolitan community, she sees no point in going to church.

One Type 7 respondent brought up in California recalls that when he was a small boy grace was said at meals and prayers were said at bedtime. The family, nine in all, went to church without fail every Sunday—"and there was no getting out of it." On the other hand, "if you asked me *why* we all went to church, I wouldn't be able to tell you. As a matter of fact, I can't even remember discussing religion in my house." His parents' love of animals and his father's reverence for nature made a lasting impression on him, but their religious views remained a mystery, though he sensed that his father had "more of a spiritual view of God than a 'person' view—that's just the feeling I got." In Sunday school he learned some rudiments of the Christian faith, but he stopped attending church shortly after confirmation, and his parents offered no resistance. "It's kind of like my parents said, 'OK, fine, you're confirmed; you're a member of the church now.'" Neither he nor any of his six brothers and sisters are currently active in a church.

> My brother Tom, the oldest boy, he had a kid and he thought, "You know, from your upbringing, she really ought to be exposed to some kind of church." But then all the rest of us said, "Well, *why*? What did it do for me?" My brother Harold came to that point too. I think he tried going to church for a short period of time. But it didn't work. And now his wife goes to church with the kids.

Today this man does not "believe in a single almighty God," but he does believe that "this is all too special, too detailed an existence to be random," and he finds the doctrine of reincarnation appealing.

It seems clear that many people in our sample were confirmed without having a good understanding of the Christian faith or a genuine commitment to it. A few respondents told us that they had been reluctant to be confirmed. A thirty-five-year-old technician remembers the double bind he experienced as he contended with his doubts about the faith and the pressures that were on him to affirm it publicly:

> At that age you just don't all of a sudden say, "Mom, Dad, I really don't want to join the church, and I know that all the people my age and all of your friends' kids are joining, but I don't know if I believe that now." I don't think any child could say that to their parents at that age.

At the time, however, he saw no real alternative to going ahead with confirmation. "If you don't do it, you're very, very strange; your parents are going to be very upset." He decided to perjure himself. At a retreat in the mountains of Maryland,

> we met with the minister and everything and talked about life, and it was really kind of funny because I knew what he wanted to hear from me. I didn't know if I really believed that, but I knew what to say. And that's one thing that I didn't particularly like about the Presbyterian church, saying "OK, you're a member and you're promising to do this, and this is the way you feel at age 14." It's too early. I didn't even know *me*, and how could I really know everything else that was going on?

Lay Liberalism Revisited

The most striking finding from the in-depth interviews we conducted with people classified as Type 7 is how closely their thinking about issues of faith resembles that of the lay liberals we encountered among active Presbyterians. As we observed earlier, on matters of faith the sharpest differences among our confirmands are between fundamentalists and religious agnostics rather than between those who are churched and those who are not.

Like the lay liberals who are active Presbyterians, Type 7s are reluctant to impose their own religious views on their children. Ann Brooks lets Kevin and Stephanie know what she believes, but she never tries to convince them that her beliefs are true. Type 7s also resemble other lay liberals in not discussing religion with their friends and in seldom discussing it with members of their immediate families. As an accountant told us, "if someone wants to hear about what I believe or is interested in learning about it, that's fine; but I don't try to influence anyone." The religious tolerance zones of Type 7 respondents are extremely broad. None of them offered religious arguments against the teachings of Catholics, Buddhists, or Muslims, though a few criticized the exclusivism of Christian fundamentalists and one condemned Islamic fundamentalists for condoning the assassination of those who disagree with them.

Our interviews with those classified as Type 7 enable us to pinpoint more precisely the problems that lay liberals have with orthodox versions of the Christian faith. The three most often mentioned problem areas are the lack of religious authority, the relativity of religious truth, and uncertainty about an afterlife.

Problem 1: The Lack of Religious Authority. The key to lay liberals' uncertainty about religious truth is their deep ambivalence concerning the authority on which claims to the truth of Christianity rest. On what foundation does one build a faith? To what does one turn to make decisions of ultimate importance?

Historically, the scriptures have been the ultimate religious authority for Protestant Christians. However, many lay liberals, whether churched or not, told us that they could not accept the Bible as a reliable authority. Barbara Hickman speaks for most of those who think this way. Barbara is a thirty-three-year-old mother who lives with her husband and two small children in a suburb near Washington, D.C. She has recently decided to move her part-time computer programming business to her home so that she can care for her children. Her religious background resembles Marcia Wilson's. Both of Barbara's parents were active, serious-minded Presbyterians and she did not curtail her own church participation when she was in her teens. Unlike Marcia, however, Barbara began doubting what she had been taught about Christianity and she dropped out of church life. It has been a long time since either she or her husband, a former Catholic, has attended church.

Barbara still reads the Bible now and then because "it is inspirational." But she is "very annoyed by people who want to take it literally and use it to show other people what to do. I don't like that." The Bible may work as a source of inspiration, but it cannot be turned to for ultimate authority.

A thirty-five-year-old computer operator recounted the disillusionment she experienced when she was introduced to other religious systems in a college anthropology class:

And I thought, it's like all these societies have a reason for creating these beliefs, and maybe these religions aren't the real thing. I mean it's like growing up you were told, "This is the Bible. It's sacred. There is a God. You believe the Bible. God told men to write this book." And you believe that. But when you see all the rest of this and you think, "Well, no. The men wrote the book, but they wrote from the perspective of the day that they were living in."

The belief that the institutional church might be a source of ultimate authority—a largely pre-Reformation notion—was rejected by everyone in the study except a few fundamentalists, and those persons respected the authority of specific teachers and clergy, not the church as an institution.

A forty-one-year-old social service administrator exemplified the widespread ambivalence among Baby Boomers when she spoke about the paucity of available bases of religious authority:

Basically, I don't think there are any religious authorities. Perhaps Christ was as much of one as we have ever had, in a lot of ways. That doesn't mean to me that he was divine. The problem is when you start getting into the spiritual kinds of authority you are accepting *so much* on faith. So *no*, I would say that there is no one that I feel is an authority, because I don't have the faith that I need to believe.

If there are no ready sources of authority for truth claims, then where should one turn when making the crucial decisions of life? We put this question to Barbara Hickman, who replied:

It's hard. What do you base it on if you don't have a religion? A lot of things you kind of just fall into, I think. You make a decision based on what you know. You try to be true to your own values.

Barbara was one of many Type 7 respondents who turned to her own resources, in her words, to "what you know," to make religious decisions. She has come to the disconsoling conclusion "that I don't think there's any way—though it distresses me greatly—to ever know the truth about life *at all*, to ever really know the truth about why we're here and why the world is the way it is." She acknowledges that some people have overcome their existential distress by making a "leap of faith," but she would feel dishonest doing so. She believes that everyone needs a sense of purpose. Since she no longer believes that God imparts that sense, "you have to summon up your own purpose." Hers is "helping other people and giving of yourself to other people." In spite of her skepticism she has not abandoned the values instilled in her by her family and church. For lay liberals like her, preferences in religion are like preferences in art; since no agreed-upon authorities exist, questions of good or bad art and religion need to be decided by each individual on the basis of personal feelings. There is little else to go on.

Problem 2: The Relativity of Religious Truth. If neither the Bible nor the church is the ultimate religious authority, what is? A Muslim would answer that the Qur'an is such an authority, and a Mormon would point to the revelations that Joseph Smith claimed to receive, but none of our Baby Boom confirmands who doubt the authority of the Bible have accepted a different authority. Instead, they incline toward relativism in matters of religion. One lay liberal we interviewed declared that

> I don't think that you can ever say what's true and what isn't. To me, there is no way of being able to factually say, "This is absolutely the truth." You have to do it on faith, and if you take it on faith, how can you prove it? You might know it within yourself, but it's not something provable.

So strong is the skepticism about any religion's claims to ultimate truth that most Type 7 respondents oppose sending missionaries to convert people to Christianity. Many respondents made the distinction between missionaries who *serve* and those who *convert*. A forty-one-year-old airport manager made such a distinction when he was asked whether missionaries should be sent to convert people:

> Convert? No. Educate? Yes. I think that's probably part of the reason that some of the wars are going on—the attempt of conversion rather than education. Let them be simply *aware* of other people in the world besides them, and not have to believe exactly the same as the next person believes. It would probably be a lot more peaceful. Conversion, I think, is forcing someone to do something *foreign*.

Some Type 7 respondents posit the existence of a universal truth underlying all religious teachings, some doubt that we will ever know the real truth even if it exists, and some reject the notion of religious truth altogether. Many of those we interviewed voiced more than one of these views. Barbara Hickman has no firm convictions on the subject. "I'm not saying that there's no truth in any religion," she told us, "because I don't really know." She has no objection to others making a leap of faith, "if it makes your life happier, sure; if it makes you better toward your fellow man."

Another interviewee admitted her skepticism about the existence of ultimate truth while affirming her personal preference for Presbyterianism. When we asked her about religious truth, her initial response was that "ultimate truth is an individual thing" that is "within yourself," though she went on to say that "the religious influence, the educational influence, the political influence, and experiences" can help a person discover it. After a pause and a laugh, she exclaimed, "I'm not sure if there *is* a truth!" As for her own preference,

Well, I think that I basically have cast my lot with the Presbyterian church —I guess. I still believe the things I was brought up to believe. But I'm not so sure that ultimate truth is in any one religious doctrine. I think maybe each religious doctrine has a great deal of truth to it.

When pressed, most Type 7 respondents concluded that the issue of ultimate truth may be insoluble. As a result, it was not a matter of overwhelming concern. "I may never know" what religious truth is, a thirty-five-year-old management trainee told us.

I guess I just think about it, and if I don't have an answer then, I let it be until I can think about it again. *Perhaps* an explanation will come at some point in time. I'm comfortable with saying, "I don't know and that's OK, and we'll reconsider it again later."

Problem 3: The Afterlife. Although none of the persons classified as Type 7 have traditional convictions concerning heaven and hell, their views about the afterlife are quite diverse. Asked whether there is an afterlife, Barbara Hickman replied, "I'd say a pretty unequivocal no—at this point." A thirty-seven-year-old engineer has different views:

I do think there's *some* place we go. I don't know where it is. I don't think we go there and stand around drinking Pepsi either. You know, I don't think we go there and maintain ourselves as we are now—have whole conversations and have memories and whatnot. It doesn't even make sense to me.

Like many Type 7s we talked to, this man is attracted to the doctrine of reincarnation. He speculates that the afterlife is "going to be more like a continuum."

The Hindu idea of reincarnation, I like that idea. It seems reasonable. Maybe when you die your energy is used up in some other form. Maybe some of it as animals. Maybe some of it as free-energy fields or something. I don't know. Some life form.

An accountant we interviewed became intrigued with the doctrine of reincarnation after reading books written by Edgar Cayce, the late psychic who did much to popularize it.

You have a purpose in life and until you get correct what you are here for, you will come back until you *do*. And then once you do, you would move on because there are other planes of existence where you have other things to learn.

Despite her attraction to this teaching, neither she nor anyone else we talked to is firmly convinced of its truth. For most who mentioned the topic, reincarnation was a matter of bemused conjecture rather than one of real conviction. It seemed more plausible than the Christian idea of heaven and hell, partly because it fits better with scientific notions of energy and cycles, and partly because it strikes many as more fair and just than certain traditional notions of the afterlife.

These three problems—the lack of religious authority, the relativism of religion, and uncertainty about the afterlife—were the biggest philosophical obstacles to faith among Type 7 persons. While not everyone expressed these doubts, about two-thirds did. These issues underlie the ambivalence that many Type 7 persons have had about religion in general and church participation in particular, and they have been instrumental in keeping many from rejoining congregations.

The Moral Code

Like the lay liberals who are active Presbyterians, Type 7s agree on the importance of the shared moral code we described in chapter 4. Time and again, the respondents brought up the topic without any prompting on our part, and they linked it with religion. The views expressed by a thirty-five-year-old businessman are typical of most of those who rarely if ever attend church but who describe themselves as religious. In his opinion, what is especially praiseworthy about Christianity is "just its basic belief that humans are supposed to be good people. Don't go out of your way to be mean to people." He admires Buddhism as well. "I don't see the Buddhists going out saying, 'Kill anybody that's not a Buddhist.' It's, 'Let them be whatever they want to be.'" Type 7 respondents consider any religion to be acceptable if it is tolerant of outsiders.

Another businessman defined the very essence of religion as morality. In response to our question as to whether "there is something out there that's got to guide us all, that is important for all of us to know about," he answered, "Yeah. Try not to hurt people. Don't lie to people. Do unto others as you want done to you, basically." A woman who believes in the afterlife told us that the best way to prepare for it is to "be a good person. Be *fair* to others and *just* to others. And I think that you should do the best that you can do in this life." In her opinion, God has no favorite religion, but God does expect people to be basically moral. A similar view was expressed by the person who told us that "probably as long as I'm doing the right thing, being fair and all, and trying my best," everything will be "all right" in the hereafter. This was also the position of the schoolteacher who believes that "if somebody, no matter what religion they are, is trying to be a good person, then that's all that really matters!" Many Type 7 respondents would agree with the man who considers Jesus an excellent "role model—showing how to live."

We asked Barbara Hickman about her overall objective in life, and she replied that it is "living the best I can every day, and striving to be a better person, and striving for good rather than the downfall of things. That's my purpose." As we have seen, Barbara is not really convinced that her "purpose" in life reflects the mandate of a transcendent spiritual authority. She cannot make a *religious* leap of faith, but she and the many like her have no trouble making a *moral* leap of faith. Her awareness of religious pluralism and her exposure at college to the critical study of religion have undermined her confidence in the existence of religious truth. But she and all the other lay liberals we interviewed in depth accept the basic moral code. They are like Calvin Caletti, the agnostic who assumes that moral standards "sort of stand up on their own." Calvin also believes that there may "be some inherent good in you" that facilitates the making of proper moral choices. He might agree with the Type 7 respondent who thinks that "you don't have to ask anybody" the right way to live. "I mean it just comes from within you. You'll know; you'll just instinctively know." For him, the basic moral code is inscribed in the human heart and is revealed to us subjectively.

Comfort Zones

Like the active Presbyterians in chapter 4, very few Type 7 respondents have been members of any religious body other than the Presbyterian church (8 percent of Type 2s and 12 percent of Type 7s). A few people talked about psychic powers and extrasensory perception and, as we have seen, even more talked about reincarnation. But otherwise the New Age themes—such things as past life regressions, channeling, crystal healing, and mental self-cultivation—were not taken seriously. Few, if any, seem to have adopted New Age religious perspectives on ultimate truth. Furthermore, no one reported having been a member of the Hare Krishna organization, the Unification Church, or other well publicized "cults" of the 1970s.

The religious comfort zones of Type 7s are as narrow as they are for most active Presbyterians. Most would be comfortable in a Methodist or Episcopal church, though several had reservations about Episcopalian ritualism and Methodist attitudes toward alcohol. We encountered the same personal aversion to Catholicism, Mormonism, fundamentalism, and fundamentalist-style Baptist churches that we encountered among Type 2s and 3s. The Mormons were criticized for their strictness and their undue control over people's lives, while the Catholics were criticized for being too medieval in rules and outlook, for praying to Mary, for being too controlled by priests, and for being unreasonable regarding birth control and the role of women.

A typical complaint concerning overly strict religions was voiced by a thirty-seven-year-old legal secretary from California:

> I sent my kids to a Mormon camp. They enjoyed it, but the more I found out about the Mormons the more I was sorry that I got them involved. They are extremely strict and they give you the distinct message that their way is *the* right way and that you're in trouble if you don't do it their way. That is a message that I don't buy. I don't like for anyone to hard-sell their religion. And once the Mormons have you, they don't let you go. They had people come to the house, which is a no-no for both me and my husband.

In view of their religious outlooks and their aversion to strict, "hard-sell" churches, why is it that so few of the lay liberals in our sample have become Unitarians or members of the liberal branch of the Society of Friends? These bodies appeal to people who derive gratification from involvement in a church community but who feel uncomfortable with conventional Protestantism. In the entire sample, however, there were no Friends and only one Unitarian. Moreover, in the United States as a whole, these religious bodies have not grown in recent decades. In fact, the Unitarian-Universalist Association has suffered membership declines since the mid-1960s just as have the mainline denominations.

The lack of interest in Unitarianism among the lay liberals in our sample suggests that this denomination may also lie outside the comfort zone of the vast majority of people who were raised as Presbyterians. Perhaps other respondents who have attended Unitarian services reacted the way this forty-one-year-old woman did:

> Something was missing. In some ways they were better Christians maybe than a lot of people in my mom's Presbyterian church. I think they were more actively involved in their community doing things to serve people. Perhaps I didn't give it enough of a shot. I only went for a while. But I wasn't comfortable with that group of people. They had prayer, but you almost felt like you weren't talking to anyone. It was pretty hard to pray. You were almost losing the spirituality or something. I felt like it was more like a gathering of psychologists. There was no sense of divinity, or something greater. They never mentioned Christ.

No Type 7 respondent we talked to is looking for a church that is *more* liberal on theological or social issues than the average Presbyterian congregation. Type 7s, for example, were not more likely than others in the sample to criticize the churches for ignoring social justice issues or for recognizing only the masculine aspects of God. If our results can be generalized, few Baby Boomers drop out of the Presbyterian church because they are looking for a different *kind* of religion; most drop out because they assign religious activities a low priority in their lives. Long-term dropouts who describe themselves as religious are not hostile toward the Presbyterian Church. Church involvement is simply not very important to them.

Complaints Against Churches

Type 7 respondents did voice many criticisms of specific churches, but they were not noticeably different in volume or content from the criticisms voiced by active Presbyterians or others who are currently involved in church life. Some interviewees felt socially snubbed at their church. "I just didn't like the people up there at Gilmore Church at all," one person told us. "Very snobby, more well-to-do people." "I don't want *no part* of it," a working-class woman exclaimed as she described how her home church had changed while she was in the armed services. "When I came back from the Navy, I walked in our church and I saw how the people snubbed you, they looked at you the way you were dressed, and all."

Hypocrisy was among the most common complaints voiced against churches. The charge of hypocrisy is not a criticism of what the churches stand for; it is a charge that the members do not live according to the standards they profess. Some considered the snubbing of social inferiors at church to be hypocritical. "Why do the members really go?" one person asked.

> Are they really going for the fellowship? I know that there was a strong social aspect at Mt. Gilead Church. It bothered me. That's not really what the purpose of church is.

Ann Brooks related several instances of more serious misconduct by the leaders of her former church, including the seduction of a church secretary and the misappropriation of church funds. "I think there are so many examples of people who are clearly ego-driven in their efforts to be religious leaders," one man told us. He is especially critical of religious leaders who profit financially or who "use religion to preach some political philosophy." He would be much less suspicious of "the little parish priest somewhere in a really poor area who is not just a priest but also a counselor, friend, helper."

Most charges of hypocrisy focused on the failure of church people to abide by the basic moral code. Barbara Hickman, however, traces her disillusionment to a discovery, around the age of seventeen, that the members of her church seemed to take the Christian faith itself with a grain of salt. As a girl, she took her faith quite seriously. She was even involved with Young Life for a time during her high school years. Barbara grew puzzled when she sensed that the members of her home church "weren't being *forceful* enough" in professing the faith:

You know, if this is really the *truth*, if Christianity was really the way that people had to live their lives and really should, then those people weren't pushing it. They didn't really seem to *believe*. I mean, they enjoyed the church, but church and religion seemed kind of separate. As I became more religious, it bothered me.

Marcia Wilson voiced a gentler complaint of the same sort about many mainline congregations, including her home church. In her experience, many "wonderful, healthy churches" manage to mute the "simple message that there is a God who died for you and if you believe in him you will live forever." Marcia perceived this only in retrospect, after her own faith had deepened. Barbara Hickman, on the other hand, perceived it while she was still in high school, and it troubled her a great deal. She arrived at college already disillusioned about church life, and after taking courses in philosophy and in the critical study of religion she abandoned her faith.

We heard a variety of other specific complaints about churches. One person told us that he dislikes all large, impersonal organizations, including churches that "empire-build" and lose a "one-on-one sense of community." A few people had experienced difficulty at church after being divorced, and a woman in an interracial marriage said that she could never go to a Presbyterian church now, since she and her husband would not feel accepted.

Since the criticisms Type 7 respondents had about churches were not substantially different in kind from the criticisms voiced by respondents who are currently active in a church, the complaints, taken by themselves, cannot be considered an inventory of the basic causes of the decline of the mainline churches. The man who dislikes large churches could have found a small church if he had really wanted to. Betty Taylor complained about the social snobbery and hypocrisy at her home church, but she is an active Presbyterian today. If Barbara Hickman had attended a Bible college instead of a secular institution, or if she had taken the Old Testament survey course taught by the "incredibly powerful woman" who taught Marcia Wilson, Barbara might have reaffirmed her faith.

Values in Churchgoing

Since the overwhelming majority of Type 7 respondents are lay liberals for whom religion is not a central life interest, the likelihood of their becoming active again in a church is governed partly by factors other than the strength of their own faith. In the interviews the Type 7s told of four positive values they saw in churchgoing. By far the most important value has to do with children, as we have seen. One viewpoint was almost unanimous in our interviews: young children should have religious education. Ninety-six percent of both the entire sample and the Type 7s said this.

The most common view was that children need basic moral training and also sufficient exposure to the Bible and religion that they know what it is and can make their own decisions about it. Without exposure they cannot evaluate the religions in our society today.

Already we have described Ann Brooks, who is the mother of two small children and is now looking for a church. We interviewed several others like her. Barbara Hickman had religious education of her children very much on her mind. She believes her children need religious education, but she and her husband aren't ready for churchgoing:

> Religious education is a question that's really hard for us. We don't go to church. Religious education is important, but it's just that I don't know if I should profess things to my kids that I don't believe, you know, if I should take them for religious training when it's for things that I don't believe in. So that's the problem! Even though I think that it may be good for them. . . . I do probably think that religious training is *good*, but I don't know if it's something that I can do right now.

We asked her why it's important for her kids.

> I think it helps little children to have a simple view of life. I think it makes their life easier for them to believe that God is taking care of them, and it definitely makes them feel more comfortable and safe, and plus, in our society it makes them more mainstream. It makes them more like everyone else, and helps them to understand what everyone else and their friends are going through.

Barbara also liked the personal experiences available in Sunday school and wanted them for her children:

> What I'm looking for, I think, is to have my children in a community of church people, because it teaches them a connectedness with the whole world and the universe and other people, in a different way than they have in school or anywhere else. And in a loving way. . . . And I think that's important for life, whether you believe in any particular religion, or whether any particular religion is *true*. I think it's good for your life to have this connectedness to the whole world, and I want my kids to feel that there is a certain order and rhythm to the universe and to life and that they're an important part of that. And I think you get that from church. . . . Also churches emphasize charitable work—service to other people. And that's emphasized different in churches than elsewhere. We do it in the Girl Scouts, but it's not with the same feeling that it is in church.

A thirty-nine-year-old single woman had a typical perspective on this issue when we asked if she would want a child of hers to have religious instruction:

Yes, I think so, because I think there are certain valuable truths that hopefully you can glean from a Sunday school and church environment. Even though I turned my back on a lot of my upbringing, I think that I garnered the best of the messages that hopefully I can try to use in my day-to-day life. The church is another avenue that could help teach children those things. You obviously have to have it from the home. No one institution in and of itself I think can be the sole provider of the teaching of moral values.

A thirty-six-year-old teacher without children told us she wanted religious training for her children—probably Protestant. We asked whether she wanted it as a form of exposure to religion today, or as a beginning of a life of faith.

Oh, I think for the exposure, the morals, the values. Learning about God and the teachings of Jesus. And I think I would want them to have faith, to believe in God. But I think you can do that *without* going to church.

On occasion we encountered people who were opposed to religious education for their children. Allison, a thirty-seven-year-old Californian, would like to join a church and enroll her two children in Sunday school, but her agnostic husband strongly objects.

I can put it this way: He would not object to them *knowing* something about religion, or being aware of religion. He doesn't think it's something you can be totally ignorant of, because you're going to run into it sometime in your life. But he does object to giving the children a regular diet of religion or getting them involved in church on a weekly basis.

Given her husband's views, Allison does what she can to expose her children to the Christian faith. She takes them to various Sunday schools now and then and she enrolls them in summer programs operated by the local churches. And whenever possible, "we have our own little religion at home":

For example, on religious holidays, Christmas doesn't come and go with the belief that it's only about Santa Claus. We talk about why Christmas is here. I think it's too distorted for them to think that somebody just created Santa Claus to celebrate Christmas. And the same with Easter. We don't celebrate Easter as a time when the Easter bunny can bring eggs.

A thirty-seven-year-old management consultant on the West Coast told us his wife, a former Methodist, misses church life and has persuaded him that they should enroll their five-year-old adopted daughter in Sunday school in the near future. "I conduct myself *strictly* by the Ten Commandments," he told us, but he does not believe in "a single almighty God" and he has no personal interest in churchgoing. Nevertheless, "Whether I'm interested or not, I will attend, because my wife and I do everything together."

Religious education for children is by far the strongest value Type 7s see in churchgoing, even overriding their objections to churches on other grounds, and it attracts people to churches who are not interested or committed in any other way. A simple fact underlies this situation: religious and moral education is a commodity not available from any other source. Public schools do not offer it. Parents need either to provide it themselves, to turn to church-related schools (mainly Catholic), or to turn to Sunday schools.

Our interviews identified other reasons why some Type 7 people are interested in churchgoing and may return in the future. The tone of these discussions about churches was positive. Everyone agreed that churches are good for the society and good for the people who go to them. No one was negative. Our interviewees talked about churches the same way they talked about civic associations, PTAs, social movements, card clubs, and other groups. That is, such institutions are good for society, children should become acquainted with them, and consumers should pick and choose. In the words of one man: "Churches are necessary. Just like I don't play golf, but I think golf courses are necessary. I may not be into it, but I see where other people are, and if it's good for them, fine." Whatever feels comfortable.

We could identify three other values of churchgoing in the minds of the Type 7s: (1) personal support, reassurance, and help; (2) social contacts and a supportive community; and (3) inspiration.

The values of personal support and reassurance were described by a thirty-five-year-old accountant:

> I have a girlfriend who goes every Sunday. And she needs that. She is, I'd say, an insecure person, and she needs that reassurance that she *is* doing the right thing. Someone that she can talk to. She really doesn't need it; I mean, she is one of the best Christians that I know. I mean, she would do anything! But she feels the need, and I think that's great. Then she should go.

A thirty-six-year-old teacher talked of the personal support from churchgoing:

> Some people need to go to church. And I think their needs can be varied. It can be maybe because of an illness that they've suffered. They reach a place where they feel they have to pull their life together. Or maybe they haven't been living life the right way and going to church is the right way. That it will help through this illness, this suffering, or whatever. I believe there are other people who go to church, much like I did when I was younger, for social reasons, because that's their way of getting to be with other people. And then there are other people who go to church because that sermon helps them through the week. It's a cleansing to go to church.

The value of social contacts and supportive community was mentioned repeatedly. A forty-one-year-old administrator told about the supportive encounters her mother has experienced:

> For example, when my father died, she had made a lot of friendships in the choir. They were extremely supportive of her. I think the first year they kept her active, they kept her involved. She is one of these people that likes to be active and involved. I think the church helped her tremendously during this time. I don't think without the church she would have gone through the whole grieving process as well supported or as quickly as she was able to. When I look at who her friends are, they tend to be mostly church people. . . . Church is more than just being social. There's a spiritual element that you don't find in a lot of institutions. You can go and play bridge and have a great "in" with a bridge club and have a great time doing it, but you don't have anything spiritual. And you don't have the moral and ethical part and the underpinnings that create real fellowship.

We asked her if there are alternatives to churches today that serve the same function.

> I'm sure there are alternatives. But I just don't know of one that is as good. It's more than just being social. There's a certain fellowship there. It could be because a part of being a Christian is being concerned about others. Even though you may not have a real interest in knowing every aspect of their lives, there still is, you know, the fellowship in Christ. You are part of a body.

She went on to talk about the bird watchers club she belongs to. It provides social life, but not the same support as a church:

> I think that sometimes church people maybe have a little more consciousness about the needs of their fellow men than these other folks do. Like, if I got sick, I'm not sure that the bird watchers or whatever would run over and take care of me. Whereas maybe if I belonged to a church, some people might, just because that's what Christians do. Like a surrogate family sometimes.

Lastly, the values of inspiration were mentioned several times. Some interviewees told of the strength they received from worship, from religious music, or merely from the hour in church away from everyday life. Barbara Hickman believes that the religious groups she belonged to in the past "have very much made the people better toward helping others." She finds inspiration in the Bible:

> There are a lot of good things, a lot of good passages in the Bible that are inspirational. It gives you something to live by. Something to pick you up and give you hope and spur you on to do good things, and be the best you can.

She also misses the sense of "connectedness with the whole world and the universe and other people," that churches impart. Other groups impart it too, but the churches do it "in a different way—and in a loving way." Barbara admires the religious life even though it may not be attainable for her.

> The religious life is very *appealing* to me, and it's very attractive, because it seems very good. Maybe that's more where I'm heading—a spiritual life as somehow separate from religion. . . . I still think it's possible that there's some type of spiritual force to the whole universe, but that it's something that's probably very difficult to think about and write down, but it might still be moving us somehow. I don't know. That would be nice!

A forty-one-year-old single woman told of spiritual values in church:

> I find that when I do go to church, which I am still doing occasionally, it reminds me of things that I need being reminded of, that sometimes I don't think of. You know, sometimes I start feeling sorry for myself for some reason, and I go to church, and say, hey, I don't have any reason to feel sorry. I can get up each morning! . . . Or maybe reminding me of the larger picture, that there's a lot more out there besides just me that one should be concerned with. It's psychological maybe. Maybe instead of a psychologist sometimes it's good to go to church!

Skeptics and the Church

Despite their rejection of the exclusive truth of Christianity, many Type 7 respondents do believe in a supernatural power or force. Other Type 7s, however, are skeptical of all religious claims. In chapter 4 we encountered a few skeptics who are active Presbyterians, which should come as no surprise in view of the fact that many Type 7 respondents return to church when they have children. But our interviews suggest that, in general, skeptics are less likely than other lay liberals to become involved again in a church. Calvin Caletti does not find worship services offensive, but he feels hypocritical singing the hymns and reciting the Lord's Prayer. The Californian who went backpacking with his father as a boy was angry when, after he joined the Marine Corps, the authorities refused to record his religious preference as "none." In boot camp he resented being forced to attend church.

> This CO here, he's saying, "You're gonna go to church." So I went to church, went to a Presbyterian service. Just *hated* it. We sang "Onward Christian Soldiers," and I thought to myself, "God, I feel like a terrible hypocrite sitting here."

On subsequent Sundays he sampled the services of other denominations, but he liked them even less than he liked the Presbyterian service. If he should ever return to church, it will be to a mainline congregation, but basically all religious bodies he knows about are outside his comfort zone.

Barbara Hickman is also uncomfortable in a religious setting in which she would feel like a hypocrite.

> At different times in my life I really tried hard to be what other people said. But now I decide for myself. Like, I don't go to church, and I don't put myself in situations where I need to be believing what other people are saying. That's what I think would be hard about going back to church.

A thirty-five-year-old woman told us she would prefer that her daughter learn about religions from courses taught in the public schools. In her opinion, Sunday schools present a one-sided view of a particular faith and do not provide a range of options from which children can make their own religious choices. "When you get into specific Sunday schools you get one person's opinion," she complains, "and it is biased toward that church." But "in a public school they would teach *different* views." Since the schools in her community do not offer courses about religion, this woman has attempted to provide a range of choices for her own daughter by sending her to Sunday school at churches of different denominations.

Calvin Caletti might endorse this woman's proposal that the public schools teach courses about religion. Calvin does not oppose his wife's taking their sons to Catholic CCD classes, but he wishes they could take a course in comparative religions instead. Neither he nor the woman just quoted would object if their children decided not to adopt a religion.

We conclude that few skeptics without children are likely candidates for recruitment to any religious body. Moreover, as we have seen, many skeptics who do have children have serious misgivings about becoming involved once more in a church. In chapter 4 we reported that active Presbyterians have lower levels of church attendance than their parents had, and we argued that their children's levels are likely to be even lower. Many Type 7s will become active again in a mainline church in order to provide their children with a religious education, but given their lay liberal outlook on religion, their children are not likely to become deeply committed churchgoers.

According to our data, those least likely to belong to or attend church are the unmarried, married people without children, people who have moved a hundred miles or more from their childhood community, and people who live in the West. The unmarried are under no pressure from their spouses to go to church. People without children do not have to worry about providing them with a religious education. Those who have moved far from home are less susceptible than others to pressures from family and old friends to maintain their church involvement. People who live in the West are under less community pressure to go to church than they are if they live elsewhere. Pressures such as these seem especially important in determining whether lay liberals participate in church. They are less important for persons like Wayne Sanders or Marcia Wilson, who have deeply internalized faiths.

Type Eight: Nonreligious Persons

The eighth and final type is those who are not church members, do not attend as often as six times a year, and call themselves "not religious." Our sample had 39 such persons, comprising 8 percent of the total.

The nonreligious, like Type 7s, are disproportionately men—56 percent are male compared with 46 percent in the whole sample and 42 percent of active Presbyterians. Like Type 7s, they had lower than average involvement in Sunday school, church, and youth programs during high school. Their fathers had the lowest church attendance rates of any of the eight types; 38 percent of their fathers attended weekly, compared with 43 percent among Type 7 respondents and 59 percent among active Presbyterians. Their mothers' weekly attendance, however, did not differ from the average. They reported low rates of church attendance and Presbyterian youth group participation while in high school. Calvin Caletti is a typical nonreligious person. He grew up in a family with a churchgoing mother and a nonreligious father.

Type 8 respondents were more likely than others to have rebelled against their religious training during junior or senior high school; 30 percent said they had rebelled, compared with 17 percent overall. Furthermore, over a third had religious doubts prior to confirmation, with fully 85 percent saying they have at some time "doubted most religious teachings." This contrasts sharply with the 37 percent rate for all others.

The nonreligious Baby Boomers also stopped attending church at an earlier age than did others who dropped out. Thirty-one percent of the Type 8 respondents dropped out by the time they were seventeen, as opposed to only 14 percent of the other groups. Most Type 8 persons left the church between the ages of fifteen and twenty. The predominant reason they gave for leaving was their religious doubt or loss of faith. Once again, Calvin Caletti is typical of Type 8 persons. During high school he became a thoroughgoing doubter, and he has remained one ever since.

The educational and occupational histories of Type 8 persons are not unusual relative to the rest of the sample. They attended college at the same rate as others. Like Type 7s, they are a little more likely than the sample as a whole to be single and a little less likely to be in their first marriage. They share with the other unchurched types a tendency to have fewer children than do people who belong to and attend a church. They are, however, a bit more likely than Type 7s to have one or more children living at home (68 percent vs. 62 percent). Along with Type 7 respondents, they have moved farther away than average from their hometowns.

Now 64 percent live more than 100 miles away, compared with 50 percent overall.

Of all the Baby Boomers, the nonreligious are the least convinced of the value of religious education for their children. In this respect they differ markedly from Type 7 respondents. Only 71 percent of the nonreligious (compared to 96 percent of Type 7s) would like their children to have a religious education. Despite this marked difference, the proportion of the two types whose children actually attend Sunday school is almost identical, and surprisingly low. Of those with children living at home, only 28 percent of Type 7s and 29 percent of Type 8s have enrolled them in Sunday school. By contrast, 80 percent of the active Presbyterians who have children are sending them to Sunday school.

As we saw in chapter 3, both Type 7 and Type 8 respondents are almost unanimous in their rejection of the teaching that salvation is available only through Jesus Christ. Type 8s differ sharply from Type 7s, however, in the percentage affirming that Jesus is God or the son of God (11 percent vs. 58 percent), that there is a divine judgment after death (5 percent vs. 38 percent), that there is no life after death (41 percent vs. 10 percent), and that God had some hand in writing the Bible (47 percent vs. 89 percent). Whereas Type 7s contain a high proportion of lay liberals who believe in a supernatural power of some kind, Type 8s incline strongly toward skepticism and agnosticism.

Both Type 7s and Type 8s are overwhelmingly liberal on the Morality Index, though the former are a little more conservative than the latter, especially on issues of sexuality. The nonreligious are also the most politically liberal of all the eight types, though they are not markedly more liberal than the Type 7s. Moreover, of all the eight types they are the most likely to reject the authority of institutions to regulate people's beliefs and values. Virtually all the nonreligious agreed with the statement, "An individual should arrive at his or her own religious beliefs independent of any churches or synagogues" (92 percent compared with 63 percent overall). Most agreed that "In the realm of values, the final authority about good and bad is the individual's conscience" (79 percent compared with 53 percent overall).

Becoming Agnostic

An inability to accept what the church taught them underlay the decision of most Type 8 respondents to stop attending. Religious skepticism and disbelief that churches *can* help a person discover the ultimate meaning in life make it very unlikely that they will return to a mainline church or, indeed, to any form of organized religion. These respondents are not "religious searchers" who have sampled other groups: only 2 percent of the nonreligious have ever been active in a denomination other than the

Presbyterian. Moreover, the great majority began doubting religious teachings by the time they were in their teens, and many—especially the males—had doubts even earlier.

A forty-two-year-old salesman in South Carolina (we will call him Jesse) is one of these males. He was reared in a churchgoing town he describes as "provincial." "Everybody would go to church," he remembers. "That was just expected, that was the norm." His mother and father were loyal Presbyterians, and when he was a boy they saw to it that he attended Sunday school and church on a regular basis.

Jesse liked being with his friends at church, but Sunday school and worship services bored him. "The sermons seemed to be the same song," he remembers. "It was the same thing over and over again." He understood what the church taught but he became skeptical at an early age, and after confirmation, with no opposition from his parents, he stopped attending church. Well before leaving home for college he had given up the last vestige of Christian belief. Since then, his views have changed very little. In his opinion, traditional Christian teachings have become "outmoded."

Jesse was never a believer, but Sue North was. Sue is a thirty-eight-year-old homemaker who lives with her husband and two small children in a remodeled farmhouse a few miles outside a conservative Michigan town. She grew up a firm believer, but like Barbara Hickman she became concerned as a teenager about the seeming hypocrisy of the members of her church. "I knew people who went to church faithfully every Sunday," she explained, "who in my estimation, were not Presbyterian the other six days of the week." It disturbed her also that although Presbyterians "supposedly believe" in predestination, no one at her church, including the minister, ever mentioned the subject. After graduating from high school and enrolling in college at the age of eighteen, Sue "left church altogether and never went back."

A thirty-seven-year-old college teacher exemplifies the early questioning often reported by Type 8 persons:

> I remember very clearly in fourth grade, questioning back and forth with my Sunday school teacher. I thought it seemed unfair and unreasonable that there should be missionaries to save people who might not have ever known about God or Jesus. I thought it was *totally* unreasonable that people who were raised with a particular kind of religion, whether they be Jewish or Buddhist or whatever, weren't going to be saved just because by happenstance they were that religion. I used to get very irate about this.

When she was in her teens she "talked at *great* length" about religion with her best friend, a Jewish girl who rejected all the distinctive tenets of Christianity. As a result of these talks, Lisa had become an agnostic by the time she went away to college.

None of the nonreligious respondents we interviewed attributed their skepticism to anything they learned or experienced while at college. In fact, in the entire sample only a handful of those we talked to at length told us that college had changed their religious beliefs. Some analysts of church decline have argued that liberal arts courses undermine Christian faith by emphasizing the diversity of cultures and the relativity of values and beliefs.[3] Among both Type 7 and Type 8 respondents, doubts concerning the validity of orthodox theology generally arose *before* college. This finding is in accord with Allan Bloom's observation that the freshmen he teaches at the University of Chicago arrive there already believing in the relativity of religious and moral truth.[4] The relativist perspective is no longer restricted to a small circle of intellectuals and academics but has become very broadly diffused within the American middle class.

Meaning and Morality

The nonreligious respondents we interviewed in depth no longer think very much about God, the afterlife, or the ultimate purpose of human existence. "If I can't explain something," a thirty-five-year-old management trainee told us, "then it might just be good enough to say, 'I don't know.'" She left the church when she stopped worrying about the meaning of life, and "then I felt comfortable." When pressed, others replied to similar questions in ways that resembled the answers lay liberals gave us. We heard opinions that God might be a form of "energy," that all religions have something in common, that ultimate truth is an individual matter, and that the most valuable part of religion is the support it gives to the basic moral code.

The nonreligious resemble Type 7 respondents in their lack of hostility toward churches or religion in general. We heard complaints about hypocrisy, but they were no more frequent among Type 8 than among Type 7 respondents. Sue North assured us that she is "not against religion—I think it's very good for some people; I just don't think it's necessary for me."

Sue, like most Type 7s and 8s, insists on the right of people to make decisions about religious truth for themselves without being constrained by the traditional authority of Bible and church. She believes that "the ultimate truth type of thing is something that each person has to develop within himself. I think it is a very individualistic thing." Therefore she rejects any church which has standards for belief. "I don't like the organized religion stuff. My biggest bone of contention is the *organized* part of it. The idea that we have to be constrained in what we believe." She is not troubled by problems of meaning, human suffering, or justice. Rather, she stresses individual choice, education, and exploration: "There is *so much* to life!"

Sue also resembles other respondents of these two types in rejecting conventional moral restraints against abortion and certain forms of sexual activity. She wants people to be free to make their own decisions about these matters. "I am for abortion. I don't have any problem with that. It's a personal preference," she declares. She adamantly opposes any attempt to restrict a woman's freedom to make the choice herself.

> It's an issue of choice. . . . You know, I do things because I want to do them. I am a law-abiding person. I don't break the law, and I don't hurt anybody. So, I want to be able to choose the way I want to choose, and I feel strongly enough about it that if it is going to become an issue, I'll take to the streets.

The defense of individual freedom is a fundamental political value for Sue. The "heavy responsibility" she and her husband took on with their decision to have children has also made her "feel responsibility to try to make my part of the world, or what I can influence in the world, as good as possible so that the kids can have a good life." She and her husband are strong environmentalists and advocates of a simpler lifestyle. He works in a nearby city, but the North family has moved to the country, where Sue can pursue her "hobby" of producing as much of their food as possible.

Children and Religion

Most nonreligious respondents would like their children to know something about religion, but their own disbelief rules out their joining a church and makes them hesitant to send their children to Sunday school. Sue North and her husband want Matt, who is five, and his two-year-old sister, Sandy, to become "well-rounded persons, very aware of religions," but they have decided not to enroll the children in a regular Sunday school program. Instead, when Matt was smaller, they sent him to Bible school for a time, and he has recently attended a nearby nondenominational Christian preschool. As a result, Matt is asking questions of his parents about religion, and they have granted his request to say grace before meals. Sue is also giving her children a basic religious education at home. "We talk about God and about Jesus, and at Christmas we always read the story and we read parts of the Bible."

But Sue does not restrict her children's religious instruction to the tenets of Christianity. Like Calvin Caletti, she wants them "to experience different religions to get an idea of how they vary, because there is such a drastic difference between them." Ann Brooks, a religious lay liberal mother, is reluctant to press her own religious views on her children. But agnostics like Sue and Calvin are less hesitant to do so. "I try to convey to Matt," Sue told us, "my feeling that God is like an energy that is imparted to all of the world and to people." She "would try to be a corrective" to any beliefs Matt voices "that I might be against. I would just tell him what I believe, because that's all I can."

Summary

What distinguishes Types 7 and Type 8 from active churchgoers? As we have seen, the differences between them began early in life. Compared with the others, those who became unchurched more often had parents who disagreed on religious matters or whose active churchgoing did not reflect a deep faith. Few Type 7 and 8 respondents told about inspiring Sunday school teachers, ministers, choirmasters, or youth leaders who influenced them during childhood or adolescence, and those who did, like Barbara Hickman and Sue North, had offsetting disillusionments later. Compared to active churchgoers, Types 7 and 8 are less likely to accept the authority of the Bible or the church in religious matters and more likely to believe that individuals should decide on these matters for themselves. They are not hostile to religion, and they approve of the support churches give to the basic moral code, but their level of interest in religion is low.

Many Type 7s have a faith of sorts, but others tend toward skepticism. All want religious education for their children, but fewer than a third who have children are sending them to Sunday school. Type 7 Boomers who might go back to church would feel most comfortable in a mainline Protestant congregation. On the other hand, Type 8s are openly skeptical of religious truth claims and they have no need for the church. Disproportionately male, politically and morally liberal, and ambivalent about religious education for their children, they are very unlikely ever to be drawn back into the mainline churches.

Decisions to Become Unchurched

We have now seen the four types of unchurched persons. Can we summarize why they became inactive? The interviews clearly show that the people had diverse motivations regarding churchgoing, some conscious and some unconscious. All we can do in an interview study such as this is to assess the motivations we were able to perceive. We went through all the interviews with unchurched persons (Types 5, 6, 7, and 8) and tried to discern the major motivations. About 5 percent of the interviews were too sketchy to allow any judgment at all, so we left them in an "insufficient information" category.

Table 5.1 describes four main reasons for leaving church life, two related to each of two "decision points." It is an oversimplification of reality, for there were multiple smaller decision points in each person's life. For example, they chose staying or leaving in light of questions like the following. Did they leave their hometowns after high school? Were there interpersonal conflicts during high school or afterward that strained their ties to

TABLE 5.1

Four Main Reasons Unchurched Persons Leave Church Life

Percentage of Total Sample

Decision Point 1: Internalized Faith

A. Never had faith	about 7–10%
B. Had faith but lost it during high school or after	about 8–11%

Decision Point 2: Affective Ties to a Church

C. Never had affective ties	about 3–5%
D. Had affective ties but lost them during high school or after	about 20–24%

their churches? Did they have an interfaith marriage? Did they have children? Did they move frequently? What were their experiences in churches in recent years? And so on. Here we are emphasizing only the two main decision points.

First Decision Point: Internalized Faith?

The first depends on whether the person has an internalized Christian faith. The majority but not all of our sample seem to have had that at the time of confirmation. A few, especially in Type 8, told us outright that they never could believe the doctrines taught them or that they felt ongoing doubts before confirmation that were never resolved. Several said that they merely went through with confirmation to please their parents or that the ministers told them to go ahead with it even if they could not accept the teachings as they understood them. We estimated the number in category A at about 7 to 10 percent of the total sample. They are mostly in Types 7 and 8.

The concept "faith" here is an oversimplification of reality. Our respondents made many distinctions when talking about Christian teachings; for example, they often were concerned about the moral precepts the church should promote rather than its theological formulations. In trying to categorize these persons we were guided by the Core Belief Index, which asked about whether a person should live with the assumption that there is life after death, whether Jesus was divine, and whether the Bible was inspired by God. Anyone doubting one or more of these was categorized as not having an internalized faith.

When talking to persons of category A, we heard some cynicism about the confirmation process itself. Some told us it was done too early, or that it didn't mean anything, or that they merely went through the motions without revealing their true convictions to anyone. We are left wondering whether the churches are well served by a system producing cynicism in a significant percentage of its youth. Maybe these youth should have been excused from the process.

Persons in category B seemed to have had some faith at confirmation but to have lost elements of it afterward. For example, Sue North lost her specifically Christian commitment during high school and college because of her intellectual growth and her talks with a Jewish boyfriend. In many cases the process was unclear, and we had to make a judgment whether a person fit into category A or B. We estimated the size of category B at about 8 to 11 percent of the total sample. Type 8 (nonreligious) persons are almost entirely of categories A and B.

Second Decision Point: Affective Church Ties?

The second decision point concerns affective ties to other church members. Some of our interviewees never experienced warm ties to other church members; they told us that they never felt at home in their church or that the other kids at church put them down. Some persons seemed to have an internalized faith in spite of these unfortunate situations. They do not go to church now, and in the interviews they reminded us that "you don't have to go to church to be a good Christian." We estimated that about 3 to 5 percent of the total sample were in category C—that is, never had affective ties to others in the church. About 20 to 24 percent were in category D, which contains the majority of Types 5 and 6 (unchurched attenders and unchurched members).

Table 5.1 separates internalized faith and affective ties to a church, whereas in reality these factors were often concurrent and mutually influencing. For example, some persons told us that during their high school years they had grave doubts about church teachings *and* never felt at home with the other youth in the church. Others indicated that unhappy encounters with pastors and parishioners increased their sense of the church's hypocrisy, so that both factors were pushing them away from church involvement. Despite these complications, the distinction between the two decision points is visible in our interviews and the sequence is correct.

People currently unchurched because of disrupted personal relationships have stayed the closest to the church and probably are the most likely to return. By contrast, persons unchurched because of doubt are farther away and less interested.

Persons of categories A and B typically dropped out earlier than those of categories C and D. The average age for A and B was approximately nineteen years, while for C and D it was approximately twenty-two. That is, people who found they could not assent to the creedal teachings generally dropped out earlier than those who lacked affective ties to church members. We calculated the age of becoming inactive for all the unchurched people and found that it was related to their scores on the Core Belief Index. The stronger the creedal belief, the later was the dropping out. For a score of 3 (high) the average age was 22.5; for a score of 0 (very low) it was 17.8. The age of dropping out also varied by type of unchurched respondent; Type 8 persons dropped out earlier (an average of 18.6 years) than any other unchurched type. For Types 5 and 6 the average was 22.3 years.

In the next chapter we undertake a statistical analysis of specific influences on the Baby Boomers encouraging them to be churched or unchurched.

Chapter 6

Influences During Youth
and Adulthood

In the last two chapters we heard people of all our eight types tell about their lives and we highlighted some of the factors that might have influenced the religious choices they made. In this chapter we will review past studies of the factors influencing the religious beliefs and behavior of young people, and we will present the results of a statistical analysis of our own data in an effort to gain a more precise understanding of why some Baby Boomers remained Presbyterians, why others switched denominations, and why still others left church life altogether.

Past Studies of Influences on Religion of Youth

Numerous investigators have asked high school students, college students, and recent college alumni the same kinds of questions we asked our Baby Boom confirmands. We could identify at least fifty studies.[1] They have produced two main theories about influences on youth and young adults.

The first and most prominent is the social learning theory, which suggests that socialization into a religious tradition occurs when important agents (mainly parents, but also teachers and relatives) model and reinforce religious commitment.[2] Religious behavior is learned behavior like most other behavior, and the learning takes place mainly in family life. Successful religious socialization requires parents committed to the task who actively strive to do it and who furnish affective support and modeling. Socialization is much less successful when parent-child relationships are poor.[3]

Not all parents work equally hard at religious training. They also differ in their view of what the training should accomplish. Some want their children to become orthodox Christians and loyal churchgoers, while others want their children to make their own religious decisions "without any pressure." As we have seen, many Presbyterian parents are hesitant to put any pressure on their children or to tell them what they should believe, for fear of hindering them in some way; rather, the parents want to open all possible religious vistas and educational experiences so that the children can decide freely in due time. We also saw some examples of parents who send a muted signal to their children; even though they attend church, they manage to communicate the message that "religion is unimportant" or that "religious beliefs don't matter." They may not say these things explicitly, but the children receive the message all the same.

If the social learning theory is true, children with genuinely religious parents are likely to become religious and involved in church life as adults. Families with good relationships would produce children resembling the parents, and children with positive bonds to Sunday school teachers, ministers, and churchgoing friends would tend to become most committed to the church. Past research usually provides support for these predictions.

The social learning theory is most often seen as applying to a person's early years, perhaps through high school. Our study is unique in that it looks at young adults, not youth. Whereas the social learning theory would logically include young adult experiences as well as earlier experiences, past research seldom looked at the adult years.[4] The theory would predict that recent personal influence and affective bonds would have notable impact in addition to earlier ones.

The second theory has no agreed-on name, but we will call it the "cultural broadening theory." It stresses the impact of the intellectual growth and cross-cultural learning that take place during higher education. Past research on the effects of college attendance has usually shown a liberalization of social and religious attitudes. Robert Wuthnow emphasizes this theory as the main explanation for loss of commitment among mainline Protestant youth.[5] Today mainline Protestant young people attend college in great numbers, and in the process they acquire worldviews and values inconsistent with their hometown church experiences. Both classroom experiences and the extracurricular life at college have an impact, inducing a liberalization of religious and moral attitudes.

If the cultural broadening theory is true, then youth who get a liberal college education will tend to become more relativistic and individualistic in religion, and their church commitment will weaken. Those who attend church-related colleges are perhaps pulled less in this direction—though church-related colleges vary widely, and probably no general statement about their impact can be made. Youth with education in the social sciences and humanities will be more affected than those in technical or vocational fields.

This theory has the beauty of relating closely with studies of how youth change over the years. It is consistent with trends in higher education (mainly one of vast expansion in the past forty years). By comparison, the social learning theory depends on family life and cannot explain trends over the years except through changes in family life; the impact of such changes is harder to assess.

The cultural broadening theory is plausible, but it is simpler than reality. For one thing, recent studies of the impacts of college often find little effect of the kind we are interested in here, and one reason seems to be that high school students are now exposed to liberalizing curricular materials that were once used only in colleges.[6] College will have little impact on youth who arrive already immersed in the prevailing academic worldview. Another complication for the cultural broadening theory is that college education varies greatly in content and impact. Theorists tend to think of the four-year residential liberal arts college or state university as the norm, but today many students attend commuter colleges and major in vocational subjects that expose them to little or no cultural criticism. A third complication is that college cultures vary from decade to decade; for example, many colleges in the 1960s were a setting for counterculture activity.

These two theories—social learning theory and cultural broadening theory—are not in opposition. They should be seen as components of the broader theory of "plausibility structures" proposed by Peter Berger.[7] Briefly, plausibility structures are networks of persons in constant contact who hold to a common worldview and set of moral commitments; upkeep of the structures is necessary to maintain the beliefs. (We will return to this topic in chapter 7.) Both theories developed by past researchers fit this view. The theoretical task now is to show more exactly how and where these ideas apply.

Statistical Analysis of Influences

We turn now to our sample of Baby Boomers. For statistical analysis we constructed four religious outcome measures to capture distinctions in church membership, worship attendance, and denomination. They are:

(1) *Churched versus Unchurched.* As described in chapter 3, persons who are church members and who have attended at least six times in the last year are considered "churched." This variable separates the churched (Types 1–4) from the unchurched (Types 5–8).[8]

(2) *Church Member versus Nonmember.*

(3) *Church Attendance* (frequency per year).

(4) *Switches to Other Denominations.* The number of switches to other denominations was studied only for persons who are church members at present.

In our interview we asked four sets of questions about the respondents' life experiences. They include experiences in high school or earlier, counterculture experiences, college experiences, and adult experiences. We used these experiences, together with measures of current religious belief, as predictor variables of the religious outcomes.

Predictor Set I: Experiences in High School or Earlier. Our phone interview asked numerous questions about the person's early life. It provided eight variables:

(1) *Lived with Both Parents During High School.* We distinguished between the 92 percent who lived with both parents and those who lived with one or none.

(2) *Participation in Presbyterian Youth Programs.* Respondents were asked whether they participated in Sunday school, church worship, and youth-centered programs during their high school years.

(3) *Mother's Religious Preference.* This distinguishes between those whose mothers were Presbyterian and all others.

(4) *Father's Religious Preference.* A parallel measure for fathers.

(5) *Parents' Church Attendance.*

(6) *Forced to Go to Church.* Respondents were asked whether they had been forced to go to church during their adolescence even when they did not want to.

(7) *Rebelled Against Religious Training.* Respondents were asked whether they had rejected their religious training during junior or senior high school years.

(8) *Church Size During High School Years.*

Predictor Set II: Counterculture Experiences. Three questions asked whether the persons engaged in typical countercultural behavior in their late teens and early twenties. The respondents were asked if they had ever attended a rock concert, ever smoked marijuana, or ever taken part in demonstrations or marches on current issues.

Predictor Set III: College Experiences

(1) *Educational Level.* The highest level of education received, including those who had not attended college.

(2) *Humanities or Social Science B.A. vs. Other.* Among the 63 percent

with college degrees, a distinction was made between those who had been humanities or social science majors and all others.

(3) *Attended a Religious College* (for those with college degrees).

(4) *Active in Campus Christian Group.* Since the interview asked about groups such as Youth for Christ, Campus Crusade for Christ, Inter-Varsity Christian Fellowship, or a similar student group during high school or college, this variable applies to the whole sample, not just the college-goers. Most activity of this sort occurred during college.

Predictor Set IV: Adult Experiences

(1) *Ever Married.*

(2) *Married Spouse from Mainline Denomination.*

(3) *Ever Divorced.*

(4) *Number of Children* (natural or adopted, regardless of the respondent's marital status).

(5) *Miles Now Away from Hometown.*

(6) *How Often Moved in Last Five Years.*

Predictor Set V: Religious Beliefs. As described in chapter 2, we constructed six indexes of religious and moral beliefs. They intercorrelated so strongly that three could represent all:

(1) *Core Belief Index.*

(2) *Christ Only Index.*

(3) *Morality Index: Conservative Score.*

In chapters 4 and 5 we heard respondents tell of adult experiences that strongly affected their church involvement. Our information about some of these experiences came only through the in-depth interviews. For example, several young adults felt snubbed in the mainline churches in their town, and several felt out-of-touch with the mainline churchgoers. Still others, by contrast, told of finding valuable friends and social groups in their churches. Several reported disillusionment after conflict erupted in their churches, so they dropped out. A few said their family and professional life was so demanding that they had no time. Without doubt these experiences heavily influenced some persons in our sample, but since we included no measures of them in our telephone interviews we cannot assess their effect statistically. The impact of recent influences such as these is likely to be underestimated in our statistical analysis.

Findings

We first calculated correlations relating each of the predictor variables to the church involvement outcome variables. The result was clear: the strongest predictors of the Baby Boomers' church involvement are *religious beliefs*. For example, the Core Belief Index correlated with church membership at .43 and with church attendance at .45. The Christ Only Index correlated with church attendance at .52. These are very strong associations, telling us that the main influence on church commitment is core Christian belief and faith.

A second important finding was that counterculture influences had only trivial correlations with church involvement today. Whatever impact the counterculture might have had on these persons earlier, it has minimal influence on church behavior today. (As we will see, it *did* have influence on religious beliefs, which in turn are important for church commitment.)

Third, college experiences had only a trivial influence on church commitment today. Whether the respondents went to college at all, whether they attended a religious college, whether they took part in campus Christian groups, and what they studied—all had little influence on their current church involvement. (But as with counterculture experiences, college influenced religious beliefs.) The weakness of these correlations surprised us.

Fourth, adult experiences were more important than high school or pre–high school experiences. The most important adult experience was the number of children the person has. This correlated .25 with being a church member and .24 with church attendance.[9] The second most important predictor of church membership was the number of miles the person now lives away from his or her hometown; it correlated -.25 with church membership. The number of residential moves the person has made in the last five years also had an effect; it correlated -.23 with church membership, showing that persons who move frequently are less likely to be members. Also, if the person has ever been divorced, he or she tended not to be a church member, with a modest correlation of -.21. These findings strengthen the social learning theory, and show the importance of parenthood and of maintaining social bonds to other persons in Christian churches. People who have moved many miles away or who have moved frequently, for example, lost close ties to their hometown church people, and they are less church-involved now.

Two factors had an impact on whether the person has switched to another denomination. The first is understandable—whether he or she married a non-Presbyterian. It had a modest .24 correlation with switching. The second is less clear—number of children. For reasons not clear to us, persons with more children are more likely to have switched denominations, with a correlation of .23.

Influences in high school or earlier were less important than adult experiences as predictors of church membership. The most important influence in high school was the level of activity in church youth programs. It correlated .15 (weakly) with church membership now and .24 with level of church attendance. Parents' church attendance correlated .17 with the person's current level of church attendance. Several influences we expected might be important turned out not to be, including mother's and father's denominational preference, church size, and whether the young person rebelled against religious training.

To reiterate: beliefs are the principal determinant of present-day church involvement. They are considerably more powerful predictors than pre-adult experiences. Now the question arises, whether there are important influences we can identify on the development of beliefs. If they exist, they are indirectly important as influences on church involvement. To find out, we correlated the measures of life experiences prior to high school, counterculture experiences, and college experiences with the measures of current beliefs. (We did not look at the relationship between adult influences and beliefs, assuming that they would be less influential.)

These correlations turned out to be fairly weak, though they did show the importance of a few experiences. Having rebelled against religious training during high school was a predictor of universalistic beliefs (that is, not believing in Christ only) and lower scores on core beliefs. Also, counterculture experiences were moderately predictive of liberal beliefs. For example, having taken part in demonstrations correlated -.26 with belief that Christ is the only truth and -.20 with conservative moral beliefs. Attainment of higher levels of education and being a humanities or social science major in college were mildly associated with nontraditional beliefs. Overall, the strongest predictor of beliefs was the person's level of formal education; it correlated -.23 with belief that Christ is the only truth and -.26 with conservative moral beliefs. The more education the respondent has, the more universalistic and morally liberal are that person's beliefs.

Are the predictors of beliefs and church involvement different for persons from small towns than for those from large cities? Do people from small towns conduct their religious lives differently than city dwellers? To check, we divided the sample into two parts, based on whether the respondents grew up in small towns or large cities. The best cutting point was cities of 100,000, but the vast majority of the persons in the small-town category came from communities of 40,000 or less. We found that the correlations between social influences and church involvement were stronger for small-town persons. Whether the respondent married a non-mainline spouse, moved a distance away from the hometown, and moved frequently in recent years had more impact on small-town respondents than on city-reared respondents. Conversely, religious beliefs were more influential for city persons than for small-town persons. For example, the Core Belief Index correlated .50 with church attendance for city people, but only .39 for small-town people. Apparently small-town people were more embedded in a definite religious culture and a definite network of persons, and if that embeddedness was weakened, their religion changed. For small-town Boomers the cultural broadening that accompanied life changes had a negative effect on their church involvement. City people were less involved in such tight circles. For this reason, it seems, big-city people were influenced by specific *religious* motives. In the city, churchgoing is not so much "tribal" behavior as a product of deliberate decisions, thus it is more motivated by religious beliefs.

Regression Analysis

Which of these predictor variables has the strongest influence on respondents' religious beliefs and practices? This question is best answered with regressions, which can estimate the independent influence of numerous factors on a particular outcome. We assessed the importance of the four sets of predictor experiences on the religious beliefs and church involvement of our respondents.

Let us begin with beliefs. First, however, we must consider the question of when beliefs are formed. Do childhood and college experiences have an effect on them? Past research indicates that they do. Do adult experiences such as marriage, divorce, or parenthood also have an effect? Since research gives no clear answers to this question, we have taken the cautious position of assuming that adult experiences are not important in forming core religious beliefs for most people. Therefore, in assessing influences on beliefs we looked at only the first three sets of experiences—high school or earlier, counterculture, and college—on beliefs. Table 6.1 contains a summary of the results. Its estimates of effects are sequential, in that the second line is estimated *in addition to* the first line, and the third line *in addition to* the first two lines. The ordering of the lines reflects the most likely sequence in most people's lives. All of the effects were weak or only moderately strong.

TABLE 6.1

Impact of Experiences on Beliefs

	Core Beliefs	Christ Only	Moral Conservatism
Impact of experiences in high school or earlier	Medium	Weak	Weak
Impact of counterculture experiences	None	Weak	Weak
Impact of college experiences	Weak	Medium	Medium

Next we looked at the predictors of church involvement. We positioned religious beliefs after college experiences but prior to adult experiences, since this seemed the most realistic (see Table 6.2). A striking result in the table is that, when other predictor variables are taken into account, neither counterculture experiences nor college experiences have any direct

TABLE 6.2

Impact of Experiences on Church Involvement

	Member vs. Not Member	Yearly Church Attendance	Number of Switches
Impact of experiences in high school or earlier	Weak	Medium	None
Impact of counterculture experiences	None	None	None
Impact of college experiences	None	None	Weak
Impact of religious beliefs	Strong	Strong	Medium
Impact of adult experiences	Strong	Weak	Medium

effect on church involvement today. These experiences *did* have some influence on beliefs, as we saw in Table 6.1, indicating that their impact on church involvement is only *indirect*, via changes they caused in beliefs.

By far the strongest predictor of church involvement is beliefs, especially Core Beliefs and belief that truth is in Christ only. Adult experiences have modest impact—mainly divorce and having children. Divorce has a small influence discouraging church involvement, and having several children has a small encouraging effect. The single most influential adult experience is the number of children a person has.

The paramount lessons from the regression analysis are shown in Figure 6.1. The figure has two stages of causal influences flowing from left to right, depicted as arrows. Where arrows are not shown between variables, there is no influence. The first stage is the effect of early experiences, counterculture experiences, and college experiences on religious beliefs. None of these experiences is very strong, but there is a mild influence of overall level of education and a slight influence of church size—in that large churches tended to produce more liberal religious and moral beliefs. The best summary of all three influences on respondents' beliefs is "weak."

FIGURE 6.1

Influences Affecting Church Involvement

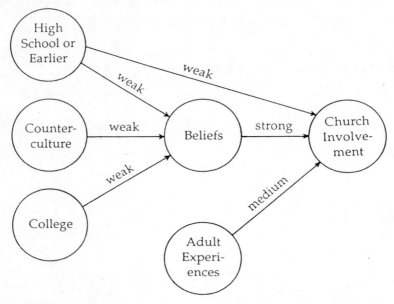

The second stage is the combined impact of early experiences, beliefs, and adult experiences, as they affect church involvement. By far the strongest influence is from beliefs (the more traditional and conservative in beliefs, the more church involvement). There are additional influences from early experiences (mainly, a positive influence from having been active in youth programs or Sunday school) and from recent adult experiences (mainly from a negative influence from divorce and a positive influence from having several children). Since Figure 6.1 does not include some of the adult experiences revealed to us in the in-depth interviews, adult experiences may in reality have a larger effect than the figure indicates, and especially on church membership.

Conclusions

What have we learned about the sources of the lukewarm church commitment of Baby Boomers? Our findings rule out any theory about the strong impact of the counterculture of the 1960s. The counterculture did have a weak impact on *beliefs*, but not on present-day church involvement. Our study also rules out any theory about the alleged strong impact of higher education, and of liberal education in particular, on present-day church involvement. To sum up, what determines whether a person in our sample is churched or unchurched today? Two factors are foremost. The first is the person's religious beliefs. The second is adult experiences and family situation—marital history and current marital status, number of children, distance of residence from the home community, and recent experiences with the church. A third and weaker factor is the carryover from childhood and youth—a history of involvement or non-involvement in youth programs and Sunday school, and the parents' churchgoing habits.

If beliefs are so important, what is their origin? Are they formed by the time of high school graduation, or do they change afterward? Without doubt both the high school years and the experiences of college (for the 90 percent who had some college) had some impact. Our statistics do not indicate conclusively which period was the most determinative. However, the in-depth personal interviews we conducted strongly suggested the greater importance of pre-college influences, and past research does the same. So we believe that pre-college experiences are more influential than college experiences.

We found evidence in our data supporting both the social learning theory and the cultural broadening theory. The specific pattern we found, which earlier research did not, was that the impact of college and the counterculture was on religious beliefs, not directly on church involvement fifteen or twenty years later. The only effect of cultural broadening that was strong enough to be noticeable was on beliefs, and they in turn were crucial for church involvement.

This two-step picture is a summary of what actually influenced our respondents to be involved or non-involved in churches today. Earlier life experiences were pertinent mainly in that they produced the respondents' religious views. Now, during their thirties and forties, these people are making decisions about church based both on their beliefs (the most important factor) and on their needs and social relationships today (the second most important).

Chapter 7

Why Mainline Churches
Are Declining

What conclusions do our findings allow us to draw about why the mainline Protestant churches have lost members and what their prospects for recovery are?

In the Introduction to this book we identified three major types of theories that have been advanced to explain the churches' decline. Two types emphasize the impact on the churches of various changes that have taken place in American life in the last several decades. The first focuses on *cultural* changes, that is, changes in people's beliefs, values, and modes of reasoning about moral issues. The second type focuses on *social structural* changes, for example, changes in gender roles, composition of the labor force, and rates of participation in community life. Both types of theory argue that church membership decline is the result of changes that originated outside the churches. The third type traces membership decline to factors internal to the life of the churches. We referred to this type as *institutional* theories, and we identified four of them.

The findings that emerged from our study of Presbyterian confirmands cast such serious doubt on the validity of some theories of church decline that we believe the theories should be discarded. On the other hand, our findings point strongly in the direction of a new explanation of the decline that integrates factors internal to the life of the churches with factors originating in the cultural and social milieu outside their boundaries.

175

Some Discredited Theories

There are four theories of mainline church decline that our data fail to support. One points to cultural factors as the main source of decline and three point to institutional factors. Let us explain.

The Counterculture and Church Decline

Our findings have made us doubt that the youth counterculture of the 1960s is a major source of mainline Protestant membership decline. We asked all the confirmands in our sample whether they had ever attended a rock concert, used marijuana, or taken part in marches or demonstrations. We found, as expected, that the Baby Boomers were much more likely than the pre-Boomers to have done so. In chapter 6, however, we reported that Baby Boomers who participated in the counterculture are only slightly less likely to be involved in church today. We did find that counterculture participants are more relativistic and more liberal regarding personal morality than nonparticipants. Yet in spite of this the church involvement of the two groups is roughly the same.

Even though direct involvement of youth in the sixties counterculture may not explain mainline Protestant membership loss, the counterculture may have had an indirect effect on the churches. The hippies came and went, but the 1960s ushered in some changes that have lasted, for example, relaxation of old norms concerning cohabitation and premarital sex. Even if a person never attended a rock concert, smoked marijuana, or went to a demonstration, he or she could still have been influenced by the new norms and sentiments of that era. We do believe that the social changes of the 1960s had an effect on church trends because it had a moderately strong relativizing effect on Boomers' beliefs.

In this context, we also doubt the importance of the recent growth of anti-institutionalism. In our survey and in other research we saw evidence of this attitude, usually couched in terms of rejection of large, impersonal, out-of-touch organizations. We found relatively few Boomers who expressed hostility toward the church itself. We did discover a generalized lack of interest in denominational or ecumenical organizations or their various projects. Rather than being anti-institutional, our respondents tended to see large-scale organizations as irrelevant to their religious lives.

Three Institutional Theories

The first institutional theory of which we are skeptical is one that is often advanced by denominational officials. It attributes membership losses to certain shifts in official denominational policies over the past generation, for instance, changes in the content of Sunday school lessons or youth group programs, the format of worship, or even the content of hymnals. A second theory, well publicized in the late 1960s and early 1970s, explains the losses as a rejection of the institutional church as socially "irrelevant" by the generation of youth that was radicalized in the sixties. This theory, which is rarely heard today, emphasizes the failure of the mainline Protestant churches to become more active in struggles for peace and justice and implies that the churches might grow once again if they joined these struggles.

The third theory makes the opposite argument. It is widely believed in the conservative sectors of the American religious community that members have been leaving the mainline churches because the national leadership and governing bodies of these denominations have been *too* involved in social action programs. Those who support this theory want the churches to emphasize spiritual nourishment, and they urge the mainline denominations to place greater emphasis on theological witness and evangelism. This perspective is regularly aired in journals such as *Presbyterian Layman* and in letters to the editor of *Presbyterian Survey*. Recently, Richard John Neuhaus, a respected analyst of the American religious scene, voiced support for it. He attributed the "dizzying decline" of the mainline denominations to the activities of "leadership elites styling themselves as 'prophetic,'" who "have worked, it seems almost deliberately, to alienate the general membership."[1]

All three institutional theories should be abandoned. We say this for several reasons. The downturn in Presbyterian membership began in the middle 1960s and has continued until the present day. The trends are long-term curves that are not affected by particular denominational events such as the controversial Confession of 1967, the Angela Davis crisis of 1971, or the merger of denominations in 1983. The downturn continued as if unmindful of particular leaders, social action initiatives, or evangelism programs. Furthermore, the Presbyterian downturn has analogues in all the mainline denominations. Such long-term, cross-denominational phenomena cannot be attributed to particular denominational leaders, programs, or institutional priorities. The trend lines in different denominations are basically the same; it is unconvincing to argue that this is because leadership and programs at the national level have been the same in all these bodies, for they have not. During the 1970s and 1980s there have even been leadership attempts at the national level in several denominations to reverse direction in hopes of stemming the decline. But nothing has changed the trends. They seemed to be unresponsive to leadership decisions. Something else was causing them.

We also doubt these institutional theories of membership decline because the issues they address almost never came up in the interviews we conducted. We heard numerous criticisms of churches, but these complaints rarely concerned such matters as the Sunday school curriculum, summer youth camp programs, confirmation classes, hymnals, evangelism, the national leadership of the Presbyterian Church (U.S.A.), or the stands the denomination has taken on controversial issues. Moreover, when we pressed our respondents about these issues, we discovered that most knew little or nothing about them. The criticisms we heard were directed almost exclusively at *local congregations* rather than at the Presbyterian Church or at mainline Protestantism as a whole. We interviewed only two confirmands who had quit the Presbyterian Church because it was insufficiently concerned with social justice, and one of them returned to the denomination when she found a socially concerned congregation. We heard a few complaints that a particular church was too liberal, but we heard no calls for programs of evangelism.

The vast majority of complaints that were voiced about churches concerned matters having nothing to do with these institutional theories of church decline. Calvin Caletti, for example, found his pastor's sermons boring. Marcia Wilson once left a Presbyterian church because its minister had become a fundamentalist. Ann Brooks criticized churches for requiring too much time and effort of their members. Numerous others, including Ann, complained about the hypocrisy and social snobbery they encountered at a particular church. The complaints we heard about particular churches did not, however, lead us in the direction of a new institutional theory of decline focusing on such shortcomings of local churches as hypocrisy and snobbery. There is no reason to believe that these failings have increased dramatically in recent years. Our findings make us doubt that unhappiness with local churches is a major cause of membership loss. Calvin Caletti left the church because he was skeptical of religious teachings. Marcia Wilson, who had a strongly internalized faith, quickly found a nonfundamentalist church to attend. Ann Brooks, a lay liberal, once quit a church in disgust with hypocrisy, but now that she has Sunday school age children, she is looking for a new one.

To sum up, we are convinced that the basic reasons for membership decline have little to do with the issues highlighted in the ongoing conflict between liberal and conservative factions in the mainline denominations, or with complaints about particular congregations, or with participation in the counterculture. Rather, the crisis the mainline churches face is a *spiritual* one. They have lost members because, over the years, *beliefs* have been changing.

Excursus: Does the Center Hold?

Our findings have implications for another widely voiced view of the predicament the mainline churches face. Many observers of American religion have reported that in recent decades these denominations have become polarized into two camps having sharply differing views on theological and moral issues. Sociologist Robert Wuthnow is the most prominent advocate of this view. Based on a 1984 nationwide survey, he argues that the two factions are roughly equal in size.[2] Some have argued that the conflicts within the mainline denominations are so severe that the churches' unity is in jeopardy. Among the issues that have divided mainline Protestants are whether homosexuals should be ordained, whether the language of worship should be "inclusive" or remain "patriarchal," and whether evangelism and new church development should be the churches' major mission.

According to some observers the controversy between right and left factions within the churches has become so intense that they no longer serve as bridges between cultural extremes. James Moorhead, for example, has recently written that "the story of Presbyterianism in the last half century suggests that such a church is destined to recapitulate within its own life the divisions of the culture." The Presbyterian Church has historically been at the very center of American culture and society, but with the culture itself disintegrating into increasingly hostile fragments Moorhead fears—in the words of William Butler Yeats—that "the center cannot hold."[3]

It is certainly true that for more than twenty years liberal and conservative interest groups have been vying for influence in the governing bodies of all the mainline denominations, and that these bodies have often been the scene of acrimonious disputes. In view of this, it is noteworthy that the Baby Boom confirmands we interviewed know little or nothing about the national leadership of the Presbyterian Church (U.S.A.) or about the pronouncements and policy commitments of its General Assembly. For them, the church is primarily the local congregation, a place for worship, spiritual nurture, religious education for children, and participation in a supportive community exemplifying the basic moral code.

Our sample of confirmands does contain two types of people who differ sharply from one another on theological, moral, and political issues. These two types are the fundamentalists (Type 1) and the nonreligious (Type 8). However, together they comprise only 14 percent of the total, and none of them attend mainline churches. The active Presbyterians, who comprise 29 percent, represent a diversity of views, but they cannot be described as polarized, for they show little tendency to align themselves consistently with either the religious right or the religious left. Marcia Wilson, for example, supports abortion rights but opposes the ordination of homosexuals. Most active Presbyterians do not object to gay ordination, but on the other hand most favor prayer in the public schools. Many who believe that Jesus is the son of God also affirm that all the different religions are equally good ways of helping a person find ultimate truth. In short, the majority of active Presbyterians are "liberal" on some issues and "conservative" on others. This is shown in the large proportion who scored "mixed" on the Morality Index.

What is more, very few of the active Presbyterians we interviewed in depth are involved in organized efforts to promote one or another position on controversial issues. The great majority, for example, favor many of the positions advocated by feminists, including abortion rights and an Equal Rights Amendment to the U.S. Constitution; yet in our interviews no one told us that he or she was committed to achieving feminist objectives in the life of the congregation or through church-sponsored programs for women's rights. Only one or two complained about the use of noninclusive language in worship or about the fact that most clergy are males. If our findings can be generalized, then most Baby Boomers who are active in mainline churches hesitate to raise their voices at church about issues that might create disharmony.

The absence of polarization among the active Presbyterians in our sample suggests that at the congregational level the mainline Protestant churches continue to serve as "bridging institutions." They moderate the conflict between traditional orthodoxy and secularism by accommodating a variety of theological and moral perspectives.[4] Indeed, by stressing the importance of tolerance, lay liberalism provides the theological framework that allows many mainline church members to make this accommodation. In sum, our findings suggest that the center *has* held at the level of the congregation. Conflict over currently controversial issues erupts in congregations now and then, but the chief focal points of mainline disharmony today are in its national agencies and governing bodies where the ideological elites contend among themselves. If the religious center is collapsing, it is doing so at the higher echelons of the church.

Kelley's Thesis

The institutional theories we found unconvincing pertain to leadership, policies, and programs of the past three decades. All refer to relatively recent institutional factors rather than to longer-term trends. The institutional theory we find more persuasive applies to a longer time period, perhaps all of the twentieth century. In the Introduction we presented Dean Kelley's theory of church decline, which appeared in his 1972 book, *Why Conservative Churches Are Growing.*[5] It is usually summarized by the proposition that "strong churches grow, whereas weak churches decline."

When we began this study we were unclear about the usefulness of Kelley's theory in explaining why the mainline churches have lost members. The Hartford Seminary Foundation project on church decline, in which one of us (Dean R. Hoge) participated, had conducted a partial test of Kelley's theory that yielded very high correlations between indicators of the "strength" of major denominations and their growth rates in recent decades. But it was not clear whether these indicators represented the true causes of variations in growth rates or whether something else was the cause.

The Hartford project focused its search for the causes of church decline on noninstitutional, or contextual, factors specific to the 1960s and 1970s. Still, it was difficult to ignore the very strong correlations that had been found between denominational "strength" and the rate of change in denominational membership. Kelley had emphasized that the mainline denominations were not set apart by distinctive lifestyles or values from the rest of middle-class America. "We believe Kelley is right," Hoge wrote, "when he says that denominations most embedded in the surrounding culture are most subject to favorable or unfavorable shifts in that culture. These denominations benefitted from a favorable cultural context in the 1950s but suffered in the late 1960s."[6]

The findings from our study of Presbyterian confirmands and from other recent research have convinced us that Kelley was right to describe the mainline Protestant denominations as weak and to emphasize the critical importance of *belief*—or "meaning," as he puts it—in creating and sustaining strong religious bodies. Moreover, Kelley's explanation of how and why strong religions tend to become weaker over time not only provides important insights into the processes at work, it also enables us to understand recent mainline Protestant decline as a special case of the operation of a general principle.

Strong Churches

The strength of organizations, whether religious or secular, depends on the extent to which they can mobilize their members' resources, including their enthusiasm, their energy, their time, their money, and their influence, for the attainment of shared objectives. The strongest organizations are able to define goals that take precedence in their members' lives over any other interests they might have. The weakest organizations, on the other hand, rank low on their members' lists of personal priorities and can command only small amounts of their time, energy, and other resources. Religions of highest strength are, in Kelley's words, agencies for "transforming men and groups into vigorous, dynamic, conquering movements."[7] In their early days, the Anabaptists, the Methodists, and the Mormons were religions of this sort.

What are the conditions that make religions strong? The most important condition, according to Kelley, is the presence of a compelling teaching concerning the ultimate purpose and destiny of humankind. Kelley refers to such teachings as *meanings*. Meanings claim to offer the exclusive truth concerning human existence. In the name of this truth, meanings make *demands* on people. They ask people to stake their time, their fortunes, and even their lives on their trust in God or some other ultimate power. Kelley uses an economic metaphor to emphasize the demands that the meanings espoused by strong religions make:

> There is as realistic an economy in the realm of meaning as in that of commodities, but the currency is different. In both cases, it obtains its value from the guarantees that undergird it: what has been invested in it, what backs it up. In the realm of meaning that backing, that guarantee or validation, is a personal and social earnestness shown in the investment by real people of time, money, effort, reputation, and self in the meaning and the movement that bears it. What costs nothing, accomplishes nothing. If it costs nothing to belong to such a community, it can't be worth much.[8]

Strong religions are also characterized by the "shoulder-to-shoulder solidarity" of those who have committed themselves to the movement. The followers "are linked together in a band of mutually supportive, like-minded, equally devoted fellow believers, who reinforce one another in times of weakness, persecution, and doubt."[9] They must also be willing to subordinate their personal desires and ambitions to the shared goals of the group. Strong religions require not only commitment and solidarity, but also what Kelley refers to as "traits of strictness." They need mechanisms for reassuring their members of the exclusive truth of their teachings, for enforcing orthodox professions of belief, and for maintaining distinctive standards of conduct and demeanor that set the followers apart from outsiders. Prospective members must be carefully screened and dissidents must be corrected or expelled. Recently, economist Laurence Iannaccone has shown that strictness helps sustain a religion's strength by purging the "free riders" (those who enjoy the church's benefits without contributing) from its ranks and deterring new free riders from joining.[10]

Peter L. Berger has identified a related mechanism by which religions remain strong. He develops the concept of "plausibility structures," which consist of networks of fellow believers in constant contact with each other. All religions must maintain plausibility structures if they are to remain strong. Through continuous contact among believers, and particularly through the conversation it involves, members' confidence in the plausibility—the rightness and truth—of the shared meaning system is constantly affirmed. In other words, talking about the faith, sharing it, and dispelling any doubts or challenges to it that may arise, help perpetuate both belief and commitment. According to Berger,

> Each conception of the world of whatever character or content can be analyzed in terms of its plausibility structure, because it is only as the individual remains within this structure that the conception of the world in question will remain plausible to him. The strength of this plausibility, ranging from unquestioned certitude through firm probability to mere opinion, will be directly dependent upon the strength of the supporting structure.[11]

Both Kelley and Berger emphasize the difficulty of integrating the next generation into the plausibility structures of the faith. Unless the youth are firmly socialized into its tenets and standards, the strength of the religious community will eventually ebb away. The Old Order Amish, for example, voluntarily segregate themselves from outsiders and restrict their contacts with the "world" to those that are absolutely necessary. All plausibility structures are partly sustained by this "tribal behavior." But there is a complication. Many strong religions, as Kelley points out, also seek contact with outsiders because they are eager to make converts. If they are to avoid challenges to the plausibility of their faith, such spreaders of the good news must do more talking than listening; they must create "a flood of outgoing messages that swamps any incoming ones."[12]

Among the members of our sample of Presbyterian confirmands, only the fundamentalists and a few other active churchgoers like Marcia Wilson have the zeal and commitment found among the adherents of strong religions. They are the only ones who are truly excited about their faith or put the church and its mission near the top of their list of personal priorities. No one from any of the other types told us, as Dan Fuller did, that he would rather quit his job than quit his church. The fundamentalists have by far the highest rates of church attendance and participation in other church activities. Moreover, none of the other churched types approach the degree of solidarity, or consensus, that the fundamentalists have on matters of belief and morality. We did not ask our respondents about their circles of close friends, but since the fundamentalists spend so much time in church-related activities, we consider it very likely that their closest friends are also fellow believers.

Both Kelley and Berger emphasize the importance of integrating the next generation into the plausibility structures of the faith. Unless the youth are firmly socialized into its tenets and standards, the strength of the religious community will eventually ebb away. As Kelley puts it, "A culture which cannot hand on its shared meanings through time will not survive."[13] The fundamentalists and religious conservatives in our sample are also determined to socialize their children in the faith, and many are educating their children within its plausibility structure by sending them to Christian schools or teaching them at home. In sum, they are participants in strong churches.

Weak Churches

Weak churches are at the opposite end of Kelley's continuum. Such churches do not teach one clear-cut, compelling message with a claim to absolute truth. Instead, they are open to a variety of interpretations of the tradition they represent and are not hostile to other traditions. They are receptive to the exploration of divergent views and to the tenet that "no one has a monopoly on the truth." Furthermore, the views they do purvey, or accommodate, are not "meanings," but "notions." Kelley uses this old Quaker term to refer to "ideas that do not require anything of those who espouse them but can be bandied back and forth like verbal playthings." Unlike meanings, notions make no demands on people's time or energy. They do not "have the power to change lives, to recruit movements, to explain things convincingly."[14]

Because weak churches are unable to mobilize the energies of their members for shared purposes, their group life is characterized by lukewarmness, indecisiveness, a "reluctance to espouse one's personal beliefs or to impose them on others," "no effective sharing of conviction or spiritual insight," a preference for individuality rather than conformity, and negligible enforcement of collective standards.[15] The members of weak churches tend to regard their religious commitment and their church as but one among several interests competing for their time and effort. Consequently, many of them are not in church every Sunday and are reluctant to get involved in a round of time-consuming obligations surrounding the church or its mission. Because of the multiplicity of their personal commitments, they do not confine their social contacts to those who share their religious views. Religious plausibility structures hardly exist for them.

Churches such as these are congenial settings for people who have an interest in religion but who also value individuality and are repelled by faiths that demand total commitment and conformity to a constricting lifestyle. Weak churches cannot be strong precisely because they are unable to make the demand of total commitment, or to make it successfully. Individualism, relativism in matters of faith, a diversity of viewpoints on many issues, and openness to alternative perspectives all make for weak religious organizations. Such churches, Kelley argues, are always susceptible to losing whatever commitment their members may have.

One of the most striking findings about the active Presbyterians among our sample of Baby Boom confirmands is the low level of their commitment to the church and its programs. Whereas the fundamentalists have the highest level of church participation of all the four "churched" types, active Presbyterians have the lowest. Whereas fundamentalists tend to be of one mind concerning theological and moral issues, active Presbyterians espouse a variety of views. Our in-depth interviews suggest that the great majority of active Baby Boom Presbyterians subscribe neither to the traditional Presbyterian standards contained in the Westminster Confession of Faith and the Shorter Catechism, nor to any of the more contemporary theological formulations espoused by denominational leaders.

Some of the active Presbyterians we interviewed can be described as evangelicals, but many more hold theological views that we have described as "lay liberal." Although lay liberalism has several different versions, its defining feature is the rejection of the claim that Christianity, or any other faith, is the only true religion. Lay liberals have no compelling truth, no "good news," to proclaim, and few of them share the views they do have with their friends and acquaintances. When it comes to religion, lay liberals do not participate in strong plausibility structures. They respect people's right to make the religious choices they feel comfortable with, so long as their choices do not violate the basic moral code. They want religious education for their children, but they are reluctant to instill in them their own religious views. Lay liberals are uncomfortable with any religion that makes high demands on its members and tries aggressively to make converts.

Lay liberalism does not offer *meaning*, in Kelley's sense of the word. Our findings show that belief is the single best predictor of church participation, but it is *orthodox* Christian belief, and not the tenets of lay liberalism, that impels people to be involved in church. What is more, lay liberals do not seem driven to find meaning in Kelley's sense. None of them we talked to were seriously grappling with questions concerning the ultimate nature and purpose of human existence. Most lay liberals have wearied of pursuing these questions, and some seem reconciled to never knowing ultimate truth. Lay liberalism, and the individualism and the tolerance of diversity that it celebrates, make civility and cooperation in human relations possible in a pluralistic society, but they also make for weak churches. They are particularly suited to a membership that is fully engaged in such a society, largely because they easily coincide with science and university-based intellectualism.

Another notable finding from our interviews is that lay liberals who are active Presbyterians do not differ sharply in their religious views from the people who are not involved in a church but who describe themselves as religious. There is, in short, no clear-cut "faith boundary" separating active Presbyterians from those who no longer go to church. To be sure, unchurched yet religious people (our Type 7) include some who verge on outright skepticism and who would feel uncomfortable reciting confessions and singing hymns at church, but most Type 7s would feel comfortable in a Presbyterian or other mainline church, and in fact prefer such a church to any others. Very few ever joined another church. Clearly, these people are not repelled by mainline Protestantism and are not searching for a faith that provides them "meaning." Given their low level of interest and involvement in organized religion, they simply do not receive enough benefits from the church to invest time and energy in it.

Sociologist Reginald Bibby, who has studied Canadian religion extensively, reports findings concerning Canadian church dropouts that are quite similar to ours. Although he does not use the term "lay liberalism," he found that Canadians tend to pick and choose their religious opinions from a "cafeteria" of available options. For example, many Canadians "believe in God but are not sure about the divinity of Jesus or the nature of life after death." Even though church participation in Canada has declined precipitously since World War II, "few are disenchanted and turning else-where" for new systems of meaning.[16] Canada is not, therefore, a religious "field ripe for harvest." Bibby's study of inactive Anglicans in Toronto, for example, revealed that they had "generally favourable views of the Church." When asked, however, what the Church might do to lure them back, the most common response was that it could do nothing. An inten-sive study of dropouts from the United Church of Canada "did not find *any* who stressed loss of confidence in the Church or theological conflict as reasons for leaving."[17]

The findings from our study of Baby Boom confirmands strongly sup-port Kelley's contention that the mainline Protestant churches are inter-nally weak as religious bodies. But why have they become weak? Kelley's theory also addresses that question.

How Churches Become Weak

Kelley's theory of how strong churches become weak is based on the assumption that all organized social life, including religion, needs constant maintenance to avoid running down. He uses the concept "entropy" to refer to the dissipation, or loss, of energy devoted to religious purposes that tends to occur because of the competition of other interests and needs in individual members' lives.[18]

Strong religions mobilize energies by their dramatic, compelling teach-ings and by the personal magnetism of their founders. Repeated reinforce-ment of the teaching in the face-to-face conversation of strong plausibility structures and the strict enforcement of standards are among the means such religions adopt to keep the energy level high. But unless special countermeasures are taken, the strength of a new religion tends to weaken from one generation to the next. As Kelley puts it, there tends to be a "lukewarmness in the children of believers and *their* children."[19] More-over, strict enforcement of standards requires an extra output of energy that may be difficult to mobilize among a generation somewhat less com-mitted than the founders were. A religion can take a number of steps to counter, if not overcome completely, the processes of dissipation. Revivals and awakenings have sometimes pumped new energy into old religions. A more reliable strategy is to withdraw into ghetto-like isolation from the larger society, where strong plausibility structures can be maintained un-contaminated by outside messages. Orthodox Jews and Old Order Amish have done this.

A more common way of ensuring conformity to group standards, how-ever, is to institute a strong system of authority with a vested interest in enforcing them. This was the strategy adopted by the Roman Catholic Church. But Kelley observes that a recourse to authoritarian enforcement is itself a sign of the cooling of religious ardor among the laity. "In the beginning of a strong religious movement, strictness is not a quality imposed from without so much as arising spontaneously among the adherents." *Stringency* is the form strictness takes "when all the members feel a personal and direct responsibility" for upholding group standards. As time goes by, however, "these qualities do not arise so spontaneously," and some groups resort to a form of strictness that Kelley calls *stricture*, which is a "discipline imposed by the stern leader upon shamed and sheepish members."[20] When this discipline is relaxed, as happened in the Roman Catholic Church after Vatican II, the organization's strength dissipates much more rapidly. Dean Hoge has used the model of a river and a dam in explaining the changes in American Catholicism in the 1960s. The underlying pressures for change had been building up for a decade or two, but when Vatican II opened the floodgates for the desired changes, they poured out pell-mell with astonishing speed. Two conditions explained the rapid change—the high level of pent-up pressures for relaxation of old standards, and the sudden opening of the doors.[21]

Two tendencies embodied in many religious movements accelerate the dissipation. The first tendency is summed up in "Wesley's law," which has been widely cited by students of religion. John Wesley, the founder of Methodism, wrote that "wherever riches have increased, the essence of religion has decreased in the same proportion. Therefore, I do not see how it is possible for any revival of religion to continue long."[22] As the faithful grow richer, the competition with other interests in their lives becomes more intense, and religious fervor flags.

A second tendency that accelerates the cooling of ardor and the relaxation of group standards is the missionary enterprise itself. Kelley emphasizes that strong new religions seek to grow. A certain proportion of the population is always eager for "meaning" and for the demands it makes. But they are not the majority. Kelley asserts that people who are receptive to high-demand movements are not numerous:

> Perhaps one in a hundred or one in a thousand. For the interest and allegiance of these few, the movements of a given hour compete. . . . We may suppose that *the higher the demand a movement makes on its followers, the fewer there will be who respond to it.*[23]

Perhaps the religions with the very highest demand cannot grow at all, since the price is too high. Recently Iannaccone, in a formalization of Kelley's ideas, has shown that a religion can be so demanding that it cannot grow because virtually no one would be willing to bear the cost of belonging.[24] Both Kelley and Max Weber assume that there are different markets for religion within human populations. The market for high-demand faiths is much smaller than markets for more lenient faiths.

If this is the case, then any strong religion that wishes to grow beyond the limits of the high-demand market must be willing to lower the costs of membership. There is an abundance of historical evidence that this is precisely what many British and American religious movements have done in the past two centuries in an effort to add members. In a classic essay, sociologist Bryan Wilson has shown that not all religious sects grow; those he labels "conversionist" sects are the ones that transform themselves from small, high-demand, world-rejecting movements into large, lenient, accommodated denominations.[25] Kelley cites historian Franklin H. Littell, who observed that "in order to build up mass memberships," many American churches "progressively relaxed the standards of membership for those coming in from the outside," with the result that "the churches became filled with baptized pagans, who soon far outnumbered those who had gained and kept some understanding of the obligations of discipleship."[26]

We can now see that the usual understanding of Kelley's theory concerning the relationship between religious strength and religious growth is too simple. Kelley does argue that weak, lenient churches are liable to decline, but he does not argue that strictness always makes for growth. A strict church may decline if it fails to meet the changing needs of its constituents. One of us (Donald Luidens) has recently shown that several conservative, and presumably strict, Presbyterian denominations have actually lost members during most of the twentieth century.[27]

The Presbyterian Case

The Presbyterian Church has never isolated itself from the culture and public institutions of American society. Ever since the first Presbyterians arrived in America they have participated actively in the economic, educational, and political life of the nation. For many generations, by virtue of their strategic location "at the center" of American life, they and other mainline Protestants exercised a formative influence on its culture. Moreover, Presbyterians, along with Episcopalians and Unitarians, tended to be better educated and more affluent than the average American. Presbyterians stressed those traits of "industry and frugality" that John Wesley described. They also placed a high value on education, not only for their ministers, but for the laity as well. Presbyterians have been at the forefront in establishing colleges across the land.

But these proclivities do not sustain strong churches in a pluralistic and open religious environment. For many generations, their dissipatory potential was offset in several important ways. In the first place, Christianity in general and mainline Protestantism in particular long enjoyed such influence and prestige that the credibility of its tenets easily survived the occasional public attacks by such critics as Tom Paine and Robert Ingersoll. In the second place, Presbyterianism, like many other mainline bodies, benefited from the revivals and awakenings that occurred periodically during the eighteenth and nineteenth centuries. On the institutional level, Presbyterians were generally careful not to accept into full membership converts who had only a rudimentary understanding of the faith, and they took special care in the instruction of their own children. Moreover, Presbyterians placed a greater emphasis on maintaining doctrinal standards than did many other mainline bodies.

New Challenges

By far the most serious challenge the Christian religion has faced in recent centuries is the questioning of its most basic traditional teachings that emerged in educated circles on both sides of the Atlantic during the nineteenth century. Anyone who believes in the theory of biological evolution or that the Bible was the work of men influenced by the social and cultural forces of their times cannot simultaneously affirm all the tenets of the Christian faith as understood by leaders of most of its branches in the United States as late as 1800. During the eighteenth century, attacks on traditional Christian belief had affected the thinking of a small but influential elite; but in the nineteenth century, both science and historical scholarship provided new arguments against orthodox belief, and as the years went by, many in the rapidly expanding circle of educated people were persuaded by them. Suspicion grew that the meanings provided by orthodoxy are illusory. The attempts by theological conservatives within the mainline denominations to stem the tide of skepticism about traditional belief proved largely unsuccessful.

In both Europe and the United States, this suspicion affected Protestants before it affected Catholics. One reason, of course, was that the pope and the hierarchy of the Roman Catholic Church strongly resisted the new intellectual currents and used their authority to institute "strictures" to keep the laity from being influenced by them. In the United States the Presbyterians and other mainline Protestant denominations were unable to insulate themselves from Darwin's theory of evolution because they respected the critical methods of science and placed a high value on openness. They were even less able to insulate themselves from the new critical studies of the Bible because these studies were undertaken in Europe by Protestant scholars. Peter Berger has observed that "there is no comparable case in the history of religion before the Protestant one in which people from within a tradition to which they were personally committed turned upon it the full arsenal of critical scholarship and let the theological chips fly where they might."[28]

The very openness of mainline Protestantism to new intellectual developments had the unintended consequence of exposing that religious community at an early date to the relativizing effects of what Berger and other sociologists refer to as the process of *modernization*. This process involves an increasing division of labor among the various functional branches of society, a division that deprives religious institutions of much of their traditional superintendency of social life. Moreover, scientific and technological advances facilitate travel and communication, thus breaking down the boundaries that once separated most people from the rest of the world. As a consequence, the traditional plausibility structures that once assured people that their beliefs and ways of life were superior to any others have been weakened because they can no longer protect their members from receiving messages from the outside world. In short, modernization brings pluralism, and with it comes the relativism of which Berger writes:

> Modern consciousness . . . has a powerfully relativizing effect on all worldviews. To a large extent, the history of Western thought over the last few centuries has been one long effort to cope with the vertigo of relativity induced by modernization. Different analysts may opt for different proof texts for the start of all this. A pretty good one would be Pascal's statement that what is truth on one side of the Pyrenees is error on the other. As this insight became more widespread and more profound, the question as to who is right as between the sides of the Pyrenees attained a particular urgency.[29]

The Liberal Response

Groups respond in varying ways to challenges to their traditional presuppositions. Some, like the Amish and the Hutterites, are able to insulate themselves from such challenges. More commonly, the group splits into parties advocating differing responses. For example, Asian religious groups sorely challenged by western predominance split into parties in the nineteenth and twentieth centuries, ranging from total, defiant rejection of the outsiders at one extreme, to total acceptance at the other extreme, with several gradations between.[30] In the United States, Judaism is divided into three distinct branches—orthodox, conservative, and reform—differing fundamentally on what must be maintained of tradition and what should be accepted from outside. Analogous splits can be seen among Mennonites and Lutherans.

What is often referred to as the "two-party system" in American Protestantism originated over a century ago in the differing responses of Protestant clergy and laity to the challenges of modernity. One party, which came to be known as the fundamentalists, advocated an aggressive reassertion of traditional orthodoxy. The other party, known as modernists or liberals, advocated a reformulation of Christian theology so as to accommodate the challenges to the faith and restore its credibility in the eyes of educated people. Although the liberals did not agree on a uniform theology, they widely adopted a method of self-critique that subjected Christian tradition to historical and scientific scrutiny. The fundamentalists, however, accused the liberals of abandoning the very bases of Christianity itself. Sydney Ahlstrom, in his monumental study of American religious history, called the ensuing battle between the two parties "the most fundamental controversy to wrack the churches since the age of the Reformation."[31]

For several decades the major branches of Presbyterianism were dominated by traditionalists, but during the 1920s, liberals, in alliance with the more numerous moderates, laid the groundwork for the increasing prevalence of modern theological views that occurred in the decades that followed. The posture of Presbyterian seminaries, theologians, and officials shifted toward an affirmation of critical scholarship, modern science, and the historical relativity of religious thought and practice. Although some of today's Presbyterian leaders have theological positions that are decidedly conservative, most of them do not. As a result of the liberal drift, Presbyterians no longer learned much from their ministers and Sunday school teachers about the historic doctrinal standards of the church. Moreover, liberals put little emphasis on sin, judgment, and the necessity for redemption, preferring instead to emphasize ethics and Christian service. This shift was a welcome relief to many within the churches who considered the old doctrines burdensome and distasteful, but the new themes tended to blur the old distinction between the Christian life and the life of "good people" who are not Christians. Liberalism did not offer compelling reasons why nonbelievers should make a profession of faith. In Kelley's terms, liberals helped drain the faith of "meaning." In Ahlstrom's words, "they sometimes stripped away the Church's spiritual armor."[32]

Ebbing Strength

Although the mainline denominations continued to add members for decades after their shift away from orthodoxy, their growth rate was exceeded by that of more conservative religious bodies—the new pentecostal movement, for example. In the Introduction we reported the view of historian William R. Hutchison that the strength of mainline Protestantism has been slowly eroding for the better part of the twentieth century. In particular, Hutchison showed that since 1920 the proportion of Protestants who belong to denominations affiliated with the liberal-minded Federal, and later the National, Council of Churches has steadily declined. In 1920, 72 percent of American Protestants belonged to religious bodies affiliated with the Council, but by 1960 the figure was 12 percent lower, and by 1985 it had declined another 11 percent. The competitive advantage of conservative churches is not a recent development. They have enjoyed that advantage for more than seventy years.[33]

The ebbing strength of mainline denominations in the Protestant religious market was paralleled by an ebbing of their own members' commitment to the traditional standards of conduct that once distinguished evangelical Christians from outsiders. One of us (Benton Johnson) has discovered evidence of this weakening process in the *Minutes* of Presbyterian General Assemblies covering a period of seventy years. The acts and pronouncements of General Assemblies are not binding on individual Presbyterians, but the topics brought to General Assemblies by the presbyteries, the actions of the Assemblies themselves, and the response of the presbyteries to these actions provide a window into life at the churches' grass roots.[34]

A hundred years ago Presbyterians were expected to observe the Sabbath strictly, to abstain from using alcoholic beverages, to avoid "worldly amusements" in general, to dress modestly, to conduct family devotions, not to practice birth control, and not to seek a divorce unless their spouses had deserted them or committed adultery. By the mid-1960s *all* these disciplines had fallen by the wayside. In some cases, the relaxation was enshrined in General Assembly pronouncements, but in other cases presbyteries and General Assemblies simply lost interest in the subject. The latter was the fate of Sabbath observance, which was once the centerpiece of Presbyterian piety, and it was the fate of "family altar" devotions. The relaxation of some disciplines, for instance the ban on birth control, was furiously resisted when first proposed, but easily achieved a few decades later. Moreover, a careful examination of presbytery proposals and presbytery responses to General Assembly acts reveals that over the long run the relaxation of these old disciplines was genuinely *popular* within both major branches of Presbyterianism. The denominational leaders did not resist the relaxation, but neither did they foist it on the church.

That this relaxation was a dissipation process in Kelley's sense is strongly suggested by the fact that the Presbyterian Church did not adopt new disciplines to replace those they had abandoned. To be sure, over this seventy-year period an expanding segment of the Presbyterian leadership did try to enlist the churches' support for new programs to promote peace and justice. But although they succeeded in committing General Assembly agencies to such programs, no Assembly ever recommended to the local churches that members be disciplined for failure to devote time and effort to these causes. Similar disciplinary silence greeted other causes, from ecology to ecumenism. In short, the process of dissipation was not offset by the imposition and enforcement of new standards. By 1965 it was difficult to give a clear-cut answer to the question, "What do Presbyterians do that makes them different?"

The General Assembly record shows that the process of relaxation did not occur in a very short span of time, as happened in the Roman Catholic Church at the time of Vatican II. Rather, it took place in staggered fashion over several decades. Disciplines A and B were discarded earlier than disciplines C and D, which in turn were discarded earlier than disciplines E and F. No discipline that was abandoned was ever restored. The concern about worldly amusements and family altars had subsided by the middle of the 1920s, but support for Sabbath observance and national prohibition remained strong for several more years. Among Presbyterians, the dissipation process involved *sloughing off* some elements of tradition that seemed burdensome or pointless, while *retaining* other elements, at least for a time.

The "Religious Revival" of the 1950s

The mainline churches grew substantially during the 1950s. Moreover, as Hutchison has shown, during that decade there was a marked slowing of the rate at which the conservative churches increased their share of the Protestant market. During the decade of the 1930s these churches had increased their market advantage by 5 percentage points, but during the 1950s the increase had dropped to less than 2 percentage points. A decade later the rate reached 5 again.[35]

In membership terms, the mainline Protestant denominations clearly enjoyed something of a "rally" in the period immediately following World War II. Did the rally signal a slowing, or even a reversal, of the process of internal weakening? We doubt it. Johnson's study of General Assembly minutes found no evidence of either a slowing or a reversal of the relaxation of old Presbyterian disciplines during the 1950s. Moreover, many observers of the "religious revival" had grave doubts about its spiritual depth. *The Christian Century* regularly announced the statistics on membership growth as reported in the *Yearbook of American Churches*. In 1955 its editor quipped,

> But wait a minute! The *Yearbook* was talking about an increase in church members, not a decrease in sinners. It was portraying a growth in organization, not a deepening of faith. Unfortunately the carryover is not automatic.[36]

A similar uncertainty was voiced in *Christianity Today*. In 1957 its editor wrote that "it would be too much to say that the soul of the nation has undergone repentance and revival."[37] In *Theology Today*, Elmer Homrighausen of Princeton Theological Seminary recounted all the "evidences which seem to 'prove' that we are in a rising tide of interest in religion." After reviewing the growth in religious book publications, increased church membership and attendance, the enhanced appeal of Billy Graham, the proliferation of lay organizations, and so forth, Homrighausen expressed skepticism that a true "return to religion" was under way.[38]

Dennison Nash and Peter Berger were similarly skeptical of the nature of the postwar revival. They suspected that much of the numerical growth in mainline churches was a consequence of suburban expansion rather than of genuine religious reawakening.[39] They interviewed 35 suburbanites who had recently joined Congregational-Christian churches in a

Connecticut suburb. The authors found that "in 32 cases, joining was prompted by a consideration for some other person(s)." That is, no *religious* conversion or recommitment was at the core of this "surge" in decisions to take up church memberships; rather, the driving motivation for most of their subjects was a desire to join church communities with their spouses or children.[40]

Another challenge to the quality of the 1950s revival comes from our own examination of baptism and confirmation rates. We discovered that during the immediate postwar years the rate of increase of baptisms in the major mainline Protestant denominations greatly *exceeded* the U.S. birthrate. For example, whereas births in the United States increased 24 percent between 1946 and 1956, in the southern branch of Presbyterianism (PCUS) baptisms increased 110 percent and in the two northern branches (PCUSA, UPCNA) baptisms increased 100 percent during the same period.[41] We cannot believe that Presbyterian birthrates outraced nationwide rates to this extent; clearly new families with new babies were joining these churches. These findings are presented in Figure 7.1.[42]

Where did these new families come from? Undoubtedly, many came from other mainline denominations, but it is quite likely that a large portion came from more conservative denominations. We have just seen that during the 1950s the conservative churches increased their share of the Protestant market by the smallest percent in decades. Moreover, studies conducted in the mid–1960s showed that the mainline denominations had gained more members from conservative churches than they lost to them. In fact, the mainline churches' net gain from such switching was so pronounced in two surveys from the 1960s that sociologists Rodney Stark and Charles Glock actually surmised "that members of the conservative bodies are slowly draining away."[43] Unfortunately, surveys of denominational switchers have not asked them to specify *when* they switched, but two facts suggest that the bulk of the conservative-to-mainline switching occurred during the mainline church boom of the 1950s, and indeed helped create it. One fact is that recent national surveys show proportionately fewer such switchers,[44] and the other fact is that the majority of them are now over the age of fifty-five.

It is hard to believe that people from conservative Christian backgrounds who joined mainline churches after World War II were seeking a stricter, more disciplined form of Christian faith and witness. It makes more sense to assume that they were seeking a more relaxed, less legalistic, less dogmatic version of the faith. If that is the case, then the mainline church boom of the 1950s did not "strengthen" these bodies in Kelley's sense. Rather, the swelling membership rolls concealed an ongoing weakness that a few years later produced an unprecedentedly steep decline in membership. The very openness of the mainline churches that welcomed

FIGURE 7.1

U.S. Birthrate and Baptism Rates for Various Presbyterian Denominations, 1945–1989

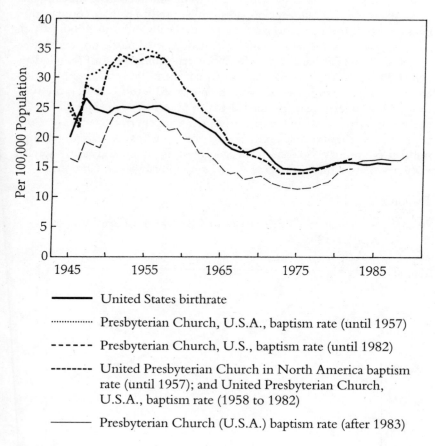

United States birthrate

·············· Presbyterian Church, U.S.A., baptism rate (until 1957)

------ Presbyterian Church, U.S., baptism rate (until 1982)

------- United Presbyterian Church in North America baptism rate (until 1957); and United Presbyterian Church, U.S.A., baptism rate (1958 to 1982)

——— Presbyterian Church (U.S.A.) baptism rate (after 1983)

newcomers during the 1950s, and made few demands on the initiates once they joined, was the basis for the subsequent decline.

In 1968, Stark and Glock reported survey data collected when membership in the mainline churches was at its peak. The data showed clear evidence of mainline church weakness. Compared with conservative church members, mainline members were considerably less likely to attend services weekly, to participate in one or more church-based activities, to limit their organizational memberships to the church and church-based groups, and to report that most of their best friends belonged to their own congregation. According to Stark and Glock, the membership of the mainline denominations was more like an "audience" than a community.[45]

The Losses Begin

Our examination of the Presbyterian baptism rates shown in Figure 7.1 revealed an influx of families with unbaptized children during the immediate postwar period. The baptism rates can be used to project confirmation rates twelve or thirteen years later, in the late 1950s and early 1960s (which is within part of the time span of confirmations used in the present study). Figures 7.2 and 7.3 present data from the major branches of Presbyterianism (UPCUSA, PCUS) allowing us to compare the actual confirmation levels during that time period with the projected levels based on the baptism rates of twelve years earlier.[46] In both branches of the church the actual number of confirmations during the early period (1958 to 1964) outdistanced the number predicted by the baptisms. Apparently a large number of young people confirmed during this period had been baptized elsewhere before their parents switched to the Presbyterian Church.

FIGURE 7.2

Actual and Projected Confirmations of Baby-Boom Presbyterians, UPCUSA, 1958–1968

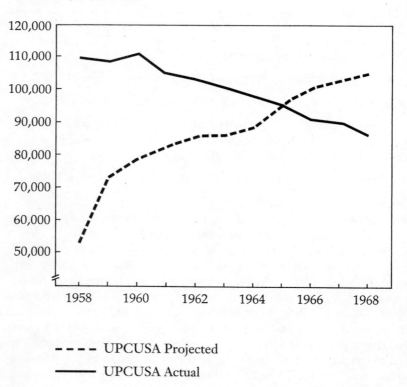

FIGURE 7.3

Actual and Projected Confirmations of Baby-Boom Presbyterians, PCUS, 1958–1968

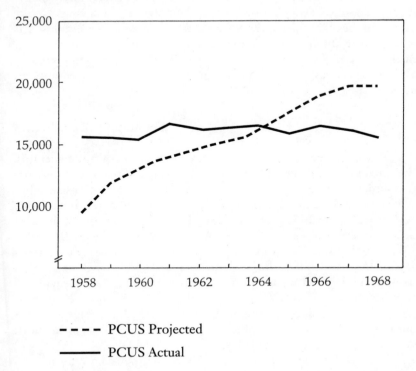

- - - - PCUS Projected

———— PCUS Actual

By the mid-1960s the baptism patterns were projecting continued steep growth of confirmation rates. But for both denominations the actual confirmation trends differ starkly from these projections. The UPCUSA confirmation level continued a decade-long decline, crossing the projected point around 1965, and then dipping far below. For the PCUS, the level remained constant, although significantly *below* the projected level, which it crossed in 1964. In both denominations, decidedly fewer people were being confirmed from among the Baby Boomers' ranks than would be expected given the earlier baptism rates. The constituency of the Presbyterian Church has therefore declined more sharply than the membership losses suggest. Not only did a sizable number of Baby Boom confirmands leave the church, but a host of Presbyterian Baby Boomers were simply not confirmed at all. Since several people we interviewed in depth told us their parents did not resist their dropping out immediately *after* confirmation, it is reasonable to suppose that many parents did not resist their children's dropping out *before* confirmation.

We suspect that the weak religious commitment of many of the Baby Boomers' parents is a factor in the recent membership decline of the mainline denominations. The mainline churches made few demands on those who flocked into its ranks during the 1950s. In effect, many members acquired only a thin gloss or "veneer" of religiosity. They were looking for churches that made low demands on them, and they found what they wanted in the mainline denominations. To some of their children, even the weak requirements of church membership seemed too burdensome or too pointless to assume. The church "boom" of the 1950s was an ephemeral one.

The Impact of the Sixties

The American cultural climate has shifted during the twentieth century in the direction of greater relativism and skepticism in matters of religion, and toward greater degrees of individualism. Acceptance of diversity in belief, lifestyle, and ethnic and racial background has broadened markedly. The shift was spearheaded by educated elites, but as the general level of education increased, especially after World War II, the shift became a broadly popular one. The leadership of the mainline Protestant churches accommodated the shift within their own ranks. The Baby Boom, which increased the demand for religious education, and the intense national anxieties attending World War II and the early Cold War period may have kept the churches full, but during that period interfaith marriage and ecumenical activities increased, and more youth attended college. In short, American society was becoming pluralistic at all levels.

In the 1960s the cultural shift returned in dramatic new forms. Although intellectuals contributed to the shift, its chief carriers were the generation of young adults born during and after World War II. It was they who flouted traditional norms concerning sexuality, marriage, and personal appearance, who challenged "establishment" authority, and who stopped going to church. Like earlier cultural shifts, this one began on both coasts, then spread to the heartland and the South. What happened quickly in the 1960s had been building up for many years. The mainline Protestant churches did not initiate the new shift, but they were unable and unwilling to resist it.

The shift toward greater personal autonomy also weakened the old expectation that respectable people should go to church, an expectation once important in American culture. In Dean Kelley's view, this expectation had concealed "the potential feebleness of the churches," but when Sabbath-observance expectations disappeared, people asked themselves why they should continue going to church, and many stopped.

Explaining Protestant Losses

In our opinion, the membership losses sustained by the mainline Protestant denominations in the United States are the result of two long-term processes. The first is the progressive weakening of mainline church life. The second is the gradual increase in relativism, individualism, and pluralism in middle-class culture—a trend that began early in the century but was arrested (and even temporarily reversed) during World War II and the early Cold War years. These two processes produced the dramatic losses that began in the mid-1960s and continue until today. By the 1960s the churches' plausibility structures had been so weakened that they could not sustain belief and commitment in the challenging new cultural setting.

Our confidence in this explanation is strengthened by findings from our sample of confirmands. Of the eight types in our sample, only the fundamentalists reported that their church attendance rates exceed those of their parents when they lived at home during adolescence. *All* the other four churchgoing types reported attending church *less* frequently than their parents did. The greatest difference was among active Presbyterians, whose rate of weekly attendance is fully 30 percentage points lower than that of their parents. We have already seen that our active Baby Boom Presbyterians have the lowest church commitment of any of our churched types; it now appears they are even less committed than their parents were.

Other, more indirect evidence, of intergenerational weakening came from our in-depth interviews. Several active Presbyterians remarked that their parents held more orthodox beliefs than they themselves held, but none told us they were more orthodox than their parents. We infer that the parents with more orthodox beliefs were more empowered by their faith. Virtually all want religious education for their own children, but many seem reluctant to impose their own religious views on them. Moreover, the religious plausibility structures of active Presbyterians seem quite weak; many told us of their reluctance to talk about religion with others. At best, their reluctance stems from a private faith that cannot be easily expressed in conventional religious language, and at worst it is because they do not want to reveal their uncertainty about their faith.

The process of weakening, judging from Johnson's study of Presbyterian General Assembly *Minutes,* has proceeded in piecemeal fashion. Not all elements of the religious tradition have been relaxed or abandoned simultaneously. What active Presbyterian Baby Boomers have abandoned is the level of church participation of their parents, and in many cases the conviction of the exclusive truth of Christianity. What they have retained is a belief in God or some spiritual force, a partiality toward mainline Protestantism, the habit of praying, the basic moral code, and a commitment to providing religious education for their children. The major difference between them and the bulk of religious dropouts is that the latter have abandoned churchgoing itself.

Presbyterian Openness

We have noted that many people in our sample are universalistic on religious matters. They have no reason to believe that Christianity is the only true religion. Such a viewpoint is a result of liberal education and cross-cultural experiences, which Presbyterians have favored for decades. Presbyterians have always insisted on a learned clergy, and they have been at the forefront in establishing colleges across the land. Today Presbyterians send their children to the finest schools and colleges. They advocate broad-mindedness and cross-cultural experiences, and most want their children to feel free to make their own decisions about religion. No wonder that the brightest and best Presbyterian youth turn out to be universalistic and liberal. What else should we expect? Maybe this is what Presbyterians really want.

For sake of illustration, let us look at the alternative. What if Presbyterians put pressure on their children not to marry anyone outside the mainline denominations, not to get a liberal education that challenges received doctrines, not to travel or study in other cultures (except perhaps in mission work), not to live or work closely with people of other faiths, and not to think for themselves in religious matters? Further, what if there were lifestyle rules concerning Sabbath observance, dress codes, alcohol use, and sexual behavior that clearly demarcated Presbyterians and set them off from others in society?

But for decades Presbyterians have been opposed to all of this. They have stood for openness, ecumenism, critical scholarship without restriction, adoption of science and higher learning, cosmopolitanism, and freedom of conscience. For decades the majority have made choices that aided their children to be world-conscious, open, autonomous, and (as a byproduct) not committed to the specific traditions of the church. The children have asked over and over what is distinctive about Presbyterianism—or even about Protestantism—and why they should believe it or cherish it. The answers have apparently not been very clear. Today Presbyterians should not bemoan the lack of faith and church commitment exhibited by their youth, since they have no one to blame but themselves. No outside power forcibly pulled their children away from the faith. No conquering army or hostile missionaries destroyed the tradition. The Presbyterians made the decisions themselves, on one specific issue after another, over the decades. They repeatedly chose openness and cosmopolitanism.

The Impact of Other Factors on Church Decline

Our findings lend support to Kelley's thesis concerning the progressive weakening of the mainline denominations. They do not support the contention that these churches have lost members because they have failed to be "relevant," or that their leadership and programs have been faulty, or that they have been excessively preoccupied with social activism.

What can we conclude about the remaining factors in our inventory of possible sources of church decline? It will be useful to look at the list in Table I.1 (p. 12). We begin with cultural factors. Regarding the first—the increase in liberal education—there is no doubt that Protestant young people have much more and better liberal education today than decades ago. Is this important? In our survey we found that college attendance is not a good predictor of church involvement today; it is only a predictor of *beliefs*, in that college graduates are more universalistic and relativistic about Christianity. We also found that the impact of college cannot be distinguished from the impact of earlier education. We can only conclude that rising education, seen broadly, has a moderate impact on religious views in a universalizing direction. Thus it is moderately important for explaining declining mainline church involvement.

Second is the rise in pluralism. Without doubt this has occurred over the past half century, and without doubt it has changed religion in America. Pluralism assaults traditional plausibility structures. We believe that it is an important historical factor explaining the problems of mainline churches.

Third is the increase in individualism. In our survey it was less telling than universalism. Its impact has probably been more on ecclesiastical authority than on biblical authority, and thus more damaging to the Catholic Church than to the mainline Protestant churches.

Individualism as a weakening of community ties has probably enfeebled church plausibility structures. As we have seen, many of the Baby Boomers believe that their personal faith need not be lived out in any formal religious organization. We do not believe this assertion, but many Baby Boomers do, and its diffusion among young adults has certainly had some effect.

Fourth is the rise of privatism. The most common meaning of privatism today is the withdrawal of personal commitment from anything outside the circle of work and family. In the 1980s we heard constantly about the "me generation" and the loss of social concern among youth. We doubt that this is important for mainline church decline, since it is a short-term phenomenon, and an understanding of the trends requires a much longer historical sweep. But if we look at privatism more broadly, including the more general modern tendencies for young adults to move to homogeneous lifestyle enclaves, it is possible that it has had some impact.. The research is unclear on this topic, and we are left to guess.

The social structural factors we outlined could not be tested directly in our survey. The most we could do was to compare the Baby Boomers with their parents' generation and to interview some of the Boomers' parents. The first factor we identified was the decline of community at the local level. We find it plausible that there was a decline, since people today travel more, move residences more readily, and enjoy more personal freedoms in decision-making. Extended families are less important today. Probably this has been important for church life, since churches depend so strongly on community ties. In our study the persons who moved far away from home tended to go church less often. Those who married non-Protestant spouses also attended less often. And those living in the West, where community is weakest, were the least church-involved. Without doubt, people go to church less if there is less community expectation of churchgoing, and as far as we can tell, such expectations have diminished. Thus we believe that community ties have weakened over the decades and that the weakening has cut down on church involvement.

Have changes in family life and the role of women been important factors in church membership decline? Research has consistently shown that families today are smaller, that people marry later, that divorce is more prevalent, and that more women are in the workforce. But do these trends have an impact on the Protestant churches? Other research on childless families indicates that motivations for adults to go to church are weaker if no children are present.[47] Whether the movement of women into the workforce affects church attendance is unclear in past research, as noted in chapter 5. We guess that these trends have some modest explanatory power in accounting for mainline membership decline.

This checklist of theoretical factors makes no pretense to be exhaustive. Given the state of research today, we cannot do more. Our main point is that we believe the dominant explanation for mainline decline is a combination of the gradual weakening of mainline churches, changes in American culture, and the churches' policy of openness to change. We lack clear evidence on specifics, but we agree with Peter Berger that any social trend as momentous as the mainline Protestant decline must surely be fueled by multiple forces.

Chapter 8

Implications for Mainline Churches

The impetus for this research was the continuing decline and marginalization of mainline Protestantism. This experience, now almost three decades long, has produced an abundance of investigations, reflections, and research studies. Denominational leaders have thought up programs for growth and have commissioned new confessional statements. New movements have emerged with their own proposals for revitalization. Church leaders have rethought Christian education and seminary training. But for the most part, mainline Protestants have not known what to do. Should they push forward on their present course, or should they try to turn back? Are the present institutions serving the Protestant community, or not? Our study has given us some new information about the options mainline Protestants actually have, and in this chapter we will look at them.

The basic question to be addressed is how mainline churches can carry out their authentic biblical and theological mission by ministering effectively to the Baby Boom generation. This is central. We are mindful that, in situations of stress, institutions sometimes change their goals for the sake of preserving their budgets and structures (what sociologists call "goal-displacement"). If the institutions are not attaining their current goals, then some incumbents will argue for changing the goals, not the institutions. That temptation must be rejected. The mission and goals of the church are based in scripture and must be kept unchanged. Of course we know that to declare this outright is far easier than to articulate it in action or to guarantee its accomplishment if one or another course of action were chosen.

Ministering to Baby Boomers is different from ministering to their elders. To begin with, they have a different approach to church life. In chapter 5 we stated that most Baby Boomers have a market view of churches. Boomers see churches as selling a product which they are free to buy or not to buy as they wish, and they feel perfectly free to change from one supplier to another if there is a reason to do so. Most feel no obligation to participate in churches at all, either because they are skeptical about one or another church teaching or because they are convinced that "you don't have to go to church to be a good Christian." Either way, they feel no obligation.

Not everyone will like this market framework for thinking about the church. But we believe it is clarifying. The question now becomes, What do the Boomers want to buy that churches have to offer? At the risk of simplification, we outlined in chapter 5 four main commodities the Boomers want. The most important is religious education for children and associated support for family life. We were amazed that 96 percent of the sample—including churched and unchurched—said they would like religious education for their own children! It was nearly unanimous. Almost all parents want religious education for their children, and most want to get it in Sunday schools. In our society today there are few alternative suppliers of this kind of education, and none are likely to appear soon. What Sunday school offers cannot be purchased anywhere else (apart from five-day-a-week religious schools). An obvious implication for churches is that they should offer first-rate religious education and youth programs. What kind of programs? As we have seen, preferences vary, but everyone stresses moral education and character education alongside the more cognitive elements of learning about the Bible and church teachings. Beyond that, lay liberals would be cautious, since they are leery of "indoctrination."

Some parents want Sunday school only for their children, and they want nothing from the church for themselves, thank you. These parents may send their kids or drop them off at church without sticking around to see what else is going on. But some will stay around and will have some exposure to what church *really* is, not just how they remembered it from their own childhood.

Second, many respondents talked about the need for personal support and reassurance. When people feel insecure, uncertain, or isolated they need help, and churches are an obvious place to look for it. Some people need to go to church to get them through the week. They need a place where they can pull their lives together, where they can get away from their home or workplace for reflection and reinvigoration. What helps them most is authentic human relationships in settings where they can speak openly and honestly without fear of rejection. Small groups within churches are often powerful in this way.

Third, many talked about a need for social contacts and a sense of community. This need seems strongest in urban settings where family and friendship ties are weak, at least for the newcomers in town. We were told that suburban living is often sterile and isolating and that churches are good places to look for contacts and ties. Churches need to be approachable to such searchers and to facilitate the development of human bonds. As one of our respondents told us, it's all right to belong to a bridge club or a bird watchers group, but those groups aren't deep enough or reliable enough really to help you when you become ill or have other needs. This person wanted ties with committed, stable, reliable people on whom she could count.

Fourth, the values of inspiration and spiritual guidance were mentioned repeatedly. People sought inspiration from the Bible and from worship services. They needed worship to be uplifting and empowering, drawing them away from petty concerns to remember the larger picture, out of self-pity to praise, adoration, and thanksgiving. They wanted devotions and music to be encouraging. Many of the Baby Boomers who are regular churchgoers told us that worship is spiritually nourishing to them.

These four needs came up in our interviews. We did not hear much talk about the lack of personal *meaning* in a deep sense, although the need is universal. Some of our respondents admitted that they had given up on finding ultimate meaning for their lives, and they doubted whether there is any that *can* be found at all. Others were resigned to expecting only short-term meanings in life, such as those found in raising a family or in serving their community. This topic was not easy to explore. In our society today one hears almost no open discussion of problems of the meaning of life, and it was slow in forthcoming in our personal interviews. Many respondents could not find words to express themselves. Nevertheless, Baby Boomers believe that churches are a primary place to turn to when facing ultimate questions. For many, this is the church's basic reason for existence. Except for the convinced secularists in the sample, most people turn to religion and the church when the questions of meaning are felt most sharply.

Again, no one else in our society deals in this commodity. Higher education is helpful but not ultimately satisfying. Status striving and consumerism turn out to be empty. Self-indulgence is stultifying. Other than religion, the main sources of deep meaning we observed in our respondents were social causes and movements. People actively engaged in helping the homeless or disadvantaged, in working to preserve nature, or in reforming the society in one way or another were the most alive and vital of the non-churched people we met. But they are a minority.

In our interviews we found an abiding sense of goodwill toward

Protestant churches. The majority of Baby Boomers who have dropped out harbor no animosity toward the church. On the contrary, they look back on their own youthful involvement as something good. Except in the cases of a small number who told horror stories about this or that disastrous church experience, there are no serious barriers preventing unchurched Baby Boomers from reconsidering church involvement.

In sum, whatever direction the church takes in the future must begin with these needs. Churches should offer high-quality Sunday school and youth programs, uplifting worship experiences, and meaningful, authentic small-group experiences. Services must include music that uplifts and devotions that touch the heart. These elements of church life are not at issue; they are necessities. But other things are at issue.

Two Basic Options

We see two options Protestant churches might choose. They were described well in 1967 by Peter Berger:

> The pluralistic situation presents the religious institutions with two ideal-typical options. They can either accommodate themselves to the situation, play the pluralistic game of religious free enterprise, and come to terms as best they can with the plausibility problem by modifying their product in accordance with consumer demands. Or they can refuse to accommodate themselves, entrench themselves behind whatever socio-religious structures they can maintain or construct, and continue to profess the old objectives as much as possible as if nothing had happened. Obviously there are various intermediate possibilities between those two ideal-typical options, with varying degrees of accommodation and intransigence. Both ideal-typical options have problems on the level of theory as well as on the level of "social engineering."[1]

These two options are a helpful way of looking at possibilities.

As we analyzed the data on the Baby Boomers, it became clear that the gospel message is not compelling to those who see it as culturally and historically relative and who are suspicious of any putative religious authority. Here is the most basic problem facing the church today. So the church is presented with two options. First, it can try to recapture traditional religious authority. Second, it can accept the fact that regaining traditional religious authority cannot be done and that churches need to proceed without it.

Recapture Authority

Authority of any kind is scarce today, and religious authority is the scarcest of all. *Church authority* is weak in American Protestantism, largely because the Reformation attacked church authority as a matter of principle. The Reformers preached *sola scriptura*, a return to scripture as the only Christian authority. This was satisfactory for Luther, but it is less satisfactory for persons today acquainted with the full force of biblical scholarship. After decades of no-holds-barred criticism, *biblical authority* today is not as firm and clear as in centuries past. Textual criticism, historicism, and new understandings of culturally conditioned worldviews have put distance between the scriptural texts and people's commitments. In this new setting many mainline Protestants have informally evolved a loosely articulated theology which we call "lay liberalism." Its chief characteristic is an unwillingness to make authoritative claims on matters of faith.

We have diagnosed the crisis of authority as being a result of the expansion of liberal higher education, pluralism, and cross-cultural awareness. Yet Protestants favor all of these. Mainline Protestants have been at the forefront of American education. They believe in broad education for their children, yet in the process of giving their children maximal exposure to cultural variety they have weakened the plausibility structures on which their children's faith rests.

One clear-cut option is to stop the process. Stop sending children to non-religious, liberal colleges. Stop the historical criticism of the Bible. Stop encouraging cross-cultural learning. Discourage interfaith marriage. Raise barriers between the denominational faith community and other people in society. Then people would know who is in and who is out, and boundaries would reappear. In sum, move the Protestant communities away from the center of the culture of higher education today, toward the encapsulated faith communities of the past. For generations some other religious groups have been doing this, for example, the Amish and the Orthodox Jews. They prove that the option is possible in reality, not just in theory.

We describe this option here to demonstrate how far-fetched it is. It calls for an about-face from a century of mainline Protestant creativity. These Protestants are proud of their colleges and universities, of their fellow members who are community and world leaders, of their religious leaders who espouse ecumenicity, racial justice, openness, and critical thinking. Protestantism has a rich heritage of liberation, intellectual achievement, and political leadership. Its young people are the best and the brightest, the most capable of leadership in tomorrow's world. It's a pity they don't go to church, but, well, worse things could happen.

So one option for the church is to strengthen its authority. It could proclaim literal biblical authority, or some approximation to it, in the neo-orthodox sense. An effective job of this would strengthen the faith and commitment of some of our Baby Boomers, but not all. The lay liberals would remain at a distance and would soon feel unwelcome. Many would leave the mainline churches and pursue their spiritual searches elsewhere. That is, if the mainline churches attempted to define themselves more distinctively, as for example by putting demands on members regarding doctrinal beliefs, it would cause dissent and splits, either locally or nationally.

Who wants to turn back now for the strength of the faith community? Who would welcome such a reclamation of authority? Not many. Lay liberals, for one, would not. The lay liberals who are outside the church would stay out, and many more who are currently involved would leave. Dean Kelley has said that an attempt to move the mainline churches back to an earlier period of authority and discipline would cause a major schism. He suggested that only one in a hundred would go along, and the rest would leave.[2] This estimate seems extreme, but we agree that only a minority would remain. Of course *other* persons would join. The new members would probably be similar to Type 1s in our sample, that is, committed and generous persons willing to devote time and money to serving Christ and helping the church, but holding expectations for the church much different from what it is now.

To accept the reclamation of authority and *still* retain large numbers of present mainline members, an alternative route must be followed. Most important, Protestant churches need more compelling answers to theological questions about truth and authority in the present-day chaotic culture. The formulations of the past will not suffice. Rather, new bases of authority claims must be generated. This is an urgent task for Protestant theologians today.

The question of biblical authority would be central to such a discussion, and one answer would be to allow diverse interpretations. An interesting instance of this is what Donald Miller has found in his studies of fast-growing Baby Boomer churches in southern California. These churches profess strong biblical authority yet leave final interpretation up to individuals without any attempt at achieving agreement or imposing official statements. The pastor gives a personal perspective on any passage and then invites the members to study, pray, ask for inspiration from the Holy Spirit, and decide for themselves. The pastor tells the people, "You read the Bible yourself! You may come out at a different place from me. This is how I read it, but you need to read it for yourself." No one tries to adjudicate individual differences. The authority of the biblical passages comes from a combination of historical text and personal ratification by the Holy Spirit. Thus biblical authority is maintained at a certain level.[3]

An important aspect of the authority problem is the distinction our respondents often made between doctrinal teachings and moral teachings. If we can distinguish moral authority from doctrinal authority—defining the former as guiding our daily behavior and the latter as dealing with heaven, earth, and ultimate reality—then moral authority remains fairly strong in the Baby Boomer sample. Moral relativity is not pervasive in our sample of Baby Boomers, and the moral authority of the Protestant church is widely accepted.

Should mainline churches define themselves more in terms of moral authority? It is worth discussing. As we found, the basic moral authority of Protestant churches is not embattled. Only when moral discussions turn to specific issues, such as homosexuality or abortion, do acute differences arise. Therefore moral authority might provide a basis for church involvement. The churches could emphasize thoughtful and responsible Christian moral living in twentieth- and twenty-first-century America. Understandings of heaven and earth, God and history, could be left to individual resolution, and clergy would acknowledge tacitly that they have little compelling to say on these matters. But the burning question is still there: how to live?

We know of some local congregations who have moved in this direction. They give foremost attention to questions about spirituality and how to live authentically in this society. In these groups, issues of social responsibility, lifestyle, and even political affiliation arise very soon, and they must be dealt with through participatory processes so that congregational unity and identity can be preserved. When this is successful, personal life and church life take on new meaning and vitality.

In our world there are many issues of near–ultimate meaning, and they have significance for churched and unchurched persons alike. The mainline churches may find a new voice of authority among Baby Boomers in addressing them. For instance, the fear of an impending environmental collapse has stimulated new groups and efforts supporting recycling, pollution control, and care for wildlife. A theology centering on ecological responsibility was very strongly advocated by representatives of the mainline during the 1992 Rio Earth Summit.[4]

Another pressing issue is the breakdown of the family. As new family configurations become more widespread, the sense of one's social location becomes increasingly difficult to sustain. Children talk blithely about step-parents, half-siblings, progeny of second and third marriages, same-sex couples, and visitation days. These changes produce a sense of crisis in many people, encouraging a turn to the church for answers.

It is appropriate for churches to encourage group discussion and action to strengthen their members in taking countercultural stands on issues such as environmentalism, family, and lifestyle. Members who do this will see themselves as in but not of the world. We hear continual debate about whether the churches should be more countercultural, and we think it should be in areas which the members today feel are central and important. The issues mentioned here would seem to be examples. Committed groups embarking on new lifestyles deserve encouragement.

In this effort to reclaim religious authority, authority should be understood not only philosophically or theologically. It is powerful in practice. For instance, people feel a sense of authority from exemplary leaders who speak and live out moral commitments. These people *embody* authority, and sociologists say they have "charismatic" authority. Examples today are Archbishop Desmond Tutu and ex-president Jimmy Carter. Anyone observing them and listening to them feels their moral power. Charismatic authority can be marvelously strong, and it needs to be nurtured by all leaders in the mainline church.

Build Church Life Without Authority

As we said earlier, doctrinal or moral authority cannot be recaptured for everyone. A good number of Baby Boomers are thoroughgoing creedal relativists, and the only way the churches can relate to them is through acceptance, at least tentative, of relativity. If mainline churches were to do this, they would have to accept the view that the Bible is at most a spiritual or moral resource and that other resources are also valuable. This viewpoint implicitly reduces the prominence of churches in comparison with other groups and movements in society, and it accepts the inevitability that church commitment of members, on average, will be weak. Without religious authority, churches are one group among others.

But even with this competition, the mainline churches have a potent product that many Baby Boomers seek. They offer religious or spiritual answers to life's questions. Churches can minister to people who see themselves as spiritual seekers—a group who are frequently found among lay liberals—so long as the churches accept them and make them feel welcome. In his book *U.S. Lifestyles and Mainline Churches,* Tex Sample says that many Baby Boomers see life as a spiritual journey.[5] Mainline churches should accept them as spiritual questers and should emphasize what he calls "journey theology." Such a theology sees life as open to new experiences and surprises, as a time of searching for spiritual truth. The notion of journey is a metaphor for growth and movement. It stresses autobiography and faith walks more than creeds and fixed doctrines, and it assumes no single religious authority, permanent identity, or boundaries. This metaphor fits our experiences with lay liberal Boomers.

Churches become important for some people when their own urges for social involvement and social change coincide with the churches' mission goals. Persons devoted to social change of many kinds will find churches attractive to them insofar as the churches are also engaged in similar efforts. Common devotion to agreed-on causes overcomes barriers, and we believe that some Baby Boomers will participate in church life from this starting point. However, their participation may be temporary and their commitments may be shaky, since the participation is based on only a few shared values. Churches hoping to capitalize on this activism should encourage their own activists to reach out to others in the community, and they should do what they can to be open.

Moving the mainline churches toward greater openness, rather than authority, would require a general expectation of weaker commitment of members to the institution. Financial giving and personal volunteering of time and energy would more likely diminish than grow. Institutional churches would need to cope with less involved, less dependable members, and maintaining a vital church life would be more difficult.

In response, individual congregations could specialize, so that some would move in one direction and others in another, as local conditions indicate. We believe this would be effective and should be encouraged. The religious marketplace operates in a complex society, and no single group will be able to reach all. The main problem with this will be the task of maintaining larger unity and keeping the peace in judicatories and denominations.

Denominationalism

What about denominations? Our research experience has guided us away from larger institutional topics such as the role of denominations. The Baby Boomers weren't much interested. In general, denominational identity within mainline Protestantism is flimsy, and commitment to existing denominational structures is very weak. Most Baby Boomers don't feel affected by denominations. When we asked about ecumenism, denominational mergers, or restructuring Protestantism, our respondents had little to say. It is partially a reflection of a broader skepticism about large institutions among young adults today, and partly an acknowledgment that boundaries between mainline denominations have faded and possibly vanished.

But critical issues face denominations. Can they maintain enough commitment to sustain the educational, mission, and support programs they now support? Can they manage to stay united while conservatives and lay liberals pull in opposite directions? Should there be more ecumenical mergers or cooperation? Will the conservative versus liberal cleavage dominate the years ahead, as some believe, forcing an institutional realignment in mainline Protestantism? These are momentous issues, and the principal contribution from our study is our conclusion that the problem of maintaining denominational commitment and support from Boomers will be a tough one. Many of the Baby Boomers we interviewed see little point in denominations and denominational identity. They will support whatever institutional structures—mainline or otherwise—are perceived to best serve their own personal needs.

Moreover, there are serious obstacles to the development and success of denomination-level programs aimed at stemming the membership losses. While mainline Protestants continue to support their congregations financially, they are sending less money to denominational offices. Furthermore, the ongoing "culture wars" among rival denominational elites stymie concerted efforts to change. Any program that would be implemented is likely to be compromised because of the conflicting explanations that the elites have of the causes of membership decline.

Finally, as we found, allegiances of mainline Protestants are principally to their local congregations, not to denominations. Successful initiatives are most likely to arise locally. Congregations in each locality, perhaps specializing as suggested above, will be in the best position to relate effectively to Baby Boomers. Individual ministries and churches, learning from successes elsewhere and adapting them to their own particular settings, hold out the greatest promise for the future of the mainline churches.

Life Goes On

What has happened in the lives of the eight Presbyterian confirmands whom we quoted by name in this book? Two years after interviewing them in depth, we telephoned to find out. Our report begins with the four we met in chapter 1 and then moves on to the others we met in later chapters.

Marcia Wilson

Marcia Wilson's life took an unexpected turn after we interviewed her. A year later her husband, Randy, was transferred by his firm to a key position in Jacksonville, Florida, and Marcia was obliged to leave her home and friends in San Antonio. She was "*so* sad" to cut her friendship ties, and she plans to make two trips a year to visit her Bible study group, her pastor, and her many other Texas friends.

Right now she is busy getting adjusted and making plans to build a new house in one of Jacksonville's more exclusive neighborhoods. She and Randy have been too busy to attend church in the last month, but Marcia has already gathered information on the major mainline Protestant churches in the city, and she will begin shopping around as soon as time permits. As in San Antonio, the minister will be the deciding factor for her.

Marcia's plans for working in a soup kitchen in San Antonio did not materialize. Instead, her desire to be of service took the form of nine months of operating a new literacy project in the local public schools. Marcia's stepdaughter is home from the mission field in Africa, having had a "wonderful, wonderful" experience there, and she is looking forward to returning within a few years. In the meantime, Randy is worried about his daughter's lack of concern for making long-range plans for her life. When it comes to career and financial matters, the daughter believes that "the Lord will provide," which Randy thinks is simplistic and naive. Marcia, who once had a successful career of her own, is inclined to agree, but her delight in her stepdaughter's Christian commitment makes her less concerned than Randy is about the young woman's future. He has still not accepted Christ as his savior.

Calvin Caletti

Calvin's life has changed very little in the past two years. He is still very much an agnostic. "My religious views are stable," he told us. "You thought I might have found Christ in some hallway?" he asked with amusement. His wife still takes the two children to Catholic religion classes and goes with them to mass on Sundays when her schedule permits. Calvin was happy to report new evidence that his sons may be forming the same attitudes toward church that he developed as a boy. They, too, are now pretending to be asleep on Sunday mornings. And they are telling their mother, "But Dad doesn't go," when it is time to leave for mass. Still, Calvin feels a little guilty about the example he is setting for them. If he did not have to work every second Sunday he might go to church more often—"not for myself," he assured us, but it would please his wife if they could attend as a family.

Calvin is not a candidate for religious conversion or renewal. The life of the spirit holds no meaning for him.

Wayne Sanders

Wayne's fundamentalist views have remained just as stable as Calvin's agnosticism. He still works part-time as a lay pastor in his nondenominational church and he still devotes most of his evenings to church work. He feels that he has grown spiritually during the past two years. His main priority in life now is bringing up his children so they will feel led by the Holy Spirit to do whatever God wants them to do.

Ann Brooks

After months of shopping around, Ann and her husband have joined a local United Church of Christ, and they now attend regularly. When she and Dave attended a Presbyterian church nearby they were turned off by the overt show of status they found there. The fur coats were particularly offensive. Although the UCC congregation is equally professional and upper middle class in its composition, its members do not put the same stock in a display of wealth and possessions.

The Brooks children, now eight and eleven, are at last enrolled in Sunday school. Ann is impressed with the Sunday children's sermon, which takes place in the front of the sanctuary with the children arrayed around the speaker. She likes the fact that the members are asked to help with scripture readings and with the junior sermons, which makes for variety and creativity. The pastor, whose informal manner puts her at ease, preaches sermons that "apply things from the Bible to our lives today."

Although Ann is active in church again, her religious perspective has not changed. She is comfortable with her questioning attitude and seems unconcerned that there are no clear answers. Her life continues to be hectic. She is still a special education teacher, and she has recently written two books on teaching children's literature. The relaxed atmosphere at her new church has given her second thoughts about becoming "roped in" to a round of church activities. There is a vacancy in the choir, and Ann may soon be helping to make Sunday worship the musical delight that she remembers so fondly from her girlhood.

Dan Fuller

Dan Fuller's independent fundamentalist church has been in turmoil, but his faith has remained firm. Not long after we first interviewed Dan the congregation called a new associate pastor, who brought along three families of his followers, bringing the church up to about 100 members. But a split soon developed and the new pastor left, taking with him the three families and half the original members. So Dan's church is now down to about 25 members. The senior pastor, whom Dan greatly admired, was devastated by the turmoil, but he is slowly regaining his vigor.

Dan is still a deacon and he remains enthusiastic about the church. He handles its finances. He and his family live at the same place, but last year he quit his job and started his own business in computer programming. Dan and his wife had prayed about the job change, and they think the Lord was leading him to start his own business.

Betty Taylor

When we talked with Betty earlier, she was giving an immense amount of time to her Presbyterian church in Michigan and was beginning to feel like cutting back. But two years later she is just as involved as ever. She has started part-time work as a medical technician, but this has not diminished her service to the church. She teaches a Sunday school class (of which her son is a member) and is now vice-moderator of the church's women's association. Next year when she is moderator she will be participating in presbytery-wide meetings.

These past two years have been a time of growth for Betty. As she puts it, "The more I learn, the more I realize that I don't know." Last summer she attended the national Presbyterian Women's annual meeting. It was exhilarating and challenging. She came home with a renewed sense of her faith, but also with a new sense of guilt about the limited ways in which she is carrying out mission. She would like to join with other parishioners in a downtown soup kitchen, but she doesn't have the time.

Betty's husband, who is a lapsed Catholic, has recently been drawn into Presbyterian church life. He began attending when the congregation added a second worship service at the same hour the children were in Sunday school. Betty is very pleased, and so are her parents, who were uneasy about her marrying a Catholic in the first place. He and Betty have become friends with the associate pastor and his wife.

Betty still feels overwhelmed with all that she is doing for the church, with how much still needs doing, and with how exhausting her life is. But all in all, she seems gratified that she is such a sturdy, reliable pillar of the congregation.

Barbara Hickman

Two years later Barbara announced to us that she and her family are now going to a Unitarian-Universalist Church. They have attended for almost a year. She loves it and her daughters do too. Her husband is wary, but he goes on Sunday mornings to be with them. Barbara thinks her girls are happy, because they feel more "with it" and less strange now that they are churchgoers. Barbara likes some of the people there, especially the minister. The people accept each other's right to have their own beliefs. She has no need to mouth any beliefs she does not really hold, or to hide her doubts and uncertainties. The church has a list of twelve things it believes, and Barbara says she honestly *does* believe all of them. Some of the others in the church are admirable people, and Barbara would like to become closer to them. She believes that most of them are there looking for community. So is she, and this church seems like a good place to find it.

Some of the church services are very moving, especially those about people's spiritual journeys. Other services tend to be political (very liberal), which she doesn't like. It is a large church, with about 600 members—really too large for Barbara's taste.

She hasn't joined, and she is not sure when she will. She needs to think about it a little more. The church puts no pressure on people to join, and many people participate without joining. Barbara and her husband make financial contributions. The girls are attending religious education classes, and Barbara and her husband help teach. If Barbara joins, she will do so as an individual, since her husband won't. Now he doesn't want to be a member of *any* church.

Barbara still wonders sometimes if she is cheating her children by not teaching them any one religion. Her Unitarian church has no set religion—that is, one which teaches about life and the world and the purpose of life. The church *does* have strong beliefs about the value of life, acceptance of all religions, and liberty. And most of the people try to live out those values.

For a while Barbara felt guilty for giving up her earlier religion and being a doubter. Now she feels it is okay to give up traditional beliefs and do her own thing. She feels less guilty. It is okay to keep seeking for something that is genuinely meaningful to you and feels right—even if the search never ends!

Barbara still ponders whether she should devote herself more to serving other people. Being a computer programmer isn't enough. She admires people like Mother Teresa who are really committed to serving the unfortunate. Maybe later in life.

Sue North

Two years later Sue said that her life continues about the same. She and her husband still live in the farmhouse in the country. Her opinions about religion and church life are still the same. She continues to be a secular humanist, committed to standards of tolerance and individualism. Her son, who had struggled with the religious content of a Christian preschool, has now graduated to the relative security of a public school's first grade. Sue's four-year-old daughter has just entered the same Christian preschool.

Sue has thought a lot about why her family has difficulty fitting in with the neighbors. She remains very circumspect about expressing her opinions to anyone. She feels as though she and her family are perceived as "different" in large measure because they are outsiders and have no extended family in the region. Also they are different since they are not farmers. Sue thinks these are probably more important factors in the eyes of the community than her divergent political and religious viewpoints. But she is not greatly bothered by the problem, and she tells herself that the distance maintained by other people is a matter of their own insular existence rather than an effort to exclude her and her family.

Appendix

Methods Used in Telephone Surveys and Personal Interviews

Pilot Study

During 1988 we tried our methods in four churches in different regions. We found that Presbyterian churches indeed do have good confirmation records, but they have no reliable records of youth ministry or youth program participants. Thus we had to base all sampling on confirmation lists. The main age of confirmation in Presbyterian churches in the 1960s was 13 or 14.

We found that every church had people who would be happy to help us find the confirmands today. Most churches have some older members who know everybody. In the pilot study we found about 70 percent of the confirmands we wanted, and about 80 percent completed the phone interviews. The pilot study included 53 phone interviews.

Sample Churches

In the final study we cut costs by clustering the sample churches geographically. We doubted that much bias would result. We divided the United States into four main regions—Northeast, Midwest, South, and West, as defined by the U.S. Census. We also divided church sizes into four levels—249 or less, 250 to 499, 500 to 999, and 1,000 or more.

We set the number of interviews at 500 for the main sample (33 to 42 years old) and 100 for the older sample (43 to 52 years old). From 1964 yearbooks of both the UPCUSA and the PCUS we found the numbers of Presbyterians that year in each church size in each region, and thereby calculated how many interviews we would need in each. They are shown in Table A.1.

TABLE A.1

Interviews Needed in Each Region and Church Size Category

	0–249	250–499	500–999	1,000+	Total
Northeast					
Age 33–42	23	28	43	42	136
Age 43–52	5	6	8	8	27
Midwest					
Age 33–42	27	28	45	73	173
Age 43–52	5	6	9	15	35
South					
Age 33–42	32	27	30	27	116
Age 43–52	6	5	6	5	22
West					
Age 33–42	8	10	20	37	75
Age 43–52	2	2	4	8	16
Total					
Age 33–42	90	93	138	179	500
Age 43–52	18	19	27	36	100

The number of churches needed in each of the 16 cells was left to be decided on the spot, so long as all churches were seen as fairly typical, and so long as all sampling of names was random. Dean Hoge took charge of the Northeast and chose Pennsylvania; Don Luidens took charge of the Midwest and chose Michigan; Benton Johnson took charge of the West and proposed sampling in Oregon and California; and Benton and Dean shared the South, with sampling in North Carolina. We decided to select one or two black churches in North Carolina to be sure the overall percentage of black interviews was correct.

During summer 1989 we met with presbytery executives in all the regions, and they helped us select representative churches fitting our criteria. The church sizes had to be for the middle 1960s, not today. We selected

23 churches for study—six in Pennsylvania, six in Michigan, five in North Carolina, one in South Carolina, two in Oregon, and three in California.

Finding and Interviewing the Confirmands

In each church we got the list of confirmands in the 1950s and 1960s, randomly selected the desired sample, and hired a member of the church to locate the target people. This was usually an older church member or a church secretary. We asked these persons to use every possible avenue, and we agreed to help find lost persons during the interview process itself. The study was announced publicly in each church. We agreed that all names of persons, churches, and towns would be kept confidential.

Finding the confirmands was the biggest problem we had. Using all possible methods we found 73 percent (see Table A.2).

During the phoning we found that some of the target persons were too old or too young to be eligible; hence they were excused and deleted from the calculations in the rightmost column of the table.

TABLE A.2

Percentage of Target Persons Found and Interviewed

	Percentage of Target Persons Found	Percentage of Interview Success Among Eligible Target Persons We Tried to Reach
Total	73	79
Northeast churches	89	85
Midwest churches	84	75
Southern churches	58	79
Western churches	58	82
Churches of 1,000+	63	79
Churches of 500–999	75	80
Churches of 250–499	78	79
Churches of 0–249	92	77

Note: This table does not include two black churches, one in North Carolina and one in South Carolina, since their confirmation records were incomplete and we had to rely partly on personal recall. We completed 15 interviews in these churches, mostly by a black interviewer on our staff.

We used all possible means to locate the target people. During the interviews we asked other confirmands of the same age if they could help us locate the lost persons, and if we knew of persons who were reluctant to be interviewed, we asked their friends to tell them how painless it was. These methods produced a few successes.

As Table A.2 shows, there was great variation in the percentage of target people who could be found in different churches. The success was best in the Northeast and Midwest. In the South we had very poor luck in one large church, which dragged down the overall percentage for the South to 58. In general the difficulties were the worst in the West, apparently because of higher transiency of people in Oregon and California.

The percentage found varied directly by church size. The small churches were by far the most successful in finding their confirmands. Most of the churches with fewer than 250 members were in rural areas or small towns, and they had the best luck—92 percent of the people located. In 3 of the 6 churches in this category, 100 percent were found. By contrast, the large churches of 1,000 or more members could find only 63 percent. The people were easiest to find in the small-town churches because of kinship and friendship ties that still existed after twenty or thirty years. Typically the confirmand's parents, siblings, or other relatives were still in the town, and a single phone call was enough to get us an address and phone number.

We expected these difficulties and made adjustments during the research process to minimize bias. In spite of the lower rate of finding the confirmands in large churches, these churches are still represented in our sample in correct proportions, because we began with larger initial lists. The quotas from each region and church size were maintained correctly; the only departure was that the interviews from the West were 7 under quota and those from the Northeast and South (combined) 7 over quota.

From the beginning we were faced with imprecise information about the confirmands' ages. Most were confirmed when they were 13 or 14, but there was much variation, and we found ourselves talking to people too young or too old for our criteria. The biggest problem was finding that people were older than we expected them to be, and it resulted in accidentally interviewing too many people aged 43 to 52. Rather than discarding these extra interviews, we enlarged the sample size of the older sample from 100 to 125 and weighted the data to eliminate biases. The weighting is described below.

The interviewing went slowly. We sent letters to all the target persons living in the United States or the Caribbean. If we had addresses for the persons, but the phone numbers were unlisted, we sent letters with enclosed postcards and asked that they mail us the number. (This seldom succeeded.) Then we tried phoning. The best interviewing times were evenings and weekends. The three of us did about half the interviews and trained hired workers to do the rest. As Table A.2 shows, the completion rate was 79 percent of those eligible persons for whom we had numbers. The other 21 percent failed for various reasons, and we tried to keep a record. The main reason was that we could not reach the person (even though the phone rang) or that we could not schedule a time for an interview. Some of these persons were unenthusiastic and hence evasive. A second reason was refusal to be interviewed. The refusal rate was approximately 8 percent, and the failure rate due to inability to reach a person or schedule an interview was about 13 percent. In addition a small number of persons were mentally incompetent, therefore excused.

The interviewing began in July 1989 and continued through October 1990. The bulk of the interviews were done in early 1990, hence for simplicity we call our survey the "1990 survey."

Biases in the Telephone Survey

Because of the inability of our helpers in several of the churches to find a high percentage of the confirmands, our data is biased in that persons with kinship or friendship ties to the church are overrepresented. Persons who are relatively sedentary are probably also overrepresented, since they could be located more easily. We believe this is related to the distance the person now lives from the home church: those living nearby were probably more locatable. In one big-city church the bias was clear: only a very low rate of persons could be found (39 percent), and those found tended to live in the greater metropolitan area. Many of the others had left the area without a trace.

A second bias, less serious than the first, became visible during the interview process. People who refused to be interviewed sometimes seemed conflicted about religious matters, worried about having their true viewpoints exposed, or somehow ill at ease with the church. By contrast, the people most eager to be interviewed were those who felt strong in the church and eager to tell of their faith. It seemed that our study was perceived by some as a kind of "checking up" on them by the church. This perception disturbed us, and we sought to dispel it. But we often failed, and it produced a modest conservative bias in our data, in that the most conventional and traditional Protestant persons are slightly overrepresented.

Weighting the Data

In sum, our data have two biases—too many people who still have ties to the home church and (we believe) tend to live nearby, and too many conventional Protestants happy in the church. All we could do to remedy these biases was to weight the data to overcome them as much as possible, and then to inform the reader of their presence.

We weighted the data in the main sample in an effort to minimize the first bias. First we calculated the percentage of target confirmands located in each of the 21 churches (not including the black churches), and we found that four had much lower percentages than all the others—three in the West and one in the South. Their average location rate was 47 percent. We assumed that all the lost persons on these churches' lists lived some distance away, specifically, more than 100 miles from the church. On this basis we weighted the data in the main sample from these four, upweighting those living more than 100 miles away and downweighting those living closer.

To illustrate: In church A we had 27 completions in the main sample, of whom 17 lived less than 100 miles away. But in that church the location rate for the main sample was only 41 percent. Based on the assumption that the lost persons live far away, we should have interviewed 66 persons (27/.41), of whom 17 lived less than 100 miles away and the other 49 lived over 100 miles away. That means .26 (17 out of 66) of the total would have been in the first group, and .74 (49/66) in the second. Our weighting factor reduced the 17 cases living less than 100 miles away to 7.02 cases (.26 of the total 27) and expanded the 10 cases from more than 100 miles away to 19.98 cases (.74 of the 27). The final weights were: Church A, .41 for those less than 100 miles ("near"), 2.00 for those over 100 miles ("far"); Church B, .55 for near, 1.25 for far; Church C, .50 for near, 1.25 for far; and Church D, .50 for near, 3.00 for far. These four churches contributed 13.6 percent of the main sample. Data from the other 19 churches were not weighted. This formula probably reduces the bias from the low location rates in these churches, but in all likelihood we still have a small overrepresentation of conventional, family-related, sedentary persons.

In the older sample (ages 43–52) we had a different problem requiring weighting. As noted above, we accidentally interviewed too many persons 43 or older, and it seemed better to weight the data than to discard the interviews. The majority of these were from Michigan, and were 43 to 48 years of age. Hence we raised the sample size to 125 and re-weighted the entire older sample to get proper proportions from each region and each age. At the same time we upweighted the males slightly and downweighted the females slightly to match the sex ratio in the main sample (46 percent male, 54 percent female).

The weights were

Males	1.057
Females	.958
Age 43–44	.781
Age 45–47	.721
Age 48–50	1.250
Age 51–52	2.273

Northeast	1.172
Midwest	.717
South	1.611
West	1.055

Each case was weighted by the product of the gender, age, and region weights.

Taped Interviews

Whereas we used strict sampling methods for the telephone survey, this was not feasible for the taped personal interviews. We made no attempt to select the interviewees in any random manner, but rather chose persons illustrating various viewpoints. We completed 40 interviews with persons selected from those in the telephone survey aged 33 to 42.

We chose persons who sounded thoughtful and interested in our project. After the telephone interviewing we asked a number of persons if they would be willing to talk with us in person. We promised anonymity. All interviews were recorded on 90-minute tapes, and the relevant portions were transcribed. In about a third of the cases we phoned the persons back later to ask more questions. Also in twenty cases we told the respondent we would like to interview one of their parents by phone, if they would recommend it. We completed 13 parent interviews.

Notes

Introduction: Understanding Mainline Protestant Rise and Fall

1. What to call those denominations which have been at the forefront of American culture since colonial days has been a matter of considerable discussion among church analysts. Mainline Protestantism is used here to include the Presbyterian, Episcopalian, Methodist, United Church of Christ (formerly Congregational), Disciples, Lutheran, and Reformed denominations.

2. George Gallup, Jr., *Religion in America, 1990* (Princeton, N.J.: Princeton Religion Research Center, 1990).

3. *Time* 66, no. 18 (October 31, 1955): 37.

4. "Resurgent Protestantism," *Newsweek*, March 28, 1955, p. 55.

5. Trend data cited here are from the *Yearbook of American and Canadian Churches* (annual edition), published by the National Council of Churches. For a compilation of Presbyterian membership trend data, see Donald A. Luidens, "Presbyterian Membership Patterns: An Omnibus Overview," unpublished paper, Hope College, Holland, Michigan, 1989. For a summary see Luidens's article "Numbering the Presbyterian Branches: Membership Trends Since Colonial Times," ch. 1 in *The Mainstream Protestant "Decline,"* ed. Milton J Coalter, John M. Mulder, and Louis B. Weeks (Louisville, Ky.: Westminster/John Knox Press, 1990), 29–65.

6. Editorial, *The Christian Century* 72, no. 14 (April 6, 1955): 411.

7. Sydney E. Ahlstrom, "Theology and the Present-Day Revival," *Annals of the American Academy of Political and Social Science* 332 (November 1960): 27.

8. "Resurgent Protestantism," 59.

9. Dean R. Hoge and David A. Roozen, eds., *Understanding Church Growth and Decline, 1950–1978* (New York: Pilgrim Press, 1979), Technical Appendix, C-1a. Data for the United Methodist Church include the Evangelical United Brethren Church in the years before merger with the Methodists.

10. Dean M. Kelley, *Why Conservative Churches Are Growing: A Study in Sociology of Religion* (New York: Harper & Row, 1972; 2d ed., 1977), 1.

11. Gallup, *Religion in America, 1990*, 45.

12. Ibid., 43–60.

13. In the mid-1970s several denominations, notably the United Presbyterian Church (U.S.A.), the United Church of Christ, and the United Methodist Church, initiated studies into the causes of their membership losses. In 1976 Hartford Seminary convened a working group of persons from these and other denominations to reflect on what was being found. With support from the Lilly Endowment, the Hartford Working Group met several times between 1976 and 1978 and published its findings in a book edited by Dean R. Hoge and David A. Roozen, *Understanding Church Growth and Decline, 1950–1978* (see note 9). The book includes research studies of individual church members, studies of congregations, and comparative studies of denominations.

14. Dean R. Hoge and David A. Roozen, "Some Sociological Conclusions About Church Trends," in Hoge and Roozen, *Understanding Church Growth and Decline*, 316.

15. William R. Hutchison, "Past Imperfect: History and the Prospect for Liberalism," in *Liberal Protestantism: Realities and Possibilities*, ed. Robert S. Michaelsen and Wade Clark Roof (New York: Pilgrim Press, 1986), 65–82; quote on p. 71.

16. William R. Hutchison, "From Protestant America to Pluralist America," *Harvard Divinity Bulletin* 19, no. 4 (Winter 1990): 13–14; quote on p. 13.

17. A comparison of the U.S. birthrate and the Presbyterian baptism rate from 1945 to 1989 is shown in chapter 7. The rates are similar except for the period between 1950 and 1965, when Presbyterian baptisms outran the national birthrate.

18. The Episcopalians have a pattern somewhat parallel to that of the Presbyterians. Like the Presbyterians, the Episcopalians had an extended period during the 1950s and 1960s of greater growth than that experienced by the rest of the nation. However, beginning in the late 1960s, they too underwent a dramatic loss of membership relative to the population's growth.

19. The United Church of Christ has a pattern similar to that of the Methodists. While not outpacing the U.S. growth rate during the period under consideration here, the UCC data show growth remarkably close to that of the total U.S. population until approximately 1960. The merger of the Evangelical and Reformed Church and the Congregational Church in 1959–1961 caused the departure of numerous congregations in 1961, resulting in a sudden drop in the membership figures. After that initial fall-off, the UCC membership continued to drop dramatically relative to the nation's growth rate.

20. Mark Chaves, in "Secularization and Religious Revival: Evidence from U.S. Church Attendance Rates, 1972–1986," *Journal for the Scientific Study of Religion* 28, no. 4 (1989): 464–77, argues that the dramatic decline in membership is related to a cohort effect. In his model, "every successive cohort coming of age since about 1940 attended church less than the cohort before it" (476). Thus he pushes the beginnings of the change to the prewar period. He agrees with us that the 1950s "revival" must be rejected as an aberration of birthrates rather than a pervasive return to religion.

21. See Hoge and Roozen, *Understanding Church Growth and Decline*, 321–23.

22. Robert Wuthnow, "Recent Patterns of Secularization: A Problem of Generations?" *American Sociological Review* 41, no. 5 (October 1976): 850–67; quote on p. 856.

23. Wade Clark Roof, "Alienation and Apostasy," ch. 5 in *In Gods We Trust: New Patterns of Religious Pluralism in America*, ed. Thomas Robbins and Dick Anthony (New Brunswick, N.J.: Transaction Books, 1981), 87–99; quote on p. 92.

24. Wuthnow, "Recent Patterns," 854.

25. See Seymour Martin Lipset and Philip G. Altbach, eds., *Students in Revolt* (Boston: Houghton Mifflin Co., 1969), esp. 495–521. Also see Dean R. Hoge, *Commitment on Campus: Changes in Religion and Values Over Five Decades* (Philadelphia: Westminster Press, 1974).

26. Daniel Yankelovich, *New Rules: Searching for Self-Fulfillment in a World Turned Upside Down* (New York: Random House, 1981). Also see Philip Blumstein and Pepper Schwartz, *American Couples: Money, Work, Sex* (New York: Pocket Books, 1983), and Landon Y. Jones, *Great Expectations: America and the Baby Boom Generation* (New York: Ballantine Books, 1980).

27. Karl Mannheim, "The Problem of Generations," ch. 7 in his *Essays on the Sociology of Knowledge* (New York: Oxford University Press, 1952), 276–320.

28. See Steven J. Cutler and Robert L. Kaufman, "Cohort Changes in Political Attitudes: Tolerance of Ideological Nonconformity," *Public Opinion Quarterly* 39 (Spring 1975): 69–81; Norval D. Glenn, "Values, Attitudes, and Beliefs," in *Constancy and Change in Human Development*, ed.

Orville G. Brim, Jr., and Jerome Kagan (Cambridge, Mass.: Harvard University Press, 1980), 596–640; Richard G. Braungart and Margaret M. Braungart, "Life-Course and Generational Politics," *Annual Review of Sociology* 12 (1986): 205–31.

29. For reviews of the research see Norval Glenn, "Values, Attitudes, and Beliefs," in Theodore M. Newcomb, Kathryn K. Koenig, Richard Flacks, and Donald P. Warwick, *Persistence and Change: Bennington College and Its Students After Twenty-five Years* (New York: John Wiley & Sons, 1967): Jeylan T. Mortimer and Roberta G. Simmons, "Adult Socialization," *Annual Review of Sociology* 4 (1978): 421–54.

30. Hoge and Roozen, *Understanding Church Growth and Decline,* 325–33.

31. Robert Wuthnow, *The Restructuring of American Religion: Society and Faith Since World War II* (Princeton, N.J.: Princeton University Press, 1988), 170.

32. See, for instance, John K. Simmons, "Complementism: Liberal Protestant Potential Within a Fully Realized Pluralistic Cultural Environment," in Michaelsen and Roof, *Liberal Protestantism,* 168.

33. Robert N. Bellah et al., *Habits of the Heart: Individualism and Commitment in American Life* (Berkeley, Calif.: University of California Press, 1985), 142–63.

34. Ibid., 221.

35. Ibid., 71–75, 335.

36. Gibson Winter, "The Church in Suburban Captivity," *The Christian Century* 72, no. 39 (September 28, 1955): 112.

37. Two series of nationwide surveys clearly depict a loss of confidence in major social institutions, which began during the 1960s and continues today. One, including six polls from 1966 to 1976, was compiled by Louis Harris and Associates. It asked respondents about their level of confidence in people running nine major institutions, including major companies, the military, Congress, and organized religion. The percentage saying "a great deal of confidence" fell from 43 to 20 during those ten years, and the percentage having a great deal of confidence in organized religion fell from 41 to 24. See *Public Opinion* 2, no. 5 (October–November 1979): 30.

The second series was compiled by the *Washington Post* from University of Michigan National Election Studies and *Post*-ABC Polls. It included eighteen surveys from 1958 to 1991. It traced how many of the people trust the government in Washington to do what is right ("always or most of the time"). The percentage was 75 in 1958 and 78 in 1964, then fell steeply to a low of 26 in 1980, and later rose gradually to 36 in 1991. See Dan Balz and Richard Morin, "A Tide of Pessimism and Political Powerlessness Rises," *Washington Post,* November 3, 1991, A1, A16–17.

38. Robert S. Lynd and Helen Merrill Lynd, *Middletown: A Study in American Culture* (New York: Harcourt, Brace & Co., 1929); Robert S.

Lynd and Helen Merrill Lynd, *Middletown in Transition: A Study in Cultural Conflicts* (New York: Harcourt, Brace & Co., 1937).

39. Theodore Caplow et al., *All Faithful People: Change and Continuity in Middletown's Religion* (Minneapolis: University of Minnesota Press, 1983), 121; see also Theodore Caplow et al., *Middletown Families: Fifty Years of Change and Continuity* (Minneapolis: University of Minnesota Press, 1982).

40. Caplow et al., *All Faithful People,* 121.

41. Ibid., 99.

42. Benton Johnson, "On Dropping the Subject: Presbyterians and Sabbath Observance in the Twentieth Century," in *The Presbyterian Predicament: Six Perspectives*, ed. Milton J Coalter, John M. Mulder, and Louis B. Weeks (Louisville, Ky.: Westminster/John Knox Press, 1990), 90–108.

43. Rodney Stark and Charles Y. Glock, *American Piety: The Nature of Religious Commitment* (Berkeley: University of California Press, 1968), 189.

44. Wade Clark Roof and William McKinney, *American Mainline Religion: Its Changing Shape and Future* (New Brunswick, N.J.: Rutgers University Press, 1987), 175.

45. William F. Starr, "The Changing Campus Scene: From Church to Coffeehouse," in *Never Trust a God Over 30*, ed. Albert H. Friedlander (New York: McGraw-Hill Book Co., 1967), 60.

46. *Minutes*, General Assembly, Presbyterian Church in the United States, 1970, p. 26.

47. Jeffrey K. Hadden, *The Gathering Storm in the Churches: The Widening Gap Between Clergy and Laity* (Garden City, N.Y.: Doubleday & Co., 1969).

48. See Dean R. Hoge, *Division in the Protestant House: The Basic Reasons Behind Intra-Church Conflicts* (Philadelphia: Westminster Press, 1976), ch. 5, pp. 119–34 for a similar discussion. In an analysis of New Jersey Presbyterians' responses to denominational financial support for the legal defense of Angela Davis—a black Communist atheist—Hoge found that there was little "voting with their feet" among members.

49. Peter L. Berger, "American Religion: Conservative Upsurge, Liberal Prospects," in Michaelsen and Roof, *Liberal Protestantism*, 19–36, quote p. 25.

50. Donald A. Luidens, "Between Myth and Hard Data: A Denomination Struggles with Identity," in *Beyond Establishment: Protestant Identity in a Post-Protestant Age*, ed. Jackson W. Carroll and Wade Clark Roof (Louisville, Ky.: Westminster/John Knox Press, 1993), 248–269.

Chapter 2: Who Are These Young Adults?

1. See esp. David A. Roozen, "Church Dropouts: Changing Patterns of Disengagement and Re-Entry," *Review of Religious Research* 21, no. 4 (Supplement, 1980): 427–50: also Wade Clark Roof and William McKinney,

American Mainline Religion: Its Changing Shape and Future (New Brunswick, N.J.: Rutgers University Press, 1987).

2. U.S. Department of Commerce, Bureau of the Census, "Marital Status and Living Arrangements," *Current Population Reports*, Population Characteristics, Series P-20, no. 445 (Washington, D.C.: Bureau of the Census, March 1989), 1.

3. Ibid., 2.

4. U.S. Department of Commerce, Bureau of the Census, "Households, Families, Marital Status, and Living Arrangements: Advance Report," *Current Population Reports*, Population Characteristics, Series P-20, 441 (Washington, D.C.: Bureau of the Census, November 1989), 4.

5. One such widely circulated work is Landon Y. Jones, *Great Expectations: America and the Baby Boom Generation* (New York: Ballantine Books, 1980).

6. "Clustering" involves selecting congregations in close proximity to each other to represent a wider geographic region. In our study, the eastern churches were located in Pennsylvania, the midwestern churches in Michigan, the southern churches in North and South Carolina, and the western churches in California and Oregon.

7. This date was chosen because it fell midway between 1959 and 1969, the years of confirmations used for selecting the main sample.

8. For an explanation of this 4 231 4 model, and for further details of the sampling and interview process, see the Appendix.

9. We thank Jack Marcum, Administrator of the Presbyterian Panel, for advising us on the comparisons and for doing the computer analysis. The 1990 Panel study is described in *The Presbyterian Panel: 1991–1993 Background Report* (Louisville, Ky.: Research Services Office, 1991).

10. U. S. Department of Commerce, Bureau of the Census, *Statistical Abstracts of the United States: 1990* (Washington, D.C.: Bureau of the Census, 1991), 134.

11. Ibid., 389–91.

12. Ibid.

13. Ibid. Comparable employment breakdowns in 1988 were 41 percent for all U.S. males employed in skilled and manual labor in 1988 and 28 percent for all U.S. females working in clerical and administrative support services.

14. In 1990, the comparable figure for all Americans 33–42 years old was 64 percent currently married, according to the nationwide General Social Survey. Twenty percent were divorced, and 15 percent were never married. The percent with children, regardless of marital status, was 78. Presbyterians are more inclined to marry and remarry than the national average. See *General Social Survey Codebook* (annual) (Chicago: National Opinion Research Center).

15. In 1990, among Americans 33–42 years old, 23 percent had experienced divorce, according to the nationwide General Social Survey. This is close to the 24 percent figure for Presbyterians.

16. For discussions of denominational switching, see especially Stark and Glock, *American Piety*, and Roof and McKinney, *American Mainline Religion*. Wade Clark Roof has a discussion of multiple switching in "Multiple Religious Switching: A Research Note," *Journal for the Scientific Study of Religion* 28, no. 4 (December 1989): 530–35.

17. This difference is not statistically significant, in part because the number of church member divorcées is relatively small (52 respondents out of 307 church members).

18. The 1990 General Social Survey included the same question about political self-definition. Among Americans 33–42 years old, 31 percent called themselves liberal, 36 percent called themselves conservative, 32 percent said they were moderate, and the rest did not know. Presbyterian Baby Boomers are slightly more conservative than average Americans of the same age.

19. Robert Wuthnow, *The Restructuring of American Religion: Society and Faith Since World War II* (Princeton, N.J.: Princeton University Press, 1988), esp. ch. 7. Also see Robert Wuthnow, *The Struggle for America's Soul: Evangelicals, Liberals, and Secularism* (Grand Rapids: Wm. B. Eerdmans Publishing Co., 1989), and Tex Sample, *U.S. Lifestyles and Mainline Churches* (Louisville, Ky.: Westminster/John Knox Press, 1990).

20. Jones, *Great Expectations*, 1–2.

Chapter 3: Where Are They? Eight Religious Types

1. The decision whether to define a person as fundamentalist was not always obvious. For example, one active Catholic insisted that his church was fundamentalist, but we did not classify him as a fundamentalist. There were about eight boundary cases which could have been put into the fundamentalist group or left in the residual "other" category. For these cases we made the decisions guided by the total interview, not just the person's description of his or her church. Persons belonging to the Assembly of God, Pentecostal Church of God, or the Church of the Nazarene were categorized as fundamentalists if they described their churches that way. For two members of independent charismatic churches, we deferred to the interviewees themselves in categorizing one a fundamentalist, the other not. The categorizing method is not precise; a safe statement is that the number of fundamentalists in our sample is between 5 percent and 8 percent.

2. The data on countercultural experiences are not shown. The percentages of the eight types who reported attending a rock concert were

(from Type 1 to Type 8) 74, 71, 69, 57, 69, 51, 80, and 81. The percentages who reported smoking marijuana were 45, 44, 44, 49, 66, 44, 59, and 60. The percentages who were in demonstrations were 19, 21, 25, 28, 25, 22, 28, and 39.

3. A 1988 Gallup poll asked the same question about whether most churches today are concerned enough with social justice. Forty-one percent of both the total sample and also of adults 30–49 years old strongly agreed or moderately agreed, compared with 31 percent in our sample (*Unchurched Americans 1988* [Princeton, N.J.: Gallup Organization], 1:44). The adults in our sample are less critical of churches for this reason than average Americans.

4. The same question about the Bible was included in the 1987 General Social Survey, which polled a random sample of American adults. We looked at the persons 33–42 years old in that survey and found that 46 percent chose the response "The Bible is God's Word and all it says is true," compared with 23 percent in our sample. In the nationwide survey 94 percent of the persons 33–42 years old chose the first or second responses, compared with 93 percent in our sample. Most Americans see the Bible as in some way inspired by God, as did our sample, but many more Americans see it as *literally* true than did our sample.

5. In 1981 a Gallup poll asked, "Do you believe in reincarnation—that is, the birth of the soul in a new body after death, or not?" Twenty-three percent said yes; among persons 30–49 years old the response was 21 percent, very similar to our finding (George Gallup, Jr., and Sarah Jones, *100 Questions and Answers: Religion in America* [Princeton, N.J.: Princeton Religion Research Center, 1989], 30).

6. Gallup Organization, *Unchurched Americans 1988*, 1:32. In an identical survey in 1978 the percentage agreeing strongly or moderately was nearly the same—80 percent of persons 30–49 years old (Gallup Organization, *Unchurched Americans Survey 1978*, vol. 1, Question 12).

7. Gallup Organization, *Unchurched Americans 1988*, 1:81. In the 1978 survey the percentage saying yes to this question was similar—75 percent of persons 30–49 years old (Gallup Organization, *Unchurched Americans Survey 1978*, vol. 1, Question 31).

8. The third and seventh items in Table 3.6 were asked in a 1985 nationwide survey of men and women. In it, 40 percent agreed that "laws making abortion legal should be repealed," compared with 21 percent in our sample. Our sample is more supportive of legalized abortion than the total American population. Also in the 1985 survey 17 percent said that society's more widespread acceptance of sexual freedom is a change for the better, compared with 13 percent in our sample, and 39 percent said it is a change for the worse, compared with 35 percent in our sample. On this item the attitudes were almost the same (*The 1985 Virginia Slims American Women's Opinion Poll,* paperback report [New York: Roper Organization, n.d.]).

9. We found 50 percent in favor of allowing an admitted homosexual man to be ordained as a Protestant minister. In a 1989 Gallup poll using a slightly different question, not distinguishing between homosexual men and women, 44 percent approved hiring homosexuals as clergy; among Protestants the figure was 39 percent. Our sample is more accepting of homosexual clergy than average Protestants (*Emerging Trends* 11, no. 12 [December 1989]: 2).

10. For making intercorrelations we scored the indexes more precisely. The *Core Belief Index* was the mean of three items, if at least two were answered, recoded: On the Bible, belief that it is God's Word or that it was written by men inspired by God yet contains error = 5; belief that God had nothing to do with it or that it is worth very little today = 1. On Jesus Christ, belief that He was God or the son of God = 5; all other responses = 1. On whether humans should assume that there is no life after death, strongly agree = 1; moderately agree = 2, don't know = 3; moderately disagree = 4; strongly disagree = 5; Cronbach's alpha (a measure of perceived homogeneity of the items) = .69. On the *Otherworldly Index*, responses to both statements were scored ranging from strongly agree = 5 to strongly disagree = 1. The statements said that the primary purpose of life is preparation for the next life and that the respondent believes in a divine judgment after death. The index score is the mean if both were answered; Cronbach's alpha = .66. On the *Universalism Index,* responses to both statements were scored ranging from strongly agree = 5 to strongly disagree = 1. The statements said that all the different religions are equally good ways to find truth and that all the great religions of the world are equally true and good. The index score is the mean if both were answered; Cronbach's alpha = .76. On the *Christ Only Index*, the responses to both questions were similarly scored from 5 to 1 and the mean, if both were answered, was the index score. The statements said that the only absolute truth for humankind is in Jesus Christ and that only followers of Jesus Christ can be saved; Cronbach's alpha = .78. On the *Individualism Index*, the responses were scored from 5 to 1, and the mean was the index score. The statements said that the final authority about good and bad is the individual's conscience and that individuals should seek out religious truth for themselves and not conform to any church's doctrines; Cronbach's alpha = .50. On the *Morality Index,* the conservative score was scored as follows: On the question about the appropriateness of premarital sex, agree = 1; disagree = 3; don't know = 2. On the question about allowing a homosexual man to be ordained, yes = 1; no = 3; and don't know = 2. On the question about making abortion illegal, agree = 3; disagree = 1; and don't know = 2. The mean, if at least two were answered, was the index score; Cronbach's alpha = .75.

For readers unacquainted with correlations let us explain that a "correlation" is a statistic indicating how strongly two variables are related. It can vary from +1 (perfect positive association) to −1 (perfect negative association). Correlations near 0 indicate no noteworthy association. Correlations stronger than about .50 indicate that the two variables are very strongly associated.

11. The item asking about a constitutional amendment allowing prayer in the public schools was used with the identical wording in a 1987 Gallup poll. It found 68 percent of American adults in favor, compared with 56 percent in our sample (*Emerging Trends* 10, no. 1 [January 1988]: 5).

Chapter 4: Four Types of Churched Persons

1. The best studies indicating this are Robert Wuthnow and Glen Mellinger, "Religious Loyalty, Defection, and Experimentation: A Longitudinal Analysis of University Men," *Review of Religious Research* 19, no. 3 (Spring 1978): 234–45; Bruce Hunsberger, "A Reexamination of the Antecedents of Apostasy," *Review of Religious Research* 21, no. 2 (Spring 1980): 158–70; and John N. Kotre, *The View from the Border: A Social-Psychological Study of Current Catholicism* (Chicago: Aldine Atherton Co., 1971).

2. Cited in Will Herberg, *Protestant—Catholic—Jew: An Essay in American Religious Sociology* (Garden City, N.Y.: Doubleday & Co., Anchor Books, 1960), 84.

3. The rates of out-marriage have risen in all American religious groups in the last few decades. See Allan L. McCutcheon, "Denominations and Religious Intermarriage: Trends Among White Americans in the Twentieth Century," *Review of Religious Research* 29, no. 3 (March 1988): 213–27.

4. For research showing that converts make the best members, see Dean R. Hoge, *Converts—Dropouts—Returnees: A Study of Religious Change Among Catholics* (Washington, D.C: U.S. Catholic Conference, 1981), 42; and Wade Clark Roof and William McKinney, *American Mainline Religion: Its Changing Shape and Future* (New Brunswick, N.J.: Rutgers University Press, 1987), 178–79.

5. Research on Protestant-Catholic marriages indicates that in about half of the cases neither spouse converts to the other religion. In the other half the numbers of conversions-to-Catholicism and conversions-to-Protestantism are roughly equal. See Andrew M. Greeley, *Crisis in the Church: A Study of Religion in America* (Chicago: Thomas More Press, 1979), 127. Our sample is similar.

Chapter 5: Four Types of Unchurched Persons

1. On nonmember attenders see Jon R. Stone, "The New Voluntarism and Presbyterian Affiliation," ch. 5 in *The Mainstream Protestant "Decline,"*

ed. Milton J Coalter, John M. Mulder, and Louis B. Weeks (Louisville, Ky.: Westminster/John Knox Press, 1990), 122–49.

2. Bradley R. Hertel, "Work, Family, and Faith: Recent Trends," paper presented to the annual meeting of the Society for the Scientific Study of Religion, Virginia Beach, Va., November 1990. On earlier research see Dean R. Hoge and David A. Roozen, "Research on Factors Influencing Church Commitment," ch. 2 in *Understanding Church Growth and Decline, 1950–1978*, ed. Dean R. Hoge and David A. Roozen (New York: Pilgrim Press, 1979), esp. p. 44.

3. See esp. Robert Wuthnow, *The Restructuring of American Religion: Society and Faith Since World War II* (Princeton, N.J.:Princeton University Press, 1988), 166–67.

4. Allan D. Bloom, *The Closing of the American Mind* (New York: Simon & Schuster, 1987), 25.

Chapter 6: Influences During Youth and Adulthood

1. For reviews of earlier studies see Robert J. Havighurst and Barry Keating, "The Religion of Youth," ch. 18 in *Research on Religious Development*, ed. Merton P. Strommen (New York: Hawthorn Books, 1971), 686–723. Also see Bruce E. Hunsberger, "Apostasy: A Social Learning Perspective," *Review of Religious Research* 25, no. 1 (September 1983): 21–38; Bruce E. Hunsberger and L. B. Brown, "Religious Socialization, Apostasy, and the Impact of Family Background," *Journal for the Scientific Study of Religion* 23, no. 3 (September 1984): 239-51; Dean R. Hoge and Gregory H. Petrillo, "Determinants of Church Participation and Attitudes Among High School Youth," *Journal for the Scientific Study of Religion* 17, no. 4 (December 1978): 359–79; Robert Wuthnow and Glen Mellinger, "Religious Loyalty, Defection, and Experimentation: A Longitudinal Analysis of University Men," *Review of Religious Research* 19, no. 3 (Spring 1978): 234–45.

2. For discussions of the social learning theory see Hunsberger, "Apostasy"; Fern K. Willits and Donald M. Crider, "Church Attendance and Traditional Religious Beliefs in Adolescence and Young Adulthood: A Panel Study," *Review of Religious Research* 31, no. 1 (September 1989): 68–81.

3. See John N. Kotre, *The View from the Border: A Social-Psychological Study of Current Catholicism* (Chicago: Aldine Atherton Co., 1971).

4. On value change among adults see Jeylan T. Mortimer and Roberta G. Simmons, "Adult Socialization," *Annual Review of Sociology* 4 (1978): 421–54; Theodore M. Newcomb, Kathryn E. Koenig, Richard Flacks, and Donald P. Warwick, *Persistence and Change: Bennington College and Its Students After Twenty-Five Years* (New York: John Wiley & Sons, 1967).

5. Robert Wuthnow, *The Restructuring of American Religion: Society and Faith Since World War II* (Princeton, N.J.: Princeton University Press, 1988), ch. 7.

6. See Alexander W. Astin, *Four Critical Years: Effects of College on Beliefs, Attitudes, and Knowledge* (San Francisco: Jossey-Bass, 1977); Philip R. Hastings and Dean R. Hoge, "Religious Trends Among College Students, 1948–79," *Social Forces* 60, no. 2 (December 1981): 517–31.

7. Peter L. Berger, *The Sacred Canopy: Elements of a Sociological Theory of Religion* (Garden City, N.Y.: Doubleday & Co., 1967).

8. We also constructed a measure in which churched persons active in mainline Protestant denominations (Types 2 and 3) were distinguished from all others. The results were so similar to the results from *Churched Versus Unchurched* that we did not report the findings. Statistical details of the analysis reported in chapter 6 can be found in the paper "Determinants of Church Involvement of Young Adults Who Were Confirmed as Youth in Presbyterian Churches," by Dean R. Hoge, Benton Johnson, and Donald A. Luidens (unpublished, 1992; available from the first author).

9. We also looked at a variable measuring presence versus absence of children, apart from their number. The *number* of children was a more powerful predictor of church involvement than the presence versus absence of children, so we dropped the latter variable.

Chapter 7: Why Mainline Churches Are Declining

1. Richard John Neuhaus, "The Church as Interest Group, Once More," *First Things* 22 (April 1992): 73.

2. Robert Wuthnow, *The Restructuring of American Religion: Society and Faith Since World War II* (Princeton, N.J.: Princeton University Press, 1988), 218–23.

3. James H. Moorhead, "Redefining Confessionalism: American Presbyterians in the Twentieth Century," ch. 2 in *The Confessional Mosaic: Presbyterians and Twentieth-Century Theology*, ed. Milton J Coalter, John M. Mulder, and Louis B. Weeks (Louisville, Ky.: Westminster/John Knox Press, 1990), 83.

4. Wade Clark Roof, "America's Voluntary Establishment: Mainline Religion in Transition," in *Religion and America: Spiritual Life in a Secular Age*, ed. Mary Douglas and Steven Tipton (Boston: Beacon Press, 1982), 130–49; quote on p. 138.

5. Dean M. Kelley, *Why Conservative Churches Are Growing: A Study in Sociology of Religion* (New York: Harper & Row, 1972; 2d ed., 1977).

6. Dean R. Hoge, "A Test of Theories of Denominational Growth and Decline," ch. 8 in *Understanding Church Growth and Decline, 1950–1978*, ed. Dean R. Hoge and David A. Roozen (New York: Pilgrim Press, 1979), 179–97; quote on p. 197.

7. Kelley, *Why Conservative Churches Are Growing*, 43.

8. Ibid., 52–53.

9. Ibid., 51.

10. Laurence Iannaccone, "Why Strict Churches Are Strong," unpublished paper presented to the annual meeting of the Society for the Scientific Study of Religion, Salt Lake City, 1989.

11. Peter L. Berger, *A Rumor of Angels: Modern Society and the Rediscovery of the Supernatural* (Garden City, N.Y.: Doubleday & Co., 1969), 36.

12. Kelley, *Why Conservative Churches Are Growing*, 81.

13. Ibid., 41.

14. Ibid., 52.

15. Ibid., 84.

16. Reginald W. Bibby, *Fragmented Gods: The Poverty and Potential of Religion in Canada* (Toronto: Irwin Publishers, 1987), 82–83.

17. Ibid., 135.

18. Kelley, *Why Conservative Churches Are Growing*, 97, 111. The word "entropy" is potentially misleading, since in physical science it refers to gradual and irreversible inanimate processes. Emile Durkheim speaks of the weakening of religious sentiments during monotonous everyday life and the need for their revivification in community gatherings; see *The Elementary Forms of the Religious Life* (New York: Collier Books, 1961), 241–46. Phillip Hammond employs "extravasation" for a similar idea, a word based on the image of water seeping out of clay vessels; see "The Extravasation of the Sacred and the Crisis in Liberal Protestantism," ch. 3 in *Liberal Protestantism: Realities and Possibilities*, ed. Robert S. Michaelsen and Wade Clark Roof (New York: Pilgrim Press, 1986), 51–64.

19. Kelley, *Why Conservative Churches Are Growing*, 104.

20. Ibid., 106–10.

21. Dean R. Hoge, "Interpreting Change in American Catholicism: The River and the Floodgate," *Review of Religious Research* 27, no. 4 (June 1986): 289–99.

22. Cited in Max Weber, *The Protestant Ethic and the Spirit of Capitalism* (New York: Charles Scribner's Sons, 1958), 175. For further analysis see Rodney Stark and William Sims Bainbridge, *The Future of Religion: Secularization, Revival, and Cult Formation* (Berkeley: University of California Press, 1985), chs. 5 and 7.

23. Kelley, *Why Conservative Churches Are Growing*, 101. Emphasis in the original.

24. Iannaccone, "Why Strict Churches Are Strong."

25. Bryan R. Wilson, "An Analysis of Sect Development," *American Sociological Review* 24, no. 1 (February 1959): 3–15.

26. Kelley, *Why Conservative Churches Are Growing*, 104.

27. Donald A. Luidens, "Numbering the Presbyterian Branches: Membership Trends Since Colonial Times," ch. 1 in *The Mainstream Protestant*

"Decline," ed. Milton J Coalter, John M. Mulder, and Louis B. Weeks (Louisville, Ky.: Westminster/John Knox Press, 1990), 29–65.

28. Peter L. Berger, *The Heretical Imperative: Contemporary Possibilities of Religious Affirmation* (Garden City, N.Y.: Doubleday & Co., Anchor Books, 1979), 70.

29. Ibid., 10.

30. Robert N. Bellah, "Epilogue," *Religion and Progress in Modern Asia,* ed. Robert N. Bellah (New York: Free Press, 1965), 168–229.

31. Sydney E. Ahlstrom, *A Religious History of the American People* (New Haven, Conn.: Yale University Press, 1972), 783.

32. Ibid., 784.

33. William R. Hutchison, "Past Imperfect: History and the Prospect for Liberalism," ch. 4 in Michaelsen and Roof, *Liberal Protestantism,* 65–82; see p. 71.

34. Benton Johnson, "From Old to New Agendas: Presbyterians and Social Issues in the Twentieth Century," ch. 8 in Coalter, Mulder, and Weeks, *Confessional Mosaic,* 208–35.

35. Hutchison, "Past Imperfect," 71.

36. Editorial, *The Christian Century* 72, no. 36 (September 7, 1955): 1011.

37. Editorial, *Christianity Today* 1, no. 2 (October 29, 1956): 22–23.

38. Elmer G. Homrighausen, "Are We in a Revival of Religion?" *Theology Today* 12, no. 1 (April 1955): 107–9.

39. Dennison Nash and Peter L. Berger, "The Child, the Family, and the 'Religious Revival' in Suburbia," *Journal for the Scientific Study of Religion* 2, no. 1 (October 1962): 85. Also see Reinhold Niebuhr, "Is There a Revival of Religion?" *New York Times Magazine,* November 19, 1950, sec. 6, p. 13; Arthur Roy Eckardt, *The Surge of Piety in America* (New York: Association Press, 1958); Paul Hutchinson, "Have We a 'New' Religion?" *Life,* April 11, 1955, 138–40; and Stanley J. Rowland, *Land in Search of God* (New York: Random House, 1958).

40. Nash and Berger, "The Child, the Family, and the 'Religious Revival,'" 93.

41. The U.S. birth figures are from the U.S. Department of Commerce, Bureau of the Census, *Historical Statistics of the United States: Colonial Times to 1957* (Washington, D.C.: Bureau of the Census, 1960), B 1–18. Baptism data are from the General Assembly yearbooks for each denomination. The UPCUSA data include figures from the PCUSA and UPCNA (antecedent groups).

42. In Figure 7.1 the annual baptism rates were calculated for each denomination based on the number of baptisms and communicant membership. Specifically, the number of infant baptisms in a given year was divided by the total number of communicants in the denomination that

year, then multiplied by 1,000. This procedure provides a consistent basis for comparing baptism rates with the national birthrate. Denominational data were calculated by Donald Luidens and are available from him.

43. Rodney Stark and Charles Y. Glock, *American Piety: The Nature of Religious Commitment* (Berkeley: University of California Press, 1968), 203.

44. Roof and McKinney, *American Mainline Religion*, 175.

45. Stark and Glock, *American Piety*, 84, 166, 167, 172.

46. The number of "actual" confirmations for the UPCUSA was calculated as follows: The annual additions based on "Profession of Faith, Reaffirmation of Faith, and Restored" were reported together in the General Assembly yearbook. Therefore it was necessary to disentangle these data. In the seven years prior to 1958, the "Restored" category was listed separately. During this period, this category represented between 9 and 11 percent of the total additions for each year. Accordingly, the 1958–1968 data were reduced by 10 percent in order to delete the "Restored" category. In addition, since adults baptized during this period were also included in the profession of faith data, the reported figures were further reduced by the number of reported adult baptisms. The results of these adjustments produce the data in Figure 7.2.

The "projected" confirmation data for the UPCUSA were based on the *infant* baptism patterns for two denominations, the PCUSA and the PCNA, from 1946 through 1956.

The "actual" confirmation data for the PCUS in Figure 7.3 were calculated by subtracting the annual adult baptism figures from the annual reported confirmation figures.

The "projected" confirmation data for the PCUS were the denomination's 1946–1956 baptism figures projected to the 1958–1968 period. At two points, averaging across two years was done to smooth out precipitous—and unlikely—shifts in the baptism rates.

47. See Dean R. Hoge and David A. Roozen, "Research on Factors Influencing Church Commitment," in Hoge and Roozen, *Understanding Church Growth and Decline,* 42–68.

Chapter 8: Implications for Mainline Churches

1. Peter L. Berger, *The Sacred Canopy: Elements of a Sociological Theory of Religion* (New York: Doubleday & Co., 1967), 153.

2. Dean M. Kelley, *Why Conservative Churches Are Growing* (New York: Harper & Row, 1972), 95.

3. Donald E. Miller is directing a large study of California churches appealing to young adults. For example, see his paper "Hope Chapel: Revisioning the Foursquare Gospel," presented to the Society for the Scientific Study of Religion, November 7, 1992.

4. Wesley Granberg-Michaelson, *Redeeming the Creation: The Rio Earth Summit: Challenges for the Churches* (Geneva: World Council of Churches, 1992); also see his *A Worldly Spirituality: The Call to Redeem Life on Earth* (New York: Harper & Row, 1984).

5. Tex Sample, *U.S. Lifestyles and Mainline Churches: A Key to Reaching People in the '90s* (Louisville, Ky.: Westminster/John Knox Press, 1990), 45ff.

Index

mobility. *see* change.
modernization, 189–90
Moorhead, James, 179
morality:
    active Presbyterians, 111
    agnostics, 35
    doctrine and morals, 208
    implications for mainline churches, 204
    lay liberalism, 122
    moral conservatives, 88
    nonreligious persons, 157–58
    religious and morality indexes, 59–61
    unchurched, 31
    uninvolved but religious persons, 143, 146, 149
Morality (conservative) Index, 91, 87, 117, 155, 170
Mormons, 35, 69 141
mothers:
    active Presbyterians, 22–24
    agnostic, 33, 36
    other churched persons, 123
    unchurched, 30
    uninvolved but religious persons, 151
motivations, unchurched persons, 159–62
Mulder, John, viii
Muncie, Ind., 14
music:
    implications for mainline churches, 205
    music ministry, 108

N

national contextual explanations of membership trends, 10
national institutional explanations of membership trends, 11
National Council of Churches, 27–28, 191
near-ultimate meaning, 209
neighborhood changes, 10–11
New Age groups, 72, 80, 144
New Rules (Yankelovich), 8

Newsweek, 1, 2
"Nicodemus rebirth," 23, 104
nondenominational churches, 69, 96, 99
nonreligious persons, 70, 79–80, 154–57, 179
"normalcy" after war, 3, 4, 6
nostalgia, active Presbyterians, 22
"notions," 184

O

occupations, change of occupations, 47
openness:
    mainline churches, 211
    openness to difference, 14
    Presbyterian openness, 200
ordination of homosexuals, 24, 91
organizations, strong churches, 181
Orthodox Jews, 207
other mainline churches, 123
Otherwordly Index Items, 60, 79–80
out-marriage, 236n

P

parents and children:
    active Presbyterians, 103, 109–11, 115–16, 119
    agnostics, 34
    church attendance, 214
    fundamentalists, 28, 99, 100
    implications for mainline churches, 204
    lay liberalism, 122
    nonreligious persons, 154, 158–59
    number of children, 40, 171, 238n
    orthodoxy, 199
    social learning theory, 163–64
    unchurched, 30, 32, 130, 132–33
    uninvolved but religious persons, 147–50, 151
    weak religious commitment, 198
    Who Are These Young Adults?, 59
Pascal, Blaise, 190
Pennsylvania, 220
personal autonomy, 198
personal support and reassurance, 150, 204

U

V

W

Y